William Coolidge Lane

Travels through the interior parts of America

In a series of letters vol. 2

William Coolidge Lane

Travels through the interior parts of America
In a series of letters vol. 2

ISBN/EAN: 9783742842398

Manufactured in Europe, USA, Canada, Australia, Japa

Cover: Foto ©Andreas Hilbeck / pixelio.de

Manufactured and distributed by brebook publishing software (www.brebook.com)

William Coolidge Lane

Travels through the interior parts of America

TRAVELS

THROUGH THE

INTERIOR PARTS

OF

AMERICA;

IN A

SERIES OF LETTERS.

BY AN OFFICER.

Τί ἂν, ἄν τις εἴποι, ταῦτα λέγεις ἡμῖν νῦν;
Ἵνα γνῶτε, καὶ φυλάξησθε ἀμφότερα.

DEMOSTH. OLYNTH.

VOL. II.

LONDON:
Printed for WILLIAM LANE, Leadenhall-Street.
M DCC LXXXIX.

delighted to honor the good conduct and bravery of the defeated, not only by the secret approbation of his own heart, which induces him to respect a gallant behaviour, even in an enemy, but because his ambition

VOL. II.   B

ambition is agreeably flattered by the conquest of those who had rendered themselves formidable by their bravery——and no doubt but from these motives, General Gates being fully sensible of the mortification attending our reverse of fortune, and not wishing to add any circumstance that might aggravate our present calamity, kept his army within their camp during the time we were piling up our arms, that they might not be spectators of so humiliating a scene.

Our situation, although unfortunate, is not the first instance of an army's capitulating, witness the convention at Closterhauven, which was so shamefully broke; and if you look farther back into history, you will find, that exactly a century ago, the army under the Duke of Saxe Eysenack, which had been considerably weakened by the losses and fatigues of the campaign, was under the necessity of surrendering to

the

the Marſhal de Crequi, who granted a paſſport, conceived in very humble terms to the Duke of Saxe Eyſenack, allowing him permiſſion to paſs with his army by a particular route, and all the officers, troopers, and common ſoldiers of the French army, were expreſſly forbid to offer the leaſt injury or inſult, either to the Duke or his army, in their return to Germany.

In this latter point General Gates imitated the Marſhal, for after we had piled up our arms and our march was ſettled, as we paſſed the American army, throughout the whole of them I did not obſerve the leaſt diſreſpect, or even a taunting look, but all was mute aſtoniſhment and pity—and it gave us no little pleaſure to find that the antipathy ſo long ſhewn us was conſigned to oblivion, elevated to that treatment which the authorized maxims and practices of war enjoin, civil deportment to a captured enemy, unfullied with the exulting air of victors.

For want of the advantages of an immediate, exact, and regular communication with the fouthern army, ill fuccefs has been the confequence. The fad event of our expedition evinces the neceffity of confiding the plan of war to a General, who might improve every conjuncture by changing difcretionally the route and fpecies of the war. If our Commander's orders had been general, and not fuch abfolute ones as could not be varied from, (of which he made us acquainted on the morning of our furrender) he would not have been under the neceffity of engaging the King's army in any hazardous attempt, as he might have recroffed the Hudfon's, and changed the war to the defenfive.

People are very apt to draw conclufions from what they think ought to be, and
form

form fyftems which circumftances muft alter. No doubt but it will be generally thought in England, as we had reduced Ticonderoga, and had only twenty-five miles to Albany, the place of our intended deftination, it was eafy to accomplifh it, without confidering the delays and impediments we have met with. This hafty kind of doctrine you muft often have been witnefs to, from the fpirited hopes and expectation of our national feelings.

Our melancholy cataftrophe will be a caution to others in power, in their directions to a General; this expedition appears to have been planned by thofe, who, fitting in their clofets, with a map before them, ridiculoufly expect the movements of an army to keep pace with their rapid ideas, not only directing general operations, but particular movements of a campaign, carried on through a country in interior defarts, and at a diftance of three thoufand thousand miles, without allowing the General who is to conduct that army, to be invested with powers for changing the mode of war, as circumstances may occur.

It was universally understood throughout the army, that the object of our expedition was to effect a junction with that under General Howe, and by such means become masters of the Hudson's river, dividing the northern from the southern provinces. You can easily conceive the astonishment it occasioned, when we were informed that General Howe's army had gone to Philadelphia, and it was the more increased, as we could not form to ourselves any idea how such a step would facilitate, or effect a junction.

It is natural to suppose, when two armies are to meet, that the northern one would advance to the southward, and the southern to the northward; or if they are

to

to meet any where about the center between each, that they would set out in those directions, much about the same time. But it should seem that those who have the direction at home of the armies upon this Continent, despising such simple and natural means of effecting a junction, dispatch the army at New York further south, and send the army from Canada in the same direction, that if both continued their course till doomsday, it would be impossible to meet. I am too much afraid those at the head of affairs too implicitly credited every report, and are continually led away by the false information of men who are interested in the deception, and are profiting by the common calamities of England and America.

The courage, resolution and patience of the army in enduring the hardships of the campaign in general, but more particularly the conclusion of it, must fully refute an

invidious

invidious charge of foreigners in general, particularly the French, that the English are unfit for the hardships of war, and though brave and intrepid in the field, are not capable of enduring fatigue, without the conveniencies of life.

Throughout the whole campaign, the men had not a morsel of bread, but mixed up their flour into cakes, and baked them upon a stone before a fire; very seldom spirits to cheer them after fatiguing days, in clearing away the woods for encampments, repairing roads, and constructing bridges; seldom fresh provisions; scanty and miserable as the allowance to a soldier is, it was reduced to half its quantity on the 3d of October. After the action of the 19th of September, the men continually slept with their accoutrements on, and after the action on the 7th, never had a tent to shelter them from the heavy and almost incessant rains that fell from that time till

the

the convention, without the refreshment of
spirits during this period; and after our
arrival at Saratoga, debarred of that very
essential to the health and convenience of
troops, water, although close to a fine
rivulet, it being at the hazard of life, in
the day time, to get any, from the number
of riflemen the enemy had posted in trees,
and at night the men were prevented, as
they were sure to be taken prisoners, if
they attempted it. All the water that the
army was supplied with was from a very
muddy spring, and what they could get out
of the holes the cattle made with their feet;
by way of luxury, and to render their provisions more palateable, when it rained hard,
the men used to catch it in their caps, to
mix with their flour.

Officers in general fared the same as the
soldiers, most of them young campaigners,
and not so provident of their liquors, rely-
ing upon a fresh supply that was following
the

the army. This was the only time in life I found money of little use: how deceived we are in our opinion, that it conſtitutes *all* our happineſs!—I was not the only one who, when drenching wet and ſhivering with cold, would have given a guinea for a glaſs of any ſpirit.

One day I thought fortune had pointed me out as one of her favorites, for my ſervant came and informed me he had met with a woman who had half a pint of New England rum to diſpoſe of, but ſhe would not part with it under a guinea. I haſtened him back for it, leſt any one ſhould offer the woman more, which I was ſenſible would be the caſe, if known. I would myſelf have given treble for half the quantity, being apprehenſive of an ague, from being continually in wet cloaths, and expoſed day and night to all weathers. You will not accuſe me of a churliſh diſpoſition, but when I obtained the rum,

neceſſity,

necessity, contrary to inclination, rendered me extremely so.

Upon our arrival at Saratoga, three companies of our regiment, one of which was that I belong to, were posted in a small redoubt, close to the creek; our situation was by no means capable of making any great defence, but merely to observe if the enemy passed the creek in any force: had they attempted it, we were to have kept up a firing during their crossing, then to have abandoned our station, and joined the main body of the army. This post was a small square redoubt, constructed with logs breast high, and the only shelter afforded to the troops was from those angles which faced the enemy, as the others were so exposed, that we had several men killed and wounded in the redoubt by the riflemen, who were posted in trees; we could discern them every morning at day-break, taking their situations upon the most lofty trees

trees they met with; by which means they commanded some of the interior parts of the redoubt. Our situation was such, that a man risqued his life if he ventured in the day time to look over the works; and to convince you how sure these men are of hitting their mark, the soldiers, out of derision, would hoist up a cap upon a stick over the works, when instantly there would be one or two shot fired at it, and as many holes through it. I have seen a cap that has been perforated with three balls. We certainly could have dislodged such troublesome neighbours, or prevented their ascending the trees, but we had orders not to fire, as it might bring on a skirmishing attack, whilst the enemy were meditating another of greater importance.

The men were so harrassed and fatigued with continually sitting and lying on the ground, all huddled in a small compass, that three days before the convention took place,

place, they complained to the Captain who commanded, that they were not permitted to fire upon the enemy, whereby they could obtain more ease, and therefore ought to be relieved, and they received for answer, when night came on it should be mentioned to the General. The Captain defired me to go to head-quarters, and when I arrived there, I found they partook of the hardships in common, for the three Generals had just laid down on their mattraffes, having only an oil-fkin to cover them from the weather; the Aid-de-Camps were fitting round a fire. I went up to your old acquaintance, Noble, of the 47th regiment, as being known to him, and related the purport of my bufinefs, which he immediately communicated to General Phillips. While he was fpeaking, I am fure I fhall never forget the eagernefs and anxiety depicted in General Burgoyne's countenance, when he ftarted from his flumber, haftily enquiring what was the matter. General Phillips informed
him

him it was a trifling bufinefs about relieving a poſt, when he lay down again to refreſh his wearied fpirits, appearing almoſt exhauſted by a continual ſtate of agitation. After receiving an anſwer that the poſt ſhould be relieved, I returned to the redoubt. The men anxiouſly expected it, but were greatly difappointed by the appearance of day-break, as knowing no relief could arrive then, and that they had another day's vexation to encounter from thefe rifle-men. It was with the greateſt difficulty the officers could prevent the men from firing at them, and this only with a promife that they ſhould have permiſſion, if they were not relieved at night. Perhaps you will fay, the foldiers had reafon for complaint, for many of them, by being kept in fuch a confined fituation, were fo cramped, that they could fcarcely walk—— but we were relieved at laſt.

During

During the time I was posted in this redoubt, Lieutenant Smith, of the artillery, came one evening to see me, and upon my relating our distress as to liquors, desired me to send my servant to him the next night, and he would send me a case bottle of rum. I now thought fortune was heaping favors on me, but to shew you what a fickle creature she is, when I sent my servant the next evening, instead of returning with the comfort I was promising myself from such an acquisition, he brought me a message, that Mr. Smith was extremely sorry he could not fulfil his promise, as a cannon shot had, in the course of the day, gone through his canteen, and demolished every thing in it.

The day before the convention took place, I was compelled to acquiesce in an action that distressed my feelings much, in making away with the little colt that my mare had dropped, as my servant told me it it would weaken my mare, that, to use the fellow's words, if *ever* we march from this encampment, she will not be able to convey your baggage; at the same time adding, from the time we had arrived there she had had nothing to eat, but the dried leaves he could gather up for her; this was the situation of the horses throughout the army. Some servants let their horses stray about in the deep ravine, where they were stationed to shelter them from the cannon shot, and so sure, as a poor horse was allured by the temptation of some refreshing grass, that grew in the meadows in great abundance, it met with instant death from a rifle shot. On the plain where we piled up our arms, there were numbers of dead horses, from the stench of which, and from the performance of so humiliating an act, you will easily imagine our haste in quitting such a spot. I remain,

Yours, &c.

LETTER XLIII.

Cambridge, in New England,
Nov. 19, 1777.

MY DEAR FRIEND,

OUR expedition, for you must pardon my dwelling on a subject so near my heart, was certainly undertaken with every prospect of success, not only from the goodness of the troops, but the excellence of the Generals. The many difficulties, though in some measure foreseen, were not expected to be such as they have too fatally proved themselves; we had hitherto considered them only what perseverance would overcome. Our progress amidst complicated impediments and innumerable distresses,

diſtreſſes, was really wonderful, and the failure muſt not be conſidered ſo ſurprizing as the perſeverance and ſpirit with which we ſtruggled againſt it.

People who judge impartially, will make a diſtinction between miſconduct and misfortune. It is true the intent of our expedition has failed—General Burgoyne was too deeply intereſted in the national honor, to ſhrink from undertaking what only appeared hazardous—who can blame him, for not executing with an army that always acted like Britons, what was impoſſible.

Throughout the whole campaign, the General has not only been the Commander of the army, but fully demonſtrated he was equally as good a ſoldier; amidſt all the hardſhips and difficulties we had to encounter, the attachment of all ranks to him was unſhaken, and during the inceſſant labors, diſappointments and diſtreſſes

we

we experienced, there was not the least murmur or discontent throughout the army; nay, so strongly attached were they to his person, that when they found patience and courage had been exerted in vain, and all hopes of success at an end, they were ready to follow him to the field, and to die with their arms in their hands. No one could exhibit stronger proofs of magnanimity, nor take bolder or more decisive measures against the enemy, when humiliating terms were proposed. It should seem that he was determined, if fate had decreed the fall and total overthrow of his little army, to perish nobly, and to leave his name unsullied to future ages.

I am yours, &c.

LETTER XLIV.

Cambridge, in New England,
Nov. 20, 1777.

MY DEAR FRIEND,

GENERAL BURGOYNE had not the advantages of prosecuting war in this part of America, attendant on Lord Amherst and General Braddock, for in the last the difficulties arising from the natural strength of the country, were for the most part removed by the friendly dispositions of the inhabitants, who chearfully exerted themselves to facilitate the movements of the King's army, at the same time supplying them with every requisite accommodation; and I am confident, when I assert,

that

that had not the Generals in the laſt war been furniſhed with theſe reſources, neither of them would have made the rapid progreſs that was accompliſhed.

The progreſs of our army was on the frontiers of the New England provinces, whoſe people are univerſally diſloyal, and furniſh ſuch immenſe bodies of militia, it is really ſurprizing that we advanced ſo far, without any co-operation with the ſouthern army.

If General Howe had his reaſons for not proceeding up the north river, and wiſhed to ſtrike terror into ſome of the provinces, I think there were none he could ſo well have directed that terror againſt, as thoſe of New England; for by a diverſion on the coaſt of Maſſachuſett's, many benefits would have reſulted: it would have kept the New Englanders at home for the internal defence of their own provinces, and impeded

impeded the levies for the continental army. Such a diversion would have been a co-operation with our army, and no doubt have prevented the misfortunes that have befallen it, the principal part of the army under General Gates being composed of the militia of the New England provinces, who must have been drawn down to the defence of the cities upon that coast, in which case our army could not have failed to overcome every possible difficulty, and have effected a junction with the detachment that was sent up the North River, under the command of Sir Henry Clinton, from which detachment it certainly was obvious, that the object of the two armies were the same, that of forming a junction.

Certainly then it behoved General Howe to see so large and important a reinforcement as our army would have been to his, in a state of perfect security at least, before he carried his so far to the southward, as

to

to deprive him of the power of support. That our army was to be considered as no other than a reinforcement to General Howe's, is evident from the very orders given out by General Carleton, at the opening of the campaign, stating, " That " his Majesty had ordered him to detach " General Burgoyne with certain troops, " who was to proceed with all possible ex- " pedition to join General Howe, and put " himself under his command;"—at the same time adding this powerful reason; " with a view of quelling the rebellion it " is become highly neceſſary, that the moſt " speedy junction of the two armies ſhould " be effected."

By the junction of the two armies, we should have been in possession of the North River, from New-York to Albany, which divides the northern from the southern provinces. General Washington would in that case have been totally deprived of the great supplies of men and provisions from the New England States; and the British army would have been enabled to make excursions into either provinces, as occasion might serve: the main part of the army might have kept Washington at bay, while a few redoubts, with the assistance of our shipping, would have preserved the entire possession of the river.

General Howe's carrying his army far to the southward, confirmed an idea the northern Provinces have imbibed, that after the affair of Bunker's-hill, and the evacuation of Boston, no Britons will ever land again upon their coast; it inspired them with new hopes, it invigorated their spirits, and greatly contributed to increase the numbers of General Gates's army, which at the time of the convention amounted to 18,000. Every candid and liberal mind will allow our resolution during the treaty of the convention was magnanimous,

nanimous, when it is confidered our army only confifted of 3,500 oppofed to fuch numbers.

It may be urged, that General Howe's going to the fouthward was to draw off Wafhington from our army. He was then at Quibble-town, 200 miles diftant from us when we met the enemy at Still-water, and General Howe's force was at New-York, which was 40 miles nearer, in fome meafure fituated between our army and Wafhington's, therefore he could not move towards us without General Howe's knowledge, nor could Wafhington proceed to Albany by water for want of fhipping and craft, or march by land in lefs than a fortnight, and that only by a road leading through a gap of a mountain. If General Wafhington had, by any forced and fecret marches, paffed this gap, before General Howe had taken poft in the Jer-feys to prevent it, he had an immenfe fleet

of

of men of war and transports, fully sufficient to have carried his whole army to Albany in a week. It strikes me very forcibly, that General Howe's taking his army round Cape Charles, 350 miles more distant from Albany than he was at New York, could by no means contribute to effect a junction; and certainly it cannot be allowed that leading Washington from Quibble-town to Philadelphia, could possibly be any diversion of the least importance in favour of our army.

If it had been the intention of General Washington to have co-operated with any army that was to oppose ours, it does not appear to me how General Howe's going to the Chesapeak, which is 600 miles distant, and leaving Washington, who was 200 nearer to us, could possibly prevent it. The only apparent means, for no doubt it was the intention of General Howe to draw off General Washington's army, and to to prevent his acting against ours, would have been to have taken post between us; it would have been a check upon him, and that detachment that was sent up the North River would not have met with the many difficulties they encountered during their progress, at Montgomery and other forts. Even admitting General Washington's army to have been far superior as to numbers, there was nothing to apprehend; it was composed of new-raised and undisciplined troops, commanded by officers of little experience, mostly corps that had been defeated in every action, strangers to victory, and greatly dispirited——that of General Howe was perfectly disciplined, commanded by brave and experienced officers, the spirits of the men exalted above the effects of fear by their numerous and recent successes, for they had carried victory and conquest with them wherever they trod.

I will

I will give you the opinion of General Wafhington himfelf, as it was related to me by Major Browne, whom I have been acquainted with fince our arrival at this place, and who was at that time in the General's fuite.

General Wafhington dreaded nothing fo much as General Howe's army going up the North River: he was fenfible of the difficulties his own muft encounter in following it; he knew the eafe and celerity by which the Britifh army would be tranfported by water; his own had to march over mountains, ravines, and ftrong defiles, and the provifions for his army would be all from the diftant fouthern colonies; he knew that it would throw a great damp upon the fpirits of the New England Provinces, efpecially their militia, and in a great meafure prevent their joining Gates's army, and infallibly have faved ours.——— This opinion being firmly fixed in his mind,

mind, when he was informed that General Howe was gone to the Chefapeak, he gave as little credit to the intelligence as we did, when the news of it was brought into our camp before the furrender; he fully difbelieved it, and concluded that fuch a meafure was too abfurd to be poffible, and acted agreeable to the opinion he had formed; for when General Howe's fleet failed from the Hook fouthward, he conceived it to be only a feint, therefore moved his army from Quibble-town to the northward, that he might more conveniently follow the Britifh army up the North River, expecting every day to hear of the General's returning, and failing his army to Albany: nor till he heard that the Britifh fleet was at the Capes of the Delaware, did Wafhington march his army to the fouthward. When he received intelligence that the fleet had ftood out again to fea, ftill fo perfuaded he was that General Howe would not act fo contrary to true policy, as to go

up

up the Chefapeak to Philadelphia, but that his intentions ftill were to go to the northward, that he marched his army to his northern poft—not before he was perfectly certain that the Britifh fleet was near the head of the Elk, did he quit that poft, and march his army to the fouthward.—Thus, you fee, the conduct of General Wafhington entirely coincided with his declared and fixed fentiments.

That fome great error has been committed, either unintentional or defigned, muft be evident to every one—where to fix it is impoffible to fay.—But time, that great difclofer of all fecrets, will no doubt reveal this, and, I hope, redeem the national honor and the national welfare.

Yours, &c.

LETTER XLV.

Cambridge, in New England,
Nov. 20, 1777.

MY DEAR FRIEND,

AFTER we had piled up our arms, and our march fettled, we moved forward, and spent the night on the spot where we had formerly erected our hospitals, of which place I sent you a drawing.

The next morning I went with another officer to visit General Frafer's grave: upon our arrival at the spot, we were struck with a contemplative filence at the awful fcene that prefented itfelf, the corpfe having

ing been taken up by the Americans, and the coffin scarcely covered over with earth. Upon recovering from our consternation, we called to some soldiers, who, with a pick-axe and shovel which happened to be in the redoubt, heaped more earth upon the coffin. The Americans had been guilty of great inhumanity in cannonading the corpse when going for interment, but disturbing it after burial would have disgraced a savage; the only reason they assigned was, that we had buried cannon, and not a corpse—a very improbable supposition. I rather imagine, and it is the best excuse, that they thought it was our money-chest.

As we crossed the river at Still-Water, we observed the army under General Gates marching to Albany, to join Putnam; the object of this junction was to give General Clinton a check, who was moving up the North River; and, to our mortification,

we

we learn, that General Vaughan had advanced as far as Æsopus, which place is but a few miles from Albany.—This fully proves what I mentioned in my laft, that a junction of the fouthern army with ours was fully intended, and had any certain intelligence of General Vaughan's advancing fo far, arrived at our camp, we in all probability fhould not have furrendered.

Our army being fo furrounded by the enemy, no certain intelligence could reach the camp; the three confidential fpies whom the General had fent, after the action of the 19th of September, to New-York, had not returned; and fince the convention, we have learnt, that one could get no farther than Albany, where he was obliged to be concealed in a Tory's houfe; another had the misfortune to be detected; and the third was Captain Scott, of our regiment,

regiment, who got safe into New-York, and who was returning with General Vaughan's detachment, which, when opportunity offered, he was to have left, and made his way through the woods to our army. I really am perfuaded, for want of intelligence that could be relied on, the failure of our expedition was compleated; and the honorable terms which have been granted were complied with so readily, because General Gates forefaw, if we had gained intelligence of any detachment being so near, we should have maintained our ground, in all extremities, notwithstanding his superiority of numbers.

In crofling the river, I had nearly loft my baggage, and those in the *batteaux* had a very narrow efcape; about the center a horfe proving very unruly, jumped over, and his hind legs hung upon the side of the *batteaux*, and very near overfet it.

After

After we had crossed, we purchased some liquors and fresh provisions of the inhabitants; this purchase convinced us of the intrinsic value of the precious ore, as the Americans received our guineas with much cordiality, and gave us paper dollars in lieu, at the rate of nine for a guinea. Here I should observe to you, that the real value of a guinea is four dollars and two-thirds of a dollar, therefore, by this exchange, we got nearly double, which shews how considerable the distinction still is, notwithstanding their great veneration for Independency and Congress, between gold and paper.

In this instance we were taught a lesson, that things, however trifling of themselves, are sometimes of moment; had we taken a view of the reverse of our situation at Ticonderoga, we should not have so greatly despised and converted to all manner of uses, the many reams of paper dollars

dollars that were taken at that place.—Myself, among many other young soldiers, experienced the laugh of the old veterans, who had carefully saved several quires, in case of any reverse of fortune, and were procuring all manner of comforts for nothing, while we were parting with our guineas.

I am sorry to observe, the reciprocal esteem that had existed among all ranks of officers, and the solace and comfort they afforded each other, during our trying situation at Saratoga, seemed now to be done away; some were so inattentive to the dignity of their character, as to contend for the *devoirs* attendant on superior rank, in a state of adversity, which, if it does not level all distinction, should at least have softened the *hauteur* of command. Contest should have lain dormant, and emulation been confined to evincing the politeness of the real gentleman, in a
situation

fituation where acts of humanity and friendfhip ought conftantly to have confpired to infure the moft perfect harmony.

As you admire frank converfation, I indulged a fhort vein of reflection on the falfe delicacy of afpiring too much; but we did not embarrafs our own feelings in dwelling on that illiberal conduct, of which the officers concerned were fo quickly afhamed, and for which, by the decency and decorum of their future behaviour, they made ample amends, as it would therefore have been ungenerous to harbour, we unanimoufly fuppreffed every idea of refentment.

An officer, during our march, had flipped away, unperceived, from the main body, too fenfible of the coynefs of that blind goddefs, Fortune, he only requefted her ladyfhip's aid to favour an innocent fraud; fhe fmiled propitious; for having gone on before, and firſt reached a ſmall village, he perſonated General Burgoyne, and with ſuch an air of confidence, and conſequence too, that in ſpite of the inquiſitive temper of the Americans (particularly the peaſants of New-England) their ſcruples were entirely ſatisfied, and being compleatly outwitted, they aſſigned him the beſt quarters. Upon our arrival at the place, after complimenting him with his ingenious device to obtain preferment, he relinquiſhed his new dignity with a good grace, and received us dropping wet, after an uncomfortable march, with much hoſpitality.

We were two days in croſſing the Green Mountains, which are a part of the chain of mountains that run through the whole Continent of America, more commonly known by the name of the Allegany Mountains: the roads acroſs them were almoſt impaſſable, and to add to the difficulty,
when

when we had got half over, there came on
a very heavy fall of snow. After this, it
is impossible to describe the confusion that
ensued; carts breaking down, others stick-
ing fast, some oversetting, horses tumbling
with their loads of baggage, men cursing,
women shrieking, and children squalling!
It should seem that I was to encounter
every unpleasant duty that can fall to the
lot of an officer, for this very day I had
the baggage guard; exclusive of being
covered with snow, and riding about after
the bat-men, to keep them together, and
to assist each other, my attention was directed to a scene, which I did not think it
possible human nature could have supported, for in the midst of the heavy snow-
storm, upon a baggage-cart, and nothing to
shelter her from the inclemency of the weather but a bit of an old oil-cloth, a soldier's
wife was delivered of a child, she and the
infant are both well, and are now at this
place.

place. It may be said, that women who follow a camp are of such a masculine nature, they are able to bear all hardships; this woman was quite the reverse, being small, and of a very delicate constitution.

After we had passed the mountains, the first township we came to was Williamstown, where we soon found how choice we ought to be of our gold, as the farther we proceeded, **we found it of greater value**, the inhabitants enquiring if we wanted any paper money, and out-bidding each other; at this place we got eighteen and twenty for a guinea. It was rather remarkable, though they depreciated their Congress money in one way, they would not in another, for we never could get them to take our hard money for any article, making an allowance for the difference of exchange.

The

The night before we came to this town, being quartered at a small log-hut, I was convinced in how innocent a view the Americans look upon that indelicate custom they call *bundling*: though they have remarkable good feather beds, and are extremely neat and clean, still I preferred my hard mattrass, as being accustomed to it; this evening, however, owing to the badness of the roads, and the weakness of my mare, my servant had not arrived with my baggage, at the time for retiring to rest; there being only two beds in the house, I enquired which I was to sleep in, when the old woman replied, " Mr. Enfign," here I should observe to you, that the New England people are very inquisitive as to the rank you have in the army: " Mr. Enfign," fays fhe, " Our Jonathan and I will sleep " in this, and our Jemima and you shall " sleep in that." I was much astonished at such a proposal, and offered to sit up
all

all night, when Jonathan immediately replied, "Oh, la! Mr. Enſign, you won't be the firſt man our Jemima has bundled with, will it Jemima?" when little Jemima, who, by the bye, was a very pretty black-eyed girl, of about 16, or 17, archly replied, "No, Father, by many, but it will be with the firſt Britainer," (the name they give to Engliſhmen.) In this dilemma, what could I do?——the ſmiling invitation of pretty Jemima—the eye, the lip, the——Lord ha' mercy, where am I going to?—but wherever I may be going to now, I did not go to bundle with her—in the ſame room with her father and mother, my kind *hoſt* and *hoſteſs* too!——I thought of that—I thought of more beſides—to ſtruggle with the paſſions of nature; to claſp Jemima in my arms—to do what? you'll aſk—why, to do—nothing! for if amid all theſe temptations, the lovely Jemima had melted into kindneſs, ſhe had been an outcaſt from the world—treated

with

with contempt, abused by violence, and left perhaps to perish!——No, Jemima; I could have endured all this to have been blessed with you, but it was too vast a sacrifice, when you was to be victim!—— Suppose how great the test of virtue must be, or how cold the American constitution, when this unaccountable custom is in hospitable repute, and perpetual practice.

We every morning look from our barracks to the mouth of Boston harbour, hoping to catch a look of the fleet of transports that is to convey us to England, to which place I now turn all my thoughts, and in expectation of soon enjoying your friendship personally, I remain,

Yours, &c.

LETTER XLVI.

Cambridge, in New England,
Nov. 25, 1777.

MY DEAR FRIEND,

ON our march to this place, we were fully convinced what powerful levies the New England states are capable of furnishing; for exclusive of those that had joined Gates, and were marched to the southward, every town we passed through was raising two or three companies, to join General Washington's army.

The wants and miseries of the inhabitants in general are inconceivable, even

to

to the conveniences of life, yet you would be furprized with what chearfulnefs they bend to them, to obtain that idol, *Independency*. In many poor habitations they have parted with one of their blankets, where they had only two, to fupply their foldiers, and although the interior part of thefe ftates have not been the feat of war, yet the diftreffes of the inhabitants are equally as great as if it had.

They have in this province, among many other military inftitutions, one of a fingular nature, that of minute-men, fo named, as they are in conftant readinefs at the firft fummons of their officers, to march at a minute's warning; they are compofed of the moft active and expert of the militia, and as an encouragement to hold themfelves always prepared to march, they are promifed never to go out of the province, but only to oppofe any enemy that appears either upon their coaft
or

or frontiers. Thefe ftates can, in the courfe of a few days, form an army of fome thoufands; their conduct in affembling at the fkirmifh at Lexington and Concord, and annoying the King's troops in their return to Bofton, fully juftifies their appellation.

If the other provinces enter as heartily into the caufe of rebellion, I am afraid we fhall find it a very difficult tafk to fubdue them; for, exclufive of all the various modes of furnifhing men and fupplies, it is in thefe provinces, in fome meafure, become a religious caufe, in which the people being enthufiafts, their clergy artfully increafe a warlike fpirit among their flock.

One of them, in my hearing, firmly afferted, that rewards were prepared in Heaven for thofe who fell in the prefent conteft, endeavoring to imprefs them with

an

an idea of the real neceffity of the war, as the defence of religious liberty: this was a moft precious and prevailing argument to delude the ignorant; he infinuated that the Roman Catholic religion was to be introduced, artfully mentioned the Quebec-act, and after pretending that he had been vifited by the Supreme Being in vifions, affured them thofe only would be accepted in Heaven, who fhould feal their lives in fo righteous a caufe with their blood.

Similar doctrine is doubtlefs made ufe of by their clergy in general. Stratagems, under the difguifed veil of fanctity and religion, are conftantly formed to encreafe our mutual animofities, for men buoyed up with fuch affurances of Heaven, will fight to defperation. In all religious contefts, we find an unexampled bravery that no dangers difconcert, and a firm conftancy that no force can withftand.

In

In our way hither we passed through a small neat town, called Worcester, where I met accidentally with one of the *Committee-men*, who was upon the examination of a poor fellow, sent from our army to General Clinton, and who very imprudently swallowed the silver egg that contained the message to the General, in the presence of those who took him prisoner: after tormenting the poor fellow with emetics and purgatives till he discharged it, they immediately hung him up. The egg was opened, and the paper taken out, on which was written, " *Nous y voici*, here we are, nothing between us but Gates." The *Committee-men* stared at each other, observing, it contained no intelligence that could be of service; one of them, however, reflected, that *nous y voici* was French, and *that* might contain a good deal. None of them understanding a word of that language, they sent to the jail for a poor Canadian, who was a prisoner, to translate it for

for them: he informed them it meant *here we are*, but as that was in English, they would not credit it. At last one very sagaciously observed, that it certainly was some private mark, or correspondence between the two Generals, and as none of them had much military knowledge, it was thought proper to send it to General Washington, who certainly would understand it better.

As we passed from this town, at a small village there were assembled a great concourse of people to see us march, who were very curious, some lifting up their hands and praying to Heaven, some admiring the soldiers, others looking with astonishment; but among the croud stood foremost an old woman, who appeared to be near an hundred, upon whom your old friend, Lieutenant M'Neil, of the 9th regiment, thought to be a little witty, in which, however, he was fairly worsted:

as this old woman attracted the notice of every one, when he passed, he said to her, "*So, you old fool, you must come and see the lions*;" but with great archness she replied, "*Lions! lions! I declare now I think you look more like lambs!*"

"The lower class of these Yankees——a propos, it may not be amiss here just to observe to you the etymology of this term: it is derived from a Cherokee word, *eankke*, which signifies coward and slave. This epithet of yankee was bestowed upon the inhabitants of New England by the Virginians, for not assisting them in a war with the Cherokees, and they have always been held in derision by it. But the name has been more prevalent since the commencement of hostilities; the soldiery at Boston used it as a term of reproach; but after the affair of Bunker's Hill, the Americans gloried in it. *Yankey-doodle*, is now their pœan, a favorite of favorites, played

in

in their army, esteemed as warlike as the Grenadier's March—it is the lover's spell, the nurse's lullaby. After our rapid succeſses, we held the Yankees in great contempt; but it was not a little mortifying to hear them play this tune, when their army marched down to our ſurrender.

The lower claſs of the New Englanders are impertinently curious and inquiſitive; at a houſe where Lord Napier was quartered, with other officers, a number of the inhabitants flocked to ſee a Lord, imagining he muſt be ſomething more than man: they were continually looking in at the window, and peeping at the room door; ſaying, I wonder which is the Lord! at laſt four women, intimate friends of the landlord, got into the room, when one of them with a twang, peculiar to the New Englanders ſaid, " I hear you " have got a Lord among you, pray now " which may he be?" When his Lordſhip,

ship, who, by the bye, was all over mire, and scarcely dry from the heavy rain that had fallen during the day's march, whispered your friend Kemmis, of the 9th regiment, whose turn for wit and jocularity you are well acquainted with, to have a little mirth with them. He accordingly got up, and pointing to his Lordship, in a voice and manner as if he was Herald at Arms, informed them, that " that was " the Right Hon. Fancis Lord Napier, of " &c. &c. &c." going through all his Lordship's titles, with a whole catalogue of additions: after he had finished, the women looked very attentively at his Lordship, and whilst he and the other officers were laughing at the adroitness of Kemmis, the women got up, and one of them lifting up her hands and eyes to Heaven, with great astonishment, exclaimed, "Well, " for my part, if that be a Lord, I never " desire to see any other Lord but the
" Lord

" Lord Jehovah," and inftantly left the room.

We were efcorted on our march by the brigade of a *General Brickett*; he was very civil, and often ufed to ride by the fide of the officers, to converfe with them. One day, as he was jogging along with our friend *Sone*, he complained to the General, that he was very uncomfortable in fuch wet weather and bad roads, for want of a pair of boots, and that thofe he had, with all his baggage, were taken in a *batteaux*; when the General faid, he would fell him thofe he had on. Sone was rather furprifed at the offer of the Brigadier General, and afked him how many paper dollars he would take; the General told him he would only part with them for gold; when *Sone* offered him a guinea for them; the General inftantly got off his horfe, and after he had taken a pair of shoes out of his saddle-bags, was proceeding to pull off his boots; *Sone* told him there was no such hurry, it would do when they arrived at the end of the day's march: He replied, he should not be long in pulling them off, and he had got a pair of country boots to put on, which are pieces of cloth folded round the leg, and tied at the knee and ancle.— Upon being requested to defer it till we got into quarters, he mounted his horse, rode forwards, and on our halt diligently searched out for *Sone*, when he compleated his bargain, and parted with his boots. So much for an *American Brigadier-General!*

Notwithstanding they are displeased with our Government, they are not so with our guineas, and although they are fighting for independency, they place very little dependence upon paper-money; for
however

however martial they are at present, still they have an eye to traffic and merchandize; what a weak state the Congress must be in, when those who are fighting for its support are depreciating its credit. I am confident that the majority of the Americans are ignorant as to the cause of the contest, and what arose from the factious views of a few designing men, expressing a displeasure to our Government, is now converted into rancor and national hatred. If I might be allowed to give my political opinion, there appears to me nothing so clear, as that the true interest of America is to live in perfect harmony with Great-Britain, for it is evident to the observation of every one, that the colonies reaped great advantages when the union subsisted; they have severely felt, and at this moment continue to feel, the bad effects of being at variance.

That they may be subdued, and an union formed upon the most permanent basis, for the interest of both countries, will, I think, coincide with your sentiments, as it does with those of

Your's, &c.

LETTER XLVII.

Cambridge, in New England,
Nov. 30th 1777.

MY DEAR FRIEND,

THE last town we left, before our arrival at this place, was Westown, where we found the most convenient inn of any on the road, it is equal to most in England, the rooms commodious, provisions good, and servants attentive; above all, the landlord is a friend to our Government, and like all of that description, has been much persecuted. He was not without his apprehensions of being sent to prison for attentions shewn to the officers who

who stopped at his house, which was nothing more than the common civility he shewed to all his guests: in short, he was deemed by the Americans a rank Tory.

The spirit of Whig and Tory is as predominant in America, as it was in England some years back; perhaps you may not have troubled yourself as to the *unde derivatur* of these two words, you will therefore pardon my explaining them: *Tory*, originally, was a name given to the wild Irish robbers, who favored the massacre of the Irish Protestants, in 1641; it was afterwards applied to all enormous high-fliers of the Church. *Whig* was a ludicrous name, first allotted to the country-field devotion-meeting, whose ordinary drink was whig, or whey of coagulated sour milk: it was afterwards applied to those who were against the Court interest, in the reigns of Charles II. and James II. and

and for the Court, in the reigns of King William and King George; the Americans apply them quite the reverse.

Our march from Weftown to this place was the moſt unpleaſant of any, as it rained inceſſantly, and we reached the barracks on Profpect Hill very late in the evening, which were unfortunately in the worſt condition imaginable for the reception of troops, being fo much out of repair, that we fuffered feverely from the inclemency of the weather; the barracks were, in fact, bare of every thing; no wood, and a prodigious fcarcity of fuel, infomuch, that we were obliged to cut down the rafters of our room to dry ourfelves.

The method of quartering was dreadfully inconvenient, fix officers in a room not twelve feet fquare, permiſſion was denied us to accommodate ourfelves with
rooms

rooms in this town, till General Burgoyne arrived, and reprefented our fituation to the Council at Bofton, when it was reluctantly granted. We laboured under many diftreffes and difficulties; every fpecies of provifions was very dear, and to add to our misfortune, could hardly be procured for money. You do not, I believe, in England, rank milk in the catalogue of luxuries, yet we were obliged, *ourfelves*, to traverfe a deep fnow for a full mile, to get a fmall quantity for our breakfafts, as our fervants were not permitted to pafs the centinels

It was underftood at the convention, that the troops were to be ftationed on Profpect and Winter Hills, and the officers were to be quartered in Bofton, and the neighbouring towns. On this fuppofition fome of the officers had pufhed forward and got into Bofton, but were immediately ordered out.

At

At present, the army is disposed of in the following manner: the English troops upon Prospect Hill, and the German upon Winter Hill; the officers have the towns of Cambridge, Myftic, and Watertown, to quarter themfelves, and a parole of about ten miles in circumference; but to preferve order and regularity among the troops, three officers of each regiment conftantly refide in the barracks.

It is no little mortification that I cannot vifit Bofton, for it is the fecond city in America, and the grand *emporium of rebellion*; but our parole excludes us from it: what makes the mortification ftill greater is, that we can go as far as the ferry at Charles-town, and are debarred croffing it.

By an officer who has joined the army from Albany, I am informed, that Lady Harriet Ackland, after fhe quitted our

army,

army, experienced great difficulties, before
she arrived at that city, the night being
far advanced before the boat reached the
enemy's out-posts, and the centinel would
not let it pass, nor even come on shore,
notwithstanding the Chaplain that accompanied her offered the flag of truce, and
represented the state of her Ladyship.
The guard, from apprehensions of treachery, and punctilious to orders, threatened to fire into the boat if it stirred before day-light. What must have been
her anxiety and sufferings, when protracted for seven or eight hours, without covering to shelter from the inclemency of the
night air, and uncertain what her hus-
band's situation might be, her reflexions
during the long, dark, cold hours, could
not impress her with any favorable sentiments of the treatment she was to expect,
from this first reception. When day-light
appeared they were suffered to land, and
conducted to General Gates, who, with
that

that humanity for which he is so conspicuous, received and accommodated her with that respect and attention her rank and merit deserved.

When you trace her through the various trying scenes since her arrival in America, she stands forth an example of female excellence—an example of patience, suffering and fortitude, exhibiting an interesting picture of that spirit of enterprize and distress, you meet with in romance, realized and conducted upon that discipline of duty and chasteness of principle, which should ever be attendant on connubial love. How little the female frame can be capable of supporting, delicate to a degree as hers is, such extreme distress; yet she soared above it, and forgot the weakness of the woman in the fondness of the wife.

We have had several disputes with the Committee-men, relative to travelling on a Sunday.

Sunday, in time of service; some officers have been taken up and confined, which has occasioned the General's interference. We are now permitted to assemble at the barracks, and attend religious duties. The select men wished to be as rigid with us as with the inhabitants, any of whom that are seen in the streets, during divine service, are compelled to go to some place of worship. Whoever shall be caught carrying a bundle is committed to prison, for the spirit of puritanism is as prevalent now in these states, as it was on their first settlement.

The established religion here, as in all the other provinces of New-England, is that of the Congregationalists, a religion different only in some trifling articles to that of the Presbyterians; there were great numbers of other persuasions, particularly of the Church of England, and at this place there is a church erected within sight of of Havard College, the feminary of thefe Congregationalifts; this gave them much offence, as they confidered it a fatal ftroke levelled at their religion. Upon this account, before hoftilities commenced, they perfecuted the minifter, who was the Rev. Dr. Apthorpe, now Rector of Croydon, obliged him to refign his cure and quit the colony; but fince the war, not only this church, but every one over the province is fhut up, nor will the inhabitants fuffer any other religion but the Congregationalifts; they were happy to feize the opportunity of fuppreffing the church of England, as it was gaining ground very faft, and therefore objected to it on the ground of praying for the King and Royal Family. Some minifters offered to omit that part, but toleration is no part of their creed, and they were happy to feize fo favourable an occafion to crufh it.

Before the commencement of the war, Arts and Sciences were making great progress in these states. In this town there is erected an University, the first ever raised in America; it is a neat brick building, containing three halls for the classes, a room for natural curiosities, another for instruments of astronomy and mathematics, and a gallery where formerly was a very valuable library, but when this place was the head quarters of General Washington, the library, as well as the instruments and other articles were removed, in which many were lost and more damaged; those that remain of the handsome collection are very few; adjoining to the college is a neat chapel.

The President of this University is a Mr. Willard, and there are only a small number of students at present, not exceeding twenty, the youth of America studying tactics in preference to the more enlightening

ing sciences. This University has been founded near an hundred years, and altho' it is not on a perfect plan, has produced a number of men of genius. It was much encouraged in its infancy, by many persons at home, particularly a Mr. Hollis, who founded the professorship for the mathematics and natural philosophy, and many other benefactions, nearly to the amount of 5000l. Neither the professors or students reside in the University; the former live in their own houses, and the latter board in the town.

The town of Cambridge is about six miles from Boston, and was the country residence of the gentry of that city; there are a number of fine houses in it going to decay, belonging to the Loyalists. The town must have been extremely pleasant, but its beauty is much defaced, being now only an arsenal for military stores, and you may suppose it is no agreeable circumstance, every time we walk out, to be reminded of our situation, in beholding the artillery and ammunition waggons that were taken with our army.

The character of the inhabitants of this province is improved beyond the description that our uncle B— gave us of them, when he quitted this country, thirty years ago, but Puritanism and a spirit of persecution are not yet totally extinguished. The gentry of both sexes are hospitable and good-natured, with an air of civility in their behaviour, but constrained by formality and precisenefs; even the women, though easiness of carriage is peculiarly characteristic to their nature, appear here with much stiffness and reserve: they are formed by symmetry, handsome, and have delicate complexions; the men are tall, thin, and generally long-visaged; both sexes have universally, and even proverbially, bad teeth, which must probably be be occasioned by their eating so much molasses, making use of it at all meals, and even eating it with greasy pork.

Conversing one day with a Virginia officer relative to the curiosity of the New Englanders, he told me, that finding he never could procure any refreshment for himself or horse, till after he answered all their questions, and they had compared them with their information, he adopted the following mode to avoid their inquisitive delays; Whenever he travelled from his own province to Boston, and alighted at an ordinary, (the name given to inns in America, and some justly merit that title) the master or mistress, and other company in the house assembled at the door, and he began in this manner,—
" Worthy people, I am Mr. ***, of Vir-
" ginia, by trade a tobacco-planter, and a
" bachelor, have some friends at Boston,
" whom I am going to visit, my stay will be
short,

" short, when I shall return and follow my
" business, as a prudent man ought to do.
" This is all I know of myself, and all I
" can possibly inform you. I have no
" news; and now, having told you every
" thing, have compassion upon me and my
" horse, and give us some refreshment."

Intelligence being brought me that some ships are seen in the offing of Boston harbour, I am hastening to Prospect-hill, to see if they are those that will be the means of conveying me to the sight of my worthy friend, and that they may be is the wish of

Yours, &c.

LETTER XLVIII.

Cambridge, in New England,
Dec. 9, 1777.

MY DEAR FRIEND,

DEPRIVED of the privilege to visit Boston, still from the view that we have of it from our barracks on Prospect Hill, I am enabled to give you a description of its situation; for its interior parts, police and government, you must be referred to those authors who have described them.

Boston is situated on a peninsula of about four miles in length, at the bottom of the bay of Maffachufett's, which reaches eight or ten miles within land ; the opening of the bay appears to be fheltered from the impetuofity of the waves, by a number of rocks, which appear above water, and by feveral iflands, moft of which are inhabited, whofe fituation is fuch, that they will not admit of more than three or four fhips to enter at the fame time.

Nature herfelf too feems to have provided for the fafety of the city, for upon this narrow channel there is an ifland, that, when fortified, no fhip can pafs it : this important poft was entirely neglected till the end of the laft century, when a regular citadel, named Fort William, was erected on it, defended by a hundred pieces of cannon, of the largeft fize and extremely well placed. When our troops evacuated Bofton, they demolifhed the fortifications, which rendered the city liable to an attack by fea, therefore the principal

principal object of the New Englanders was to put Boston and this island in such a state of defence, as to prevent its falling again into our possession; and so indefatigable were they in this business, that every able-bodied citizen allotted two days in a week, the more speedily to conclude it, as they were not without their apprehensions, that when the fleet and army were reinforced they would return; what impressed them so strongly with this idea was the demolition of the works.

About a league from this island, near the mouth of the harbour, there is a high light house, the signals from which are perceiveable at Boston, where there are beacons, as well as upon most of the heights along the coast, to spread the alarm to the inland countries of an enemy's approach. Except when a very thick fog prevails, at which time some ships might slip in amongst the islands, the town

town has always five or six hours to prepare for the reception of an enemy; and in the space of four-and-twenty hours, they can raise several thousands of militia. If ever a fleet of ours should be able to pass Fort William, it would be effectually stopt by the strong batteries the Americans have raised, both to the north and south of the town, which command the bay entirely; the harbour appears so spacious, that it will admit of six or seven hundred vessels anchoring safely and commodiously. I am informed, on that side of the city that faces the harbour, there is a very magnificent pier which extends so far into the sea, as to admit of ships unloading their cargoes, without the assistance of small craft, from whence they are deposited in warehouses, ranged along this pier.

Opposite to the northern part of the peninsula on which Boston stands, are the
remains

remains of Charles-town, which had the
same connection with Boston as the Borough has with the city of London; the
river that divides the two is not much
wider than the Thames, and it appears
rather singular, that the inhabitants never
erected a bridge, as it would have greatly
contributed to the prosperity of both, especially as it was the direct entrance from
the inland towns into Boston. Unless you
cross the ferry, you have to make a circuit of several miles, over swamps and
morasses, from this place to Boston, which
is only two miles in a direct line; no
doubt, as the Americans are become so
expert in making bridges across rivers of
greater width than this, they will, when
the contest is ended, erect one; for what
was formerly either through indolence or
individual concerns considered as impossibilities and arduous undertakings, will
now be thought matters easily accomplished.

Near

Near to the remains of Charles-town is that famous spot where so much blood was spilt, and so many brave men slain, *Bunker's Hill*, which will ever be a memento to British Commanders, against attacking works with such temerity, without a sufficient information as to their construction, and holding an enemy in too great contempt; but in this instance it was in some measure unavoidable, for had the Americans secured that post, Boston would have been untenable, as it is a high ground that overlooks and commands the whole town, the only error that appears to have been committed; was at first not endeavouring to turn their flank (which proved the means of driving them from their works) instead of attacking them in the front. The only motive that could lead to the mode of attack that was adopted, must have been upon a supposition that it was impossible, in such a small space of time, to erect

any

any works, but what might eaſily be demoliſhed by the artillery, and carried by ſtorm: Certainly our troops were much annoyed by the Americans from Charlestown; and if it had not been for the General's unwillingneſs to deſtroy it, the enemy might eaſily have been diſlodged, in which caſe, the weakneſs of their flank would have been diſcovered, and ſo many lives would not have been loſt in attacking them; their induſtry, diligence and ſilence in conſtructing the works, which conſiſted of a ſmall redoubt and ſtrong intrenchment, reaching near half a mile down to the river Myſtic, is incredible. I cannot conceive how the importance of this poſt ſhould eſcape the vigilance of our Generals, as the ſafety of Boſton depended entirely on our having poſſeſſion of it.

The beſt deſcription that I can poſſibly give you as to the engagement, is what I
gathered

gathered from Captain Drew, whom I met with at Cork, who, in that action, was wounded in several parts of the body; and, notwithstanding scarcely recovered from his wounds, was going out to join his regiment. He acknowledged himself to have never been witness to such a scene of carnage and slaughter; and, in addition to the incessant roar of cannon, discharge of musquetry, and the groans of the wounded and dying, there were great explosions from the burning of the town, from which ascended a large column of black smoke; in short, it was such a scene as cannot be described, nor can any one form the least idea of it, but those who were present. What must have been the feelings of the Generals and troops in Boston, who were spectators of this dreadful carnage, without participating? The behaviour of the British troops, was truly characteristic of that valour and intrepidity that is allowed by all nations. But the reception

reception they met with from thefe entrenchments, and the execution, which
was terrible, was fufficient to ftagger the
braveft troops;—for full half an hour,
the fire poured down upon them like a
ftream; many old veterans declared, that,
for the time it lafted, it was the hotteft and
moft bloody engagement they ever remembered.

We are anxioufly expecting the veffels,
as our fituation is not only very unpleafant
but dangerous, both to officers and foldiers; the latter of whom are in continual broils with the American guards, which
are compofed of militia, who not being
under very great difcipline, not only infringe their orders, which perhaps they do
not comprehend, or elfe ufe their authority
as they think proper; they have received
orders not to let any officer pafs without
his fide arms, and as many of them left
their baggage in Canada, others loft them
with

with their baggage, during the campaign, this ignorant people will not let any one pafs without a fword, drawling out, " I " fwear now you fhan't pafs, becaufe you " have not got a fword;" at the fame time, ftupid fools, they might perceive by our cloaths and bayonets that we were officers. Much altercation has enfued, to remedy which, the officers had paffports figned by General Heath; but this did not avail, as very few of the centinels could read. At laft it was ordered, that any officer who wanted to pafs the centinels, was to go to the American guard, where the officer fhould fend a foldier to pafs him; this did not altogether remedy the evil, as many of the officers could not make out the paffport.

When I defcribe to you the troops, you will not fo much wonder at thefe embarraffments, In marching the party to relief, you will fee an old man of fixty, and a
boy

boy of sixteen; a black and an old decrepit man, limping by his side, most of them wear great bushy wigs, in short, they would be a subject for the pencil of Hogarth; but, egad, they are ready enough in presenting their pieces, and if a soldier comes the least near them they level at him, and say. "I swear now, if you attempt to pass, I'll blaze at you."

The soldiers' wives are allowed to pass the centinels; but the other day a most ludicrous circumstance took place, by the obstinacy of an old man upon guard. He would not permit a woman, who was a true campaigner to go beyond him, great altercation ensued, in which the lady displayed much of the Billingsgate oratory, when the old man was so irritated as to present his firelock; the woman immediately ran up, snatched it from him, knocked him down, and striding over the prostrate hero, in the exultation of triumph

umph, profusely besprinkled him, not with Olympian dew, but that which is esteemed as emollient to the complexion—and 'faith, something more natural—nor did she quit her post, till a file of sturdy ragamuffins marched valiantly to his relief, dispossessed the Amazon, and enabled the knight of the grisly caxon to look fierce, and re-shoulder his musquet.

The Winter is now setting in, and as the coasting of the transports from New York to Boston is attended with delay and danger, on account of the strong winds that blow at this season upon the coast, General Burgoyne has made application to Congress for the troops to march to Providence, and to embark at Rhode Island. We are now anxiously waiting for an answer; that it may soon arrive is the ardent wish of

Yours, &c.

LETTER XLIX.

Cambridge, in New England,
Jan. 19th 1777.

MY DEAR FRIEND,

IT is impossible to describe with what a dejected mind I sit down to write, as not only the flattering hopes of shortly seeing my friend is done away, and every prospect vanished, but some years, perhaps, may elapse, before the termination of this unhappy contest.

What was intended as an accommodation to the troops, relative to their embarking at Rhode Island, has proved a most unfortunate circumstance indeed; for the Congress have not only denied that request, but have put a stop to any embarkation, till the convention is ratified at home by the King and Parliament; an event that can never happen, as it would be allowing the authority of the Congress, and the independence of the Americans. What renders our situation more distressing is, that had the transports come round to Boston, the Council would have consented to our embarkation.

The General's requisition to Congress has created suspicions in their minds (and, by the bye, no people are of such a suspicious disposition as the Americans,) that the measure proposed was merely for an opportunity of joining General Howe's army, and that we should, like themselves, be base enough to evade and break the articles of capitulation; after which we were to act in concert with that army against

against Washington; and, in support of their suspicions, or, at least, to give a colour to them, they pretend that the vessels sent to Rhode Island were insufficient for transporting the army to Europe, and that it was impossible to victual the fleet and army for so great a number, in so short a space of time. This idea must arise from the great dilatoriness in all American departments.

General Burgoyne having made complaints concerning the bad accommodation of the officers, which was not agreeable to the terms of convention, the Congress have construed that as a direct declaration, that it had been broken on their parts by a violation of its conditions, and an indication, that we consider the convention as dissolved; that, under these circumstances, when out of the limits of their power, and at large, we should make no hesitation in acting as if we were in no degree bound by a capitulation that we had difavowed under reftraint.

The Congrefs have likewife paffed fome frivolous refolutions, that the foldiers had not faithfully delivered up their accoutrements, alluding to the crofs belts and cartouch boxes. Any one the leaft converfant in military affairs, muft know they are not public ftores, but private, as being always furnifhed by the Colonel of the regiment. In fhort, the Congrefs were happy to feize any circumftance, as a pretext to favor their proceedings, and to render them juftifiable in the eyes of the world. But had they made a reference to General Gates, they would have found what little dependence was to be placed as to that accufation; for, when he obferved the men march by with their accoutrements on, he afked Colonel Kingfton, who had fettled the treaty—" if it
" was

" was not cuſtomary, on field-days, for
" arms and accoutrements to go toge-
" ther?" when Colonel Kingſton replied,
" There was nothing ſaid in the conven-
" tion that he had agreed to with him,
" relating to accoutrements; and that he
" could have no right to any thing but
" what was ſtipulated in the treaty." To
which General Gates replied, " You are
perfectly right;"—and, turning to ſome
American officers, ſaid, " If we meant to
" have had them, we ought to have in-
" ſerted them in the convention." Hence
it is evident Congreſs were ready to graſp
at any pretence, however weak, to evade
the terms of convention without incurring
the charge of a direct breach of faith.

In vain was every expoſtulation of General Burgoyne, as to the ſubſtance of his
letter, which conveyed no other meaning
than complaint of improper uſage, and a
too relaxed adherence to the articles of

capitulation. To obviate all farther difficulties, the General and Officers signed a parole, and were willing to sign any paper, the more fully to ratify the convention.

Congress were inexorable, and it was very perceivable, they would not easily recede from a measure once adopted; no explanation of securities could produce the desired effect upon their determination. The conduct of Congress upon this extraordinary transaction, is extremely visible; they had conceived an idea if our army were suffered to return to Europe, it would be easily replaced in the spring; General Howe's army being now in possession of Philadelphia, Jersey, New York, and other commanding situations, and General Washington so closely pressed at Valley Forge, that upon the arrival of such an additional force, it would turn the scale of war against them; and,

and that the next campaign must end in their final subjugation; they therefore chose to sacrifice their faith and reputation, although an infant state, by an act never excusable. This ever will be an obloquy upon America, and point out to other powers, what little dependence is to be placed upon her public faith.

Judge, my dear friend, what must be the feelings of every one, and how exasperated we must be at this treatment! we have no other hopes left but an exchange of prisoners, which, considering our numbers, will be some time before the whole can be effected. Our situation now becomes every day more and more mortifying, for, exclusive of the insults we continually meet with from the American soldiery, the officers, no doubt, stimulated by this resolve of Congress, behave very tauntingly, and Colonel Henley, who commands the troops, has been guilty of great cruelty to the foldiers. That you may form an idea as to the natural ferocity of difpofition in this man, and how deliberate he is in his barbarities, I fhall ftate a few of them.

On the 19th of laft month, he went up to the American barracks to releafe fome of our foldiers; after calling over their names, he addreffed himfelf to a corporal Reeves, of the 9th regiment, " and told " him he had been confined for infulting " a provincial officer." Reeves made anfwer, " He was forry for it; that he was " in liquor, and would not have acted " fo, had he known him to have been an " officer, and was ready to afk his pardon." Colonel Henley faid, " By God, Sir, had " you ferved me fo, I would have run you " through the body, and I believe you to " be a great rafcal." Reeves made an" fwer, " I am no rafcal, but a good fol" dier, and my officers know it." Colonel

lonel Henley then demanded silence. Reeves repeated nearly the same words, adding, "That he hoped soon to carry "arms under General Howe, and fight "for his King and country." The Colonel then replied, "Damn your King "and country, when you had arms, you "were willing enough to lay them "down." Colonel Henley then ordered silence, Reeves repeating nearly the same words, the Colonel ordered one of the guard to run him through for a scoundrel; the men of the guard not obeying his orders, he dismounted from his horse, and seizing a firelock with a fixed bayonet from one of the guard, stabbed Corporal Reeves in the left breast, and whilst he had the bayonet at his bosom, the Colonel told him, "If he said another word, he "would have it through his body:" Reeves then told him "He did not care, "he would stand by King and his country, "till he died." Colonel Henley then made

a second

a second dart at him with the firelock and fixed bayonet, which two of the other prisoners threw up, and it passed over Reeves's shoulder; at the same time one of the men said to Colonel Henley, "That
" the man was his prisoner, that he had
" better not take his life, as he could do
" with him as with the other men who
" were in his custody." Colonel Henley then returned the firelock, and ordered him back into the guard-room, dismissing the rest of the prisoners.

On the 8th instant, as some soldiers were looking at a party of Americans, where Colonel Henley was present: he ordered the soldiers to go off and clear the parade. The soldiers turned about, and went off as fast as they could; the croud being great, and the road very dirty, Colonel Henley turned about, and addressing the soldiers, said, "Damn you,
" I'll make you make more haste;" and
running

running up to a corporal Hadley, pushed his sword in his left side and bent it: he then turned about and went to the right of his party, straightening his sword as he went along—a pretty example this from a commanding officer to those under his command.

Do not be surprized after this, if you should hear of a general maſſacre of all the Britiſh troops! But what more fully ſtamps the character of this moſt ſanguinary man, and his ferocious diſpoſition, is a moſt unaccountable expreſſion he made to some soldiers, without any provocation.

Our paſſes are renewable every month, for which purpoſe the Quarter-maſter-ſerjeants of the different regiments attend at the American Deputy Adjutant-General's office; on the 16th of laſt month, as the ſerjeants attended at the office, to apply

ply for paſſes, Serjeant Fleming, of the 47th regiment, not being acquainted with Colonel Henley, took him for Colonel Keith, the Deputy Adjutant-General, ſaluted him cap in hand, and was going to addreſs him, when Colonel Henley extended his arm towards him, with his fiſt clenched, and ſaid, " You raſcals, I'll "make damnation fly out of ye; for I "will myſelf, one of theſe nights, go the "rounds, and if I hear the leaſt word, or "noiſe in your barracks, I'll pour ſhot "amongſt you, and make flames of Hell "jump out of ye, and turn your barracks "inſide out; declaring, if he was a cen- "tinel, and any Britiſh ſoldiers looked "ſulky at him, he would blow their "brains out!"

Such glaring conduct could not eſcape the notice of General Burgoyne, who applied to General Heath for redreſs, and he inſtituted a Court of Enquiry, to inveſtigate

tigate the grounds of complaint, and reported, it would be for the *honor* of Col. Henley, as well as for the satisfaction of all interested, that the judgment of a Court-martial should be taken on his conduct, during his command at Cambridge, which Court-martial is to sit to-morrow.

The weather has been very severe of late, and there has been great falls of snow, but now it is more pleasant and serene; the north winds blow very sharp, the snow is about two or three feet thick on the ground, and the inhabitants, instead of carioling, like the Canadians, have large sleighs, that will contain ten or twelve persons, which are drawn by two, and sometimes four horses, but parties of young folks are more accustomed to go a frolicking. As this is a singular custom, I shall describe it to you.

On

When the moon is favorable, a number of young men and women, to the amount of thirty or forty, set off in sleighs, about seven o'clock in the evening, to join some other party, perhaps at the distance of eighteen or twenty miles, where they dance and carouse till day-light, when they return and follow their common avocations, as if they had rested all night; it is not uncommon, an hour or two after daylight, to be awaked with the singing and noise they make, and by the number of bells affixed to the horses, on the return of some of these parties. Singular situations and manners are productive of singular customs. In England, this would be esteemed extremely imprudent, and attended with dangerous consequences; but, after what I have related respecting *bundling*, I need not say, in how innocent a view this is looked upon. Apropos, as to that custom, along the sea coast, by a continual intercourse among Europeans;

it

it is in some measure abolished; but they still retain one something similar, which is termed *tarrying*.

When a young man is enamoured of a woman, and wishes to marry her, he proposes the affair to her parents, (without whose consent no marriage, in this colony, can take place) if they have no objection, he is allowed to tarry with her one night, in order to make his court. At the usual time, the old couple retire to bed, leaving the young ones to settle matters as they can, who, having sat up as long as they think proper, get into bed together also, but without putting off their under garments, to prevent scandal. If the parties agree, it is all very well, the banns are published, and they married without delay; if not, they part, and possibly never see each other again, unless, which is an accident that seldom happens, the forsaken fair proves pregnant, in which case the man, unless he absconds, is obliged to marry her, on pain of excommunication.

The ignorance of the American officers and soldiers, and the scrupulous punctuality to their orders, which one half of them have not underftanding to comprehend, muft occafion confufion and trouble. I have hitherto endeavoured to avoid having any altercation with them; but the other evening I had the pleafure of being conducted to the guard-houfe, though not without company, among whom was Lord Balcarras, Major Mafter, of our regiment, and Major England, of the 47 regiment.

We were returning, about nine o'clock, from Profpect-hill, to our quarters in Cambridge; and about a mile from the barracks, were ftopt by a patrole; who, although we fhewed our paffes and our
fide-

side-arms, would not let us proceed; but
said, he had orders to take every British
officer or soldier up after dark. His
Lordship then informed him, "that he
was sure no such orders had been given;"
but the Corporal said, " he received those
" orders from his Captain; and that we
" must march to the guard-house." Accordingly we were escorted, though a very
cold piercing night, back to the barracks.
When we arrived at the guard, his Lordship remonstrated with the Captain, who
said, " He believed he had such orders,
" but he was not certain; however, as we
" were brought prisoners, we must re-
" main till next morning." His Lordship
then desired him to send to Colonel Ger-
rish, at Cambridge, the commanding officer, which he refused. After much altercation and some persuasion, rather than
pass the cold night without any covering,
in their bleak guard-house, he was prevailed upon to let us proceed to our
quarters,

quarters, upon our figning a parole to return the next morning at eight o'clock; the next day, when we went to the guard-houfe, they flocked round us with the fame eager curiofity to fee his Lordfhip, as they did to fee Lord Napier; we remained at the guard till it was relieved, when the Captain that came to relieve would not take charge of us, nor the other difcharge us; therefore, when the old guard was gone, his Lordfhip afked the Captain " Whofe prifoners we were?" he replied, " None of mine, and I defire you will go all of you about your bufinefs." We went accordingly. Complaint being made by General Philips to their Commanding Officer, all the anfwer he received was, that he fuppofed it was fome ignorant Captain, who had made a miftake. Thus you fee we are the fport of thefe fools. What a footing military difcipline is on in the United States!

I could

I could not so freely have communicated my sentiments, had I not an opportunity to send this by an officer going to New-York, from which place he returns to Europe, who will deliver it to you, and at the same time inform you that he left, in good health, but very low spirits,

Yours, &c.

LETTER L.

Cambridge, in New England,
Feb. 28, 1788.

MY DEAR FRIEND,

OUR attention has of late been engrossed with the trial of Colonel Henley. As the whole proceedings would be tiresome, I shall only just give you the substance of General Burgoyne's opening that prosecution, his reply, and the Judge Advocate's, with the extraordinary opinion of the Court, after the enormous crimes were fully substantiated, upon oath; when ill-treatment, misconduct, and cruelty, were indisputably proved, by such respectable

respectable witnesses as Colonel Anstruther, Colonel Lind, Major Forster, Lieutenant Vallancy, Lieutenant Bibby, and other officers. But as giving you only the heads of his speeches, would take from the energy and beauty of the General's language, I shall relate it verbatim, as taken in short-hand.

At the opening of the Court, General Burgoyne took notice of a distinction between the charge, as stated in his letter, and General Heath's order. In the letter, the general tenor of Colonel Henley's language and conduct, encouraging his inferiors, and seemingly calculated to excite them to bloody purposes, was only stated as a matter of suspicious belief; reasoning upon this principle, it was more candid to suppose one instigator of such evils, than a general, voluntary, bad disposition among the American troops; that the direct matter of charge which the
General

General pledged himself formally and officially to support, was contained in the words " behaviour, criminal as an officer, and " unbecoming a man, of the most inde-" cent, violent, vindictive severity against " unarmed men, and of intentional mur-" der."

General Burgoyne made this observation, as a security against any censure of inconsistency on his part, for not going at large into matters of inferior moment, as to the general tenor of language and conduct of Col. Henley, declaring he should confine his evidence to transactions of the 19th of December, and the 8th of January, except in cases where the behaviour of Colonel Henley, at other times, served to elucidate the principles and designs upon which he acted upon those particular days. After making this observation, as to the distinction in the charge, the General opened the prosecution.

" *Mr.*

" Mr. Prefident, and Gentlemen of the
" Court,

" I prefent myfelf as profecutor before
" you, in charges of a heinous nature
" againſt Colonel Henley;—and, before
" I proceed to adduce the evidence in ſup-
" port of them, I think it a duty to my
" ſtation, and a part of propriety towards
" the Court, to declare the principles upon
" which I act.

" If the reports in my hand, and which
" will prefently be brought to teſt upon
" oath, do not deceive me, public faith
" has been ſhaken, wanton barbarities
" have been committed, and a general
" maſſacre of the troops under my care,
" apparently threatened. In objects of
" this magnitude, where not only the
" rights of a ſingle nation, but the inte-
" reſts of human nature are concerned, the
" conduct

" conduct of the prosecution falls naturally
" (however disagreeable the office, and
" unequal the talents of the person) to him
" who has the supreme trust upon the
" spot.

" A second inducement to appear here,
" is that of private honor. I have un-
" dertaken to accuse Colonel Henley,
" in a degree that ought to affect the feel-
" ings of a soldier nearer than life. It is
" fit I stand forth, in person, to maintain
" my accusation, and if it fails in point of
" proof, to make him the fullest atone-
" ment in my power.

" I acknowledge a third impulsion upon
" my mind, equally irresistible;—grati-
" tude, esteem and affection to that meri-
" torious, respectable part of my country,
" the brave and honest British soldier—
" a private man, defenceless, because un-
" armed, ignorant of your laws, unqua-
" lified

" lified to make good his caufe in a court
" of juftice, and who has not to look for
" redrefs of injury to his own officers.—
" I confefs I am too felfifh to refign to any
" brother officer the pride and gratifica-
" tion of ftanding in the front, for the
" defence of men, faithful comrades of
" honor and misfortune,——who have
" fought bravely under my orders, who
" have bled in my prefence, and who are
" now expofed to oppreffion and perfecu-
" tion, by the abufe of a treaty figned by
" my hand.

" Thus much I thought proper to pre-
" mife, left any man fhould fuppofe me
" actuated by fo mean and paltry a mo-
" tive, as vindictive perfonal refentment,
" againft a gentleman too, of whom, be-
" fore thefe tranfactions, I could know no
" harm, and towards whom, if I had any
" prejudice, I ferioufly declare it was, from
" his general deportment, a prejudice of
" favor—

" favor—perſonal reſentment ?—No, gen-
" tlemen, I ſtand upon broader and firmer
" ground—the ground of natural rights,
" perſonal protection and public honor,—
" and I appeal to the great principles and
" land marks by which human ſocieties
" hold and are directed, and which, whe-
" ther in ſituations of amity or hoſtility,
" are eſteemed equally ſacred by the uni-
" verſal concurrence of civilized man.

" And this leads me to a momentary re-
" flection upon the order under which
" you ſit, originating from the report of
" the Court of Enquiry.

" It ſtates—*That the Court, after mature*
" *conſideration, are of opinion, that from the*
" *evidence offered on the ſide of General Bur-*
" *goyne againſt Colonel Henley, it will be moſt*
" *for the honor of* COLONEL HENLEY, *as*
" *well as for the ſatisfaction of all intereſted,*
" *that the judgment of a Court Martial ſhould*
" *be*

" *be taken on his conduct, during his command*
" *at Cambridge. The General approving the*
" *opinion of the Court, orders, &c.*

" I confess, I expected General Heath
" would have joined issue with the prose-
" cutor, in this instance, and placed the
" Court-martial upon a more enlarged
" basis than the honor of an individual,
" however respectable he may be, or the
" satisfaction of the complainants.—But
" be it as it may, my purpose is answered,
" a Court-martial is obtained, the mem-
" bers are sworn, and they are bound to
" decide."

" I know you will feel with me the
" difference between this and common
" courts; such a state of the minutes as
" would suffice for your internal convic-
" tion, after hearing the evidence, or as
" would be merely explanatory to the per-
" son who is to confirm the sentence, will
" not

"not be thought sufficient here. You
"well know the whole of this matter will
"be published, translated, considered and
"commented upon by every nation in the
"world :—not only *reality*, but *perspicuity*
"of justice must appear upon the face of
"the proceedings. You are trustees for
"the honor of an infant State, and there-
"fore evasion, subterfuge and law-craft"
(an allusion to the Judge Advocate Tudor,
who is a lawyer at Boston) " were any
"man hardy enough to offer such at
"your tribunal, would be of no avail;
"nay, were it possible any member could
"be warped unintentionally by personal
"favor, or prejudice of civil contest (good
"minds are sometimes prone to such illu-
"sions) yet here a moment's reflection
"upon the reputation of his country,
"would retrieve his reason, and what his
"prejudice would incline him to adopt,
"policy would prompt him to reject."

"Upon

"Upon the full confidence, therefore, "of the neceffary, as well as willing "juftice of the court, I fhall proceed "to call the evidence. I have neither in-"clination or powers to heighten the "facts by a previous narrative; let them "ftrike the view as truth fhall fhew them "in all the fimplicity of their horrors—a "monftrous fpectacle, from which the "mind and eye will turn afide with de-"teftation."

Here a variety of evidence fully proved the accufation of the crimes I mentioned in my laft, befides various others which you will perceive commented on, when the General clofed the charge.

After a full examination of the evidence in fupport of the profecution, the Judge Advocate made an objection to the General making any obfervations on it, arguing, that if he was permitted, it muft be upon the

the principle of indulgence, not of right; and after some little altercation between the Judge Advocate and the General, the Court acquiesced, when General Burgoyne proceeded as follows:

"*Mr. President and Gentlemen of the
"Court,*"

"It being now admitted, that in closing
" the evidence I may offer such argu-
" ments as to me shall seem proper, in
" support of the charge, and reserving to
" myself a claim of replying to the de-
" fence, I shall enter upon the first part
" of the very painful, though by no
" means difficult undertaking—painful,
" because I cannot pursue the offender
" without setting that offender in points
" of view, at which every benignant mind
" must shudder—easy in every other re-
" spect is the talk, because I will venture
" to pronounce the evidence, when ar-
" ranged and adjusted, will amount to
" such

"such a mass of proof as cannot be over-
"thrown, and will authorize and call for
"the strongest terms I can use, in my
"demand of public justice. And, Gen-
"tlemen, let me be permitted to assume
"to myself applause rather than blame,
"that the evidence has not been laid be-
"fore you in a regular series; the reason
"was, that though assured by the reports
"made to me, that the evidence would
"produce conviction upon the whole, I
"was ignorant how the testimony of the
"particular witnesses would apply, and
"point to the progession of the charges,
"because I had no previous intercourse
"with them. I declare upon my solemn
"word and honor, that I had no con-
"cern or communication, directly or in-
"directly, with any non-commissioned
"officer or soldier who has appeared at
"your bar, one only excepted, viz. Ser-
"jeant Fleming, of the 47th regiment,
"who has deposed to the salutation Co-
"lonel

"lonel Henley gave him and his comrades
"at the Adjutant General's office; the
"whole matter appeared so very impro-
"bable, that I not only sent for the Ser-
"jeant, to warn him of the sacredness of
"an oath, and the crime of intemperate
"zeal that led to bearing false witness;
"but also I thought it my duty to enquire
"minutely into his character.—I found
"the man firm and uniform in asserting
"his facts; and I found his officers una-
"nimous in supporting the credit of his
"veracity."

"In every other circumstance I adhered
"religiously to the determination I had
"taken, of secluding myself from the
"witnesses, not only to guard my cha-
"racter, in this region of suspicion and
"aspersion, against the supposition of un-
"fair practices;---I besides had a scruple
"of trusting my own mind with too
"hasty prepossessions in a cause, where,
                                    "with

" with the solemn matter of a public na-
" ture, is involved the fate of a gentle-
" man, high in his military station, and
" to judge by the apparent signs of good
" wishes on this day, high in popular
" esteem.

" Thus unprejudiced I came into Court.
" I scorn to take the slighter matters that
" might be comprehended in the general
" words of the charge, such as personal
" incivility to the officers, expressions and
" actions of peevishness, haughtiness and
" disgust. I mean not to press, that they
" existed, or if they did, I am desirous that
" they should pass as faults of temper and
" deficiencies of manners, incident to
" man's nature, education, and habitual
" course of life; and I shall confine my
" comments, as it is my duty to do, to the
" testimonies of your minutes, and the cir-
" cumstances relating to them.

" Without

"Without departing from this principle, it will be neceffary to take a general
view of the ftate of things, previous to the
date of the grievances complained of.—
We arrived at Cambridge, paffengers
through your country, under the fanction
of a truce—in whatever capacity we had
been found in a foreign, and as you intend,
an independent ftate, we were entitled
to a perfonal protection, by the general
and moft facred laws of cuftom and
reafon; but when, to the promulgated
law of civilization, are added, the un-
written principles,—or written only
upon the hearts of generous people,—
honor, refpect for the brave, the hofpitable wifhes that ufually prefs to the relief of the unfortunate, the ftranger,
and the defenceless man in your power,
how will our claims multiply upon the
mind!— Sanguine imaginations conceived yet further motives for kindnefs;
there were among us men fo vain as to

"believe

" believe, that notwithstanding the sepa-
" ration between us, the different duties
" we now maintained, the prejudices of
" political zeal, and the animosity of civil
" war—yet still the conflict over, it might
" be remembered we once were brothers,
" and the more especially, as it was im-
" possible, by the convention of Saratoga,
" that the generality of us should ever op-
" pose America in arms again.

" We were led into these delusive hopes
" by the very honorable treatment shewn
" us by General Gates, by that we re-
" ceived from you, Mr. President,—(who
" was a Brigadier General Glover) when
" you conducted us upon the march, and
" by that we afterwards found from the
" worthy member of the Court near you,
" (a Colonel Lee) who had the imme-
" diate command in this district upon our
" arrival, and to whom, most happily

" for

"for us, the command is now again
"devolved."

"The first symptom we discovered of
"any uncandid design, was the mode
"established for correcting errors and dis-
"turbances in the troops of convention;
"men were taken up, imprisoned and
"otherwise punished by the American
"troops, without any prior reference to
"their own officers. I very well know with
"how much slight and severe derision my
"sentiments have been treated on this
"subject, but I still insist, that after tak-
"ing up men for faults, to have applied
"to the officers of the convention troops,
"in the first instance, for their punish-
"ment, would have been confonant to
"every principle of decorum and good
"policy, not meaning to deny, that upon
"any proof of partiality or connivance,
"or undue lenity, it then became a pro-
"per and indispensible duty of General
"Heath,

" Heath, to take the distribution of justice
" into his own hands."

"The contrary maxim having been
" established, let us examine, in point of
" time, though the last in the proceed-
" ings, that burst of independency, scur-
" rility and impiety, from Colonel Henley
" to the Quarter-master Serjeants at the
" Adjutant-General's Office. It is not
" without difficulty I can frame my
" mouth to read the words, as they were
" delivered upon oath, by that very re-
" spectable witness, Serjeant Fleming,—
" *You rascals, &c. I'll make damnation fly*
" *out of you, and I will myself one of these*
" *nights go the rounds, and if I hear the*
" *least word or noise in your barracks, I'll*
" *pour shot amongst you, and make flames of*
" *Hell jump out of ye, and turn your bar-*
" *racks inside out.*"

" The

"The Court will remember, that when
"this evidence was given, it rather ex-
"cited laughter in some part of the au-
"dience, than any serious condemnation;
"this day it seems to make a very dif-
"ferent impression——the minds of all
"around follow me while I contend, that
"expressions so wild, so unfit, so unpre-
"cedented, from the mouth of a Gentle-
"man, argue the most horrid passions
"boiling in the breast——the very enthu-
"siasm of rage and malice.-----I defy any
"man to divest himself of that idea; it
"will attend the mind through the whole
"course of the proceedings, and cast a
"shocking glare over every subsequent
"transaction, of fore-thought intention,
"and bloody resolution."

"It is very material to observe, that
"this demonstration of Colonel Henley's
"mind was on or about the 16th of
"December, and it was no longer than
"till

" till the 19th, before he confirmed by
" an overt-act, the principles he had
" profeſſed."

" The ſtabbing of Corporal Reeves is
" proved by the evidence of Corporal
" Buchanan, Alexander Thomſon, and
" Robert Steel.

" I ſhall quote indiſcriminately from
" the teſtimony of theſe witneſſes, becauſe
" though one may recollect a few ſhort
" paſſages or words more than another,
" there is not a ſhadow of contradiction,
" and I am confident, there never was an
" inſtance where truth was laid before
" a Court by united evidence, more per-
" ſpicuouſly."

" It has been ſworn, "*That on the morn-*
" *ing of the 19th of December, Colonel*
" *Henley went to the barracks, on Proſpect*
" *Hill, to releaſe ſome Britiſh ſoldiers, who*
were

" were prifoners; that having paraded them,
" he read over their crimes, and coming to
" Reeves, told him he was confined for in-
" fulting a Provincial Officer. Reeves made
" anfwer, he was forry for it; that he was
" in liquor, and would not have acted fo,
" had he known him to have been an Officer."

" I paufe here to apply to the feelings
" of the Court, whether a more decent,
" proper and fatisfactory excufe could
" have been conceived——what did it draw
" from the Colonel?——" Had it been me
" you ferved fo, I would have run you through
" the body, you rafcal." Continue the comparifon between the language of the Colonel and the Corporal:——" Sir, I am no
" rafcal, but a good foldier, and my officers
" know it; and I hope foon to be with General
" Howe, and fight for my King and country."
What did this produce from the Colonel?
" Damn your King and Country, and an
" order to the guard to run him through
" the

" the body---not a hand nor a heart could
" be found for the butchery. The Colonel,
" enraged at the virtuous difobedience of
" his men, leaps from his horfe, feizes a
" firelock with a fixed bayonet, and ſtrikes
" at the man's heart. I call upon the
" Gentleman of a learned profeſſion near
" me, to inform the Court, when he
" fums up the evidence at the clofe of the
" trial, whether this act would not con-
" conſtitute malice properiſe in law. I
" mean, that admitting, for the fake of
" argument, that there had been fuch
" provocation given, as would have juſti-
" fied a man having an offenfive weapon
" to make ufe of it inſtantly, which would
" have been only manflaughter, whether
" the intermediate act of difmounting a
" horfe, and taking a firelock from the
" other, implying time for recollection,
" would not have conſtituted the act of
" wilful murder, had the man died. Con-
" fider now, Gentlemen, what followed :
" the

"the brave Corporal, in the inſtant ex-
"pectation that his words would coſt
"him his life, perſevered, "*I don't care, I
"will ſtand by my King and my Country till
"I die!*" The action would have charm-
"ed a brave man; it would have been a
"ſpell upon his arm, and kept the ſtroke
"ſuſpended beyond the power of witch-
"craft—what effect had it upon the Co-
"lonel? To provoke a ſecond ſtab, which
"was only diverted by the intervention of
"the man next him, who caught hold of
"the bayonet and threw it up."

"Gentlemen, when I ſay the perſever-
"ance of the Corporal ought rather to
"have pleaſed than provoked, I ſpeak
"not vaguely or romantically---I feel
"conſcious proof of the truth, and when
"I conſider the actions of a Waſhing-
"ton---when I meet in the field a Gates,
"an Arnold, a General Glover, and ſee
"them bravely facing death, in ſupport
"of

" of their principles—though I would
" shed my last blood upon a different con-
" viction, I cannot withhold from the
" enemy the respect due to the soldier;
" and the immediate conflict over, he
" robs me of my anger, and seizes my
" good will.

" Gentlemen, in the different parts of
" the examination upon this fact, many
" questions have been asked by the pri-
" soner, by the Judge Advocate, and by
" the Court, respecting the appearance of
" the prisoner's temper. Was he not in
" a mild mood?---Did he not seem good
" humored?-----Mild murder------Good
" humored murder-------are phrases, I
" fancy, will not convey any clear mean-
" ing, till men change their ideas of that
" crime! We hear, it is true, sometimes,
" as a sort of proverb, to mark the utmost
" malignity and treachery of a man smil-
" ing in your face while he cuts your
                                " throat;

" throat; but, I believe, such smiles were
" never produced as excuses or extenua-
" tion of guilt. These questions, there-
" fore, as I conceive, can have no ten-
" dency but to insinuate, that Colonel
" Henley's passion was entirely raised by
" the immediate provocation he received.
" I am ready to join issue upon this argu-
" ment, and if the gentlemen will rest his
" cause upon it, I will relinquish the
" proof established of Reeves's decency
" and consistency, and give him latitude
" for all the provocation he can suppose,
" short of personal assault, and the ne-
" cessity of self-defence, which I am sure
" will not be pretended---transpose, if he
" pleases, the time when Reeves is prov-
" ed to have talked about Ring Hancock,
" and bring it back to the instant where
" it was attempted to be introduced as a
" substantial matter of provocation. He
" shall add insolence of gesture to abusive
" terms, and under all these fictitious
      " circumstances,

" circumftances, I will take the judgment
" of the Court, whether Colonel Henley,
" with full powers to imprifon, and to
" punifh by regular, decent, legal proceed-
" ing, has a fhadow of juftification for
" making himfelf, in his own perfon,
" party, judge and exccutioner." De-
ferring the conclufion till another opportunity, and willing to embrace the very
favorable one that occurs. I remain

Yours, &c.

LETTER LI.

Cambridge, in New England,
March 6th 1778.

MY DEAR FRIEND,

WITHOUT any preface, I shall proceed to finish the General's addrefs, as if no delay had intervened.

" From the 19th of December, the hands
" of Colonel Henley were imbrued in
" blood, till the 5th of January; but it
" evidently appears upon your proceed-
" ings, that the influence of his example,
" and the encouragement of his precepts,
" failed not to operate. As the firft
                                    " proof

" proof of it, I requeſt the attention of
" the Court to the teſtimony of Colonel
" Lind, concerning the poſition of the
" centry, which was ſuch as muſt neceſſa-
" rily affect every paſſenger upon the
" public road, whenever he fired; and
" at the ſame time with a readineſs to do
" miſchief, ſo marked, that he took wo-
" men for his objects, and would not
" give them time to turn round, ' *he had
' orders ſo to do.*' Let the behaviour of the
" next centry, to whom Colonel Lind
" applied, concerning the ungentleman-
" like behaviour of the officer, with his
" confirmation of the whole proceeding,
" being ACCORDING TO ORDER, be com-
" bined and compared, and it muſt uni-
" verſally ſtrike common ſenſe, that theſe
" were ſeveral parts of one determined
" plan to diffuſe the ſeeds of diſcord and
" fury, in order afterwards to countenance
" a general havock.

" But, it may be said, the orders under
" which the continental troops acted,
" were not those of Colonel Henley, but
" of a superior. Will that be pleaded?
" Was the position of the centries to kill
" or wound three or four passengers at a
" shot, the firing upon women, the refusal
" of redress to Colonel Lind, with all the
" indecent manner and language attend-
" ing---will these circumstances be al-
" ledged to have proceeded from superior
" orders ?—If so, the excuse, indeed, be-
" comes more alarming to us. It is not
" my part, at this time, to drop a consider-
" ation that would lead far on that sub-
" ject, I shall only remark, how little the
" excuse would benefit Colonel Hen-
" ley, who would still remain a cruel agent
" of—(I will use no improper terms) I
" will only say, a cruel agent of too hasty
" principles.

" Colonel

" Colonel Henley has afked, whether
" complaints were made to him of the
" tranfactions of the 22d; I believe there
" were not—but I dare fay he will recol-
" lect the reafon—other grievances of the
" moft atrocious nature, abufe of officers,
" and affaults upon their lives, were pre-
" paring to be laid before General Heath:
" they were in number, and in time, to
" have filled up a much longer interval
" than between the 19th of December
" and the 8th of January, and not brought
" before this Court, becaufe I underftood
" it to be the intention of General Heath
" they fhould be feparately enquired into.
" Enough has appeared to fhew how the
" fyftem of perfecution was preferved, and
" I come now to the tranfaction of the
" 8th of January.

" Upon a general view of that black
" day, I am at a lofs where firft to carry
" your obfervation—the field was exten-

"five, the scenes separate and successive,
"but evidently guided by one uniform de-
"sign.——In one place, a party on the
"march are stabbing and knocking out
"the brains of innocent spectators——at
"another, men, under pretence of a pri-
"soner's escape, are glutting the same
"bloody purposes upon men not pretend-
"ed to be concerned—in a third, Colonel
"Henley, in person (the British officers at
"the same time being denied admittance,
"as appears by the evidence of Lieutenant
"Bibby) is running men through the
"body with his sword.

"The first of these complicated horrors,
"in point of time, was the attack first
"with the bayonet, and afterwards with
"the butt end of the firelock. I will
"read the evidence, without a comment"
(which was the evidence of Major Forster
of the twenty-first regiment, and Lieutenant Smith of the Artillery, who deposed,

posed, that they were within thirty yards, that they neither heard or saw any provocation or insult offered, but were counting the files of the guard; that when the rear came near the British Guard-room, they observed a scuffle, and the guard passed on; upon their going over, found Trudget had been wounded, and the blood running down his face; they ordered the men to disperse, which they did immediately; that there was a free passage for the Continental troops, and not the least dispute upon that subject. " I have only
" now to remark, it is rather a prepos-
" session in favor of the Continental
" troops, to suppose that such malici-
" ous treatment could proceed from a
" general sentiment; no body of people
" are so barbarous, unless instigated, and
" now is the time to call upon the learned
" Gentleman near me, for another duty
" of his office, to expound to the Court
" the principles of law, respecting acces-
" saries

" faries and accomplices, and to fay whe-
" ther a man, by order, advice, example,
" or any other encouragement, influencing
" another to do a mifchievous act, is not
" *particeps criminis*, at an hundred miles
" diftance, as much as if prefent on the
" fpot.

" The ftabbing of Wilfon follows in
" courfe of the evidence." (he was wounded in the fide by a Provincial foldier, whilft
he was parrying off the bayonet that
another was pufhing at him) " and it
" appears, as little comment is neceffary
" upon this, as upon the former action,
" further than to remark, that in this
" cafe, Colonel Henley is found to be ac-
" ceffary, not upon circumftantial, pre-
" fumptive and argumentative, but up-
" on pofitive proof, for it is fworn the
" action was done in his fight; that he
" made no attempt to prevent it, and
" though it be alledged, and even ad-
" mitted,

" mitted, that he was at too great a dis-
" tance, yet his giving no reprimand nor
" check to the soldiers, upon seeing the
" act committed, carries as direct a con-
" viction of approbation and encourage-
" ment, as if he had given open ap-
" plause.

" The last article to mark the thirst of
" blood, is the stabbing Corporal Hadley,
" and following Winks with threats of the
" same fate.—It would be superfluous to
" expatiate upon the strength of the
" proofs, the concurrence of witnesses,
" that there was no provocation to this
" deliberation and wantonness of bar-
" barity. The intention is so clear, in
" my opinion, against the probability of
" doubt, that I should not touch a mo-
" ment upon it, were it not that a very
" grave application was made to the
" Court, by the most respectable autho-
" rity in it, to consider of the nature of

" wounds,

" wounds, as matters of the greatest im-
" portance—and question upon question
" was put to the Surgeon, in every case,
" to find whether they were dangerous or
" not.—Is it possible that any Gentleman
" can mean to measure the degree of the
" crime by the depth of the wound, and
" to argue that a man may thrust a wea-
" pon into another's breast with impunity,
" provided he does not touch a mortal
" part! If this doctrine holds good, you
" ought to establish schools of anatomy
" for the education of young officers; the
" science of dissection should be added to
" the skill of the fencing-master, to train
" the pupils to that nicety of touch, that
" can feel to a hair's-breadth between
" death and life; a sort of fiddlestick dex-
" terity, that can run divisions upon veins
" and arteries, and stop short in time and
" tune to the thousandth part of a second.
" Really, Gentlemen, I am not willingly
" ludicrous upon this subject, but it is
                                " impossible

" impossible to treat such an argument
" gravely.----I dismiss it to my learned
" neighbour, with one more injunction to
" shew the Court, in law, that where a
" man passes a sword with violence at
" another's breast, whether the wound is
" a mere puncture, or goes to the hilt, the
" intentional guilt is the same.------I have
" only one matter further to observe, upon
" the cross-questioning of the witnesses;
" it has perhaps been wished to insinuate,
" that at the time of these violent proceed-
" ings, there was cause of apprehension
" the armed troops might be surrounded
" and overcome; the troops themselves
" will hardly thank their friends for that
" idea!—What, shall it be alledged that
" the militia of America, who, animated
" by their cause, have been self taught the
" use of arms; that body, where every
" man is supposed himself to be an host—
" shall such soldiers be apprehensive of
" danger, from half their number of un-
" armed

" armed, mercenary, minifterial flaves, for
" fuch I know they think us!—No, Gen-
" tlemen, I reject with you fo injurious a
" fuppofition; I give credit to the fpirit
" and force of your militia;—I do it feri-
" oufly and upon experience, and it is
" upon that credit I found this propofi-
" tion, that it being impoffible the officers
" and foldiers fhould be induced to acts
" of violence, by any apprehenfion of
" refiftance, it follows, by the faireft de-
" duction, that either there was more pre-
" valent malignity than ever appeared be-
" fore in the human heart, or that the
" whole proceeded from direction, order,
" and a fyftematical plan.

" Little more, I imagine, need be remark-
" ed, to apply the evidence to the feveral
" diftinct terms I have ufed in the charge.
" That the whole tenor of Colonel Hen-
" ley's conduct was heinoufly criminal, as
" an Officer, will hardly be difputed, in a
" country

" country where the principles of liberty
" have been so deeply studied. An army
" is not to be borne in a free State, but
" upon the principle of defence against an
" outward enemy, or the protection of the
" laws.—The officer who makes himself
" the Arbiter of the Law, is guilty of the
" most shameful perversion of moral duty,
" and his impunity would scarcely be
" thought a very comfortable presage of
" the growing liberties of his country.

" I have also said, the Colonel's beha-
" viour was unbecoming a man.—I will
" not trifle with the time or understanding
" of the Court, to enter into definitions
" upon this term, nor will I shock the
" ears of Officers, nor even of the unfor-
" tunate person under trial, with so gross a
" term as the world in general apply to
" the act of assaulting a woman, a priest,
" or unarmed man, for they are all exactly
" in the same predicament. The sword
" drawn

" drawn for such a purpose is no longer
" the badge and distinction of a gentle-
" man; it is degraded with the imple-
" ments of the assassin and hangman, and
" contracts a stain that can never be wiped
" away.

I cannot help remarking to you, for
I was in Court that day, at the conclusion of this last sentence, the Colonel
changed color, and appeared bursting
with rage; but to proceed——

" Gentlemen," says the General,—" I
" have now gone through the material
" parts of the proceedings; whether the
" offences are resolved into vindictive
" resentment, or more deep design, or
" both, it must still appear wonderful
" that a general massacre did not ensue.—
" By the patience and the discipline of
" the British soldiers, those horrors have
" been avoided; but whatever the escape
" may

" may have been upon our part, it is
" tenfold more material on yours. We
" might, *perhaps*, for the struggles of the
" desperate are hard----but, *perhaps*, we
" might have been sacrificed to the last
" man—we should thus have paid a sol-
" dier's debt, which we have often risqued;
" our fall would have been revenged, and
" our memories attended with pity and
" honor.----But for America, the trans-
" actions would have remained a foul and
" indelible blot in the first page of her
" New History, nor would any series of
" disavowal and penitence, nor ages of
" rectitude in government, purity in man-
" ners, inflexible faith, or the whole ca-
" talogue of public virtues, have redeem-
" ed her in the opinion of mankind."

Here the Court was struck with much awe, and seemed to be impressed with a resolve to act impartially-----but to return to the General's speech——

" Now,

" Now, Gentlemen, confider the words
" of the order under which you fit----re-
" form the opinion of the Court of En-
" quiry, and fay, whether it is the *honor*
" of Colonel Henley, or the honor of
" America, by which your minds ought
" to be impreffed, when they proceed to
" judgment in this caufe. I clofe with
" that confideration, as far as I can im-
" imprefs it upon your breafts-----I truft
" they are replete and pregnant with juf-
" tice, honor, and duty to your profef-
" fion; and above all, with that glorious
" whig principle, the words of which are
" become almoft a general motto in this
" country, and the genuine fubftantial
" practice of which I fhall ever revere in
" any country, *a due fenfe of the general*
" *rights of mankind.*" I truft you have all
" thefe qualities, and in that perfuafion,
" I cannot doubt what will be the iffue
" of the caufe."

" After

After the General had finished, the evidence for the prisoner was adduced, which went fully to substantiate the evidence of the witnesses for the prosecution, making only this addition, that Reeves, &c. gave great provocation.— After the evidence for the prisoner was finished, Colonel Henley read a paper, which he had signed, attested by the Judge Advocate, and declined saying any thing further in his defence.

Mr. President and Gentlemen of the Court.

" I have particular reasons, and in *my*
" *own* apprehensions very sufficient, for
" declining to say a single word, in answer
" to the illiberal abuse thrown upon me,
" and the palpable dishonor done to my
" country, by General Burgoyne, in this
" Court.----It is, Mr. President, a new
" thing under the Sun, and, taken in all
" its

" its circumstances, totally without ex-
" ample

" The Judge Advocate will sum up the
" evidence with ability and impartiality.
" Such is my consciousness of having done
" nothing through this whole affair, but
" what the honor and safety of my coun-
" try absolutely required, that I shall rest
" entirely satisfied with your decision, be-
" ing at the same time fully persuaded,
" that the impartial public, at whose bar
" I stand, will join with you in acquitting
" me from all the injurious and illiberal
" charges of General Burgoyne, and that
" they will vindicate me for that huma-
" nity, characteristic of an American
" Officer, and with which the officers and
" soldiers of General Burgoyne's army
" have been treated, while I was honor-
" ed with the command of the Guards."

To

To this poor defence, which the Colonel and the Judge Advocate were several days in framing, with a review of the evidence in defence of the prisoner, the General made an immediate reply, which I must defer to my next, till when, I remain

. Yours, &c.

LETTER LII.

Cambridge, in New England,
March 12th, 1778.

MY DEAR FRIEND,

NO doubt, long before you receive this, you will be anxious for the General's reply to the invective defence of the Colonel.—I therefore take up my pen, and only wish this had not to cross the Atlantic to ease your anxiety.

" *Mr. President, and Gentlemen of the*
" *Court.*"
" On the day of your last adjournment,
" the Judge Advocate notified to me, that
                                                        " the

" the Court had agreed I should reply to
" Colonel Henley's defence, but had di-
" rected that the reply should be made
" immediately after the Colonel closed:
" He added, that all interested are to at-
" tend and come prepared.

" I did not judge, from the manner in
" which the Court have treated me hither-
" to, that in any instance they meant me
" uncandidly. I therefore suppose, that
" when they made it a point I should
" come prepared to answer, off hand, ar-
" guments which might have been a
" month in framing, they saw the evi-
" dence before them in so strong a view,
" that no argument, on my part, could
" be necessary----Did I want further con-
" fidence in this opinion, I could not fail
" of deriving it in a most ample degree,
" from the conduct of the prisoner, who
" has been just now constrained, by his
" situation, to substitute invective for ar-
" gument,

" gument, and to recriminate, where it
" was impossible to defend. Under the
" sanction of the Court, and the circum-
" stances of the time, this *candid* Gentle-
" man has ventured to make use of terms
" to which my ears have not been accus-
" tomed; but he is mistaken if he thinks
" to draw from me an intemperate reply;
" on the contrary, as conductor of this
" prosecution, I have rather to thank him
" for his assistance. After having furnish-
" ed me, during the whole course of what
" is called his defence, with evidence to
" corroborate the facts alledged against
" him, he at last steps forth a volunteer
" witness (the most undeniable one sure
" that ever came before a Court) to prove
" the heat of his own temper, which is of
" itself a material part of his accusation.
" This remark is the only return I shall
" at present address to the prisoner, for
" the expressions he has used; but I can-
" not quit the subject, without seriously
                                  " appealing

" appealing to the recollection of the
" Court, whether, from the outfet, I did
" not, in the moft pofitive terms, difavow
" all perfonal refentment, and whether
" the ftrongeft language which the courfe
" of my duty, as profecutor, led me to
" ufe, did not invariably arife from the
" facts, and apply to the offence more
" than to the offender. I make the fame
" appeal againft the accufation of " *hav-*
" *ing done palpable difhonor to the country*
" *in this Court.*" Is it to do palpable dif-
" honor to a country to appeal to the
" juftice of it?----It puzzles my intellects
" to conceive the meaning of this laft ex-
" preffion; but indeed, Sir, I want no
" other vindication than your filence, to
" prove that I have not abufed the lati-
" tude I poffeffed in either cafe; for would
" you, Mr. Prefident, or any member of
" the Court, have fuffered a profecutor to
" infult an unhappy man, under trial,
" with illiberal abufe? Still lefs would

L 3 " you

" you have suffered the country to be
" treated opprobiously. It is for Colonel
" Henley to reconcile with his respect to
" the Court, charges, which if founded,
" would be a general reflection upon their
" conduct.

" I understand great expectation has
" been raised of a very elaborate defence
" on the part of Colonel Henley, and ac-
" knowledge I myself little thought he
" would throw up his cause quite so con-
" fessedly, though I was always sure, that
" neither ingenuity nor sophistry, nor all
" the talents which the ablest counsel
" could assist him with, would be suffi-
" cient to effect the great leading proposi-
" tion upon which I ground myself, as
" upon an immoveable rock, viz. that the
" proofs on the part of the prosecution
" do not only remain unimpeached, but
" are augmented and enforced in the most
" material

" material parts, by the evidence produced
" in the defence.

" Gentlemen, a very few obfervations
" will fuffice to juftify this affertion.

" The firft part of the charge which the
" prifoner brings evidence to oppofe, is
" that concerning Coporal Reeves, on the
" 19th of December, and the firft evidence
" is Major Sweafey, an officer of rank and
" truft in your army, warm in the pre-
" fent unhappy conteft, and naturally
" impreffed with inclinations to favor his
" countryman, his brother officer and
" friend. Yet, with all thefe circum-
" ftances to bias (fuch is the force of
" truth and honor upon that gentleman's
" mind) he proves to be the ftrongeft wit-
" nefs of the whole trial, on the fide of
" the profecution,

"The beginning of this Gentleman's
" relation is a confirmation of all the lead-
" ing circumstances mentioned by the
" other witnesses. The first new matter
" of evidence is, that when he, the Major,
" told Reeves he was a rascal, the Corporal
" made a reply to him (not to Colonel
" Henley) he was no more a rascal than
" he was, at which he raised his whip,
" and told him, if he did not hold his
" impertinence, he would strike him.—
" One circumstance of this part of the
" evidence cannot pass observation, viz.
" that the poor Corporal had two ag-
" gressors to answer instead of one.—The
" word, and the menaces attending that
" word *Rascal*, came to his ears on both
" sides. Another circumstance is equally
" observeable, and it stands upon your pro-
" ceedings, as a record of honor to Major
" Sweasey, that his warmth of temper was
" moved at the recital of Reeves's offence,
" to give a sharp rebuke, and to use an
" opprobrious

" opprobrious expreffion, but the idea of
" chaftifement went no further than a
" ftroke with a riding-whip—Happy had
" it been for the prifoner had he followed
" fo temperate an example.

" The Major's narrative proceeds in re-
" fpect to Colonel Henley's difmounting,
" catching the firelock and ftabbing
" Reeves, in conformity to all the wit-
" neffes for the profecution, except that
" the circumftance of ordering one of the
" guard to run the Corporal through is
" omitted, and his recollection being called
" to that circumftance, by a queftion in
" the crofs-examination, he replies, " *He
" did not hear him*" (but with a candor
" and tenderness to his oath, which never
" departs from him) he adds, " *He* MIGHT
" *have given fuch an order and I not hear it.*

" The foregoing evidence, therefore,
" is not fhaken by any contradiction, but
" it

" it is immediately after augmented by an
" entire new circumstance, viz. that after
" the first thrust, upon Reeves's still talk-
" ing to Colonel Henley, he stepped back,
" and made a motion to cock the firelock,
" and added, he would blow his brains
" out, or words to that effect, when a
" British soldier took hold of the firelock
" and threw it up. I request the Court
" to take notice, that Major Sweasey, un-
" called upon by any leading question,
" remembers that act which saved Reeves
" from a second thrust, accompanied per-
" haps with fire. Can any doubt be now
" entertained of Colonel Henley's resolu-
" tion? I think I have proof they were
" obvious to Major Sweasey, at the time,
" by the very remarkable part of the evi-
" dence, " *I then got off my horse* (a con-
" duct worthy his character, expressive of
" his apprehensions and his humanity)
" *and begged Colonel Henley to send Reeves*
" *to the Guard-house.*"——The other peti-
" tioners

" tioners joined their interceflion, and the
" man's life at laft was faved.

" It may perhaps be objected to this
" argument, that Major Sweafey, upon
" being afked, in the crofs-examination,
" whether he thought Colonel Henley
" made a thruft with an intent to injure
" or to filence the Corporal; anfwers, to
" filence him; for if he had pufhed his
" arm forward, he would have run him
" through.

" And in another place he makes ufe of
" the words, " to ftill him.

" I fcorn to infinuate, that a witnefs
" of the Major's defcription meant to keep
" a falvo upon his mind, and purpofely to
" ufe any term of ambiguity. I upon my
" honor believe, that when the Major
" makes ufe of the words to filence or to
" ftill, he means to terrify him till he held
" his

" his tongue; but I beg leave to observe,
" that great difference might be made in
" the Major's opinion, between the time
" the act was committed, and the time
" his sentiments are asked in Court.—The
" conversation with Colonel Henley, the
" belief of his other friends, and the can-
" dor of his own heart now persuaded
" him, that the Colonel's intents were in-
" nocent. His own interference and in-
" tercession mark his doubts, at least at
" the time, and did they not, the Court
" will hold themselves bound to act upon
" their own opinion, formed upon com-
" bination and comparison of circum-
" stances, and not upon the opinion of
" another, which is no evidence. They
" will also recollect, that this opinion
" goes only to the first stab, and is formed
" upon its not being forcible. It does
" not appear that the Major formed any
" opinion, nor indeed could he, upon
" what force would have been the second
                                    " stab

" ſtab of a man riſing in a paſſion, had
" it not been prevented by ſeizing the
" bayonet and his interceſſion.

" It is not neceſſary to trouble the
" Court with a review of any other parts
" of this upright evidence, which is long.
" The anſwers to the croſs queſtions in
" general go to a full confirmation of the
" narrative, with this one addition and
" aggravation of Colonel Henley's con-
" duct, that the Major thinks the lan-
" guage of Reeves was addreſſed more to
" himſelf than the Colonel, till after
" the ſtab.

" Captain Wild, of the Militia, is the
" next witneſs, and confirms the excuſe
" of Reeves, and every other circumſtance
" in the beginning of the affair, as ſtated
" by the former witneſſes, and by Major
" Sweaſey, except the ſmall difference that
" Colonel Henley, not Major Sweaſey,
" firſt

" firſt made uſe of the word Raſcal. He
" mentions afterwards another new cir-
" cumſtance, that the prior witneſs had
" forgot, viz. " *Reeves turning to Buchanan,*
" *and damning him, ſaying, why don't you*
" *ſtand up for your King and Country.*——
" *Buchanan deſired him to be ſtill. Reeves*
" *replied, God damn them all, I'll ſtand up*
" *for my King and Country while I have life;*
" *if I had arms and ammunition I would*
" *ſoon be with General Howe and be re-*
" *venged.*"----He afterwards relates, in a
" very circumſtantial manner, making the
" puſh at Reeves; " Reeves ſtepped back
" one foot, but the bayonet pricked him,"
" and the lifting up the piece a ſecond
" time, and Buchanan ſeizing it and turn-
" ing it aſide.

" Upon the croſs queſtioning, the wit-
" neſs gives nearly the ſame anſwers as
" Major Sweaſey, upon the matter of opi-
" nion of Colonel Henley's intention, and
" of

" of not hearing Colonel Henley order
" a man of the guard to run Reeves
" through, before he difmounted, but
" repeating the firſt, the manner in which
" this Gentleman expreſſes himſelf is re-
" markable: " *I believe you only meant
" to ſilence him, as you ſpoke mildly, till
" Reeves ſaid, God damn them all.*" That
" Captain Wild thought the Colonel was
" in a paſſion afterwards, is clear from
" his anſwer to the queſtion, " *whether
" it is a rule in the Continental ſervice, to
" ſilence men by the bayonet or ſword;* when
" he replied, *it is not, but when a man's
" temper is raiſed, he is apt to do things he
" would not at other times.*

" I cannot quit this evidence, without
" claſſing it with Major Sweaſey's, and
" while it does honor to the witneſs, in
" point of truth and candour, it is to be
" remarked, that it is alſo exceedingly cir-
" cumſtantial, new and leading circum-
" ſtances

" ftances are remembered, none forgot,
" except the order to the guard, and the
" Court will fee by and by, why I fo folicit
" their attention to thefe remarks.

" The witneffes that follow are indeed
" of a very different fort; the Court will
" recollect the appearance of the firft,
" Corporal Dean, he told his ftory very
" fluently, with that remarkable new
" incident of provocation in Corporal
" Reeves, who, he fwears pofitively, faid
" to Colonel Henley,—" *If I am a rafcal,*
" *you are a damned rafcal*; but after all this
" fluency and recollection, upon his crofs
" queftioning, neither encouragement, nor
" admonition, nor patience, nor leading
" queftion, could draw an anfwer that
" any man could underftand; and parti-
" cularly the Court will remember his
" filence and his countenance, when preffed
" to declare his fentiments upon the obli-
" gation of an oath; I will not be fo un
" candid

" candid as positively to pronounce upon
" guilt from appearance, but it is the great
" value of parole evidence, that a Court
" may see the manner, and thence form a
" judgment upon the credibility of a wit-
" ness.—From what probable cause did the
" confusion of this man arise?—It was
" not the awe of the Court; and it is fair
" to suppose it is a weakness of under-
" standing; consequently he was a fit sub-
" subject to be tutored, and if not wilfully
" perjured, led into a belief of more than
" he actually saw and heard.

" He is followed by a string of the best
" instructed young men that ever related
" a story in public----Elijah Horton, Silas
" Moss, James Brazer, Wedsworth Hor-
" ton, and John Beny, most of them lads
" of sixteen years of age.

" I need not recall to the Court the pre-
" cision of the recital of these youths, nor

" the manner of their delivery.---It was
" the exact tone and repetition of a fable
" at school, and so well was the lesson got
" by heart, that there was not a single
" difference in the arrangement, and scarce
" a syllable misplaced. But it is not only
" in the similitude of memory these youths
" are extraordinary, they are equally re-
" markable in the precision of their for-
" getfulness, with a recollection so acute,
" as to repeat verbatim a long story of
" Corporal Reeves, and the marked ex-
" pression of " *damned rascal*" to Colonel
" Henley; not one syllable was heard by
" any British witness, nor by those atten-
" tive, circumstantial, respectable witnesses
" Major Sweasey and Captain Wild; not
" one of the whole five can remember a
" word or circumstance respecting the
" Colonel's *damning Reeves's king and*
" *country, attempting a second pass, and*
" *being prevented by Buchanan's seizing*
" *the firelock*; to all of which all the
" other

" other witnesses have positively sworn.—
" Upon the whole, I contend, that no
" contradiction of witnesses could invali-
" date their testimony more than such an
" exact conformity in circumstances, sen-
" tences and words, when it was for the
" purpose of five persons to recollect the
" same story, and an equal conformity in
" the want of recollection in circum-
" stances, that must indispensibly have
" been as manifest to their observation, as
" to that of any other witness.

" I owe an apology to the Court for
" having dwelt upon the invalidation of
" these witnesses longer than was neces-
" sary; for the weakness of their instruc-
" tor, whoever he has been, has counter-
" acted his wickedness, and it would do
" no harm to this prosecution, to give a
" full scope to their testimony, because
" there is no maxim in law more clearly
" laid down, and more generally under-
" stood,

" stood, than that *" no affront by words or
" gestures only is a sufficient provocation, so
" as to excuse or extenuate such acts of vio-
" lence as manifestly endanger the life of
" another.*

" The next matter to which the wit-
" nesses in defence have gone, is the stab-
" bing of Trudgett on the 8th of January,
" and there likewise their testimony has
" served to aggravate, instead of contra-
" dicting the charge. Serjeant Kettle, in
" particular, expressly says, he thought the
" soldiers *deserved stabbing*, as they would
" not get out of the way; and in another
" place, that laughing and sneering *as it
" were* (which he acknowledges was the
" only provocation) was sufficient to jus-
" tify stabbing.

" I shall give the Court no trouble upon
" the evidence brought to prove the *pro-
" vocation* of a rescue; the escape of
                                    " Buchanan

" Buchanan was not heard without a
" fmile in Court, nor can it be ferioufly
" commented on, except in the anfwer
" of Efell Pierce, a lad of fixteen, to
" the Judge Advocate, who afked him
" whether he thought he run the Britifh
" foldier into the body; " *I believe I did*
" (fays he triumphantly) *I pufhed as hard*
" *as I could, and with a good will—he cried*
" *out God damn you.*" This is but one of
" feveral inftances that might be felected
" from thefe proceedings, to fhew the de-
" gree of rancor to which the minds of
" the American foldiers were excited.
" Children that had fcarcely loft the tafte
" of their mother's milk, acquired a thirft
" for blood----among thofe from whom
" they took the example; the Colonel
" thinks a man deferves death if he looks
" fulky; the Serjeant thinks the fame if
" he fmiles. Good God! What is the
" value of a Britifh life, at fuch a time,
" in fuch hands.

" In

"In a former part of these proceedings, I expressed my desire that the Judge-Advocate would explain to the Court the established principles of law, respecting absent persons being accessaries to offences which they have in any manner influenced, and almost every sentence that has fallen from the last witness upon the affair of Trudgett, is a new call to press the consideration of those principles. I am persuaded the learned gentleman will not contradict me, in the few more leading propositions I shall add to those I mentioned on a former occasion, First, *"Any man advising, influencing, or countenancing another, be it by words, reward or example, to do mischief, is an accessary at a distance.* Secondly, *Though mischief is committed by different means than those proposed between instigator and perpetrator; for instance——A. persuades B. to poison C. he kills him by any other means; A. is accessary.*

" *fary*. Thirdly, *When the principal goes
" beyond the term of folicitation, if in the
" event the mifchief committed was a proba-
" ble confequence of what was ordered or ad-
" vifed; the perfon giving fuch orders or ad-
" vice will be acceffary.*

" Apply the above maxims:—Colonel
" Henley directs his men only to knock
" down any Britifh foldier, who they think
" looks fulky at them (you have feen that
" he often thought a much greater punifh-
" ment was due for fuch a crime as a fulky
" look) but we will fuppofe, he only or-
" ders them to knock a man down, or *to*
" *prick him* or *ftill him*, and a foldier fires
" down a common road, fticks his bayonet
" into one, and ftrikes at the brains of
" another with the butt of his firelock,
" Colonel Henley is a party to the mif-
" chief, whatever it may be, and upon a
" continuation of the principle laid down
" before,—" *The advice, orders or influence,*
" *are*

" *are flagitious on the part of* A---*the events*
" *falling out beyond his original intention,*
" *are in the ordinary courſe of things the pro-*
" *bable conſequence of what* B. *does under the*
" *influence, and at the inſtigation of* A.---*and*
" *therefore, in the juſtice of the law, he is*
" *anſwerable for them.*

" So much, Sir, for the enormities com-
" mitted under the orders, influence, en-
" couragement and example of Colonel
" Henley, when he was not preſent; as
" for the reſt, it is needleſs for me to fol-
" low the witneſſes brought by the Colonel
" through all the parts, wherein they ſe-
" verally and diſtinctly confirm the former
" evidence, upon the charges reſpecting
" the attempt upon Wilſon in the Colo-
" nel's ſight, and of the ſtabbing Hadley
" with his own hands.—I ſhall only re-
" mark one very ſtriking circumſtance, a
" little previous to the latter fact, which
" came out upon the ſecond examination
" of

"of that very honorable and fenfible gen-
"tleman, Major Sweafey.——After Bu-
"chanan had run away, Colonel Henley
"(having firft ordered fome men to load,
"and put himfelf at the head of the whole
"detachment) afked Major Sweafey what
"method he thought they fhould take to
"recover Buchanan: the Major faid "*the
"beft way would be to acquaint the Britifh
"Commanding Officer on the Hill, and he
"made no doubt but he would give him up im-
"mediately.*" The Major went with a
"meffage from Colonel Henley to Major
"Fofter, the Britifh officer then com-
"manding, who ordered the man to be
"fought for and confined.-----I ftate this
"circumftance to fhew, not only what
"was the proper and ready method of
"avoiding differences and ill blood in
"fact, but alfo to fhew that this method
"was proper in the judgment of your
"own temperate officers.-----The Major
"prceeds to fay, that Colonel Henley ap-
"peared

"peared perfectly satisfied with the an-
"swer he brought from Major Foster, but
"it is well worthy remark, that the vio-
"lent act of stabbing Hadley, was com-
"mitted in the interim of Major Sweasey's
"leaving Colonel Henley and his return.

"The whole stress of the evidence upon
"the defence I have not remarked upon,
"goes to one single point, viz. to prove
"provocation. I have admitted that a
"centry was knocked down, as I readily
"admit every slighter provocation alledg-
"ed, and shall not give a moment's trou-
"ble to the Court, in addition to what I
"argued and quoted in a former part of
"the proceedings upon this subject, from
"undeniable authority of law----I assume
"it to be undeniable, because I under-
"stand, gentlemen, that the criminal and
"common law of England, as well as great
"part of the Statute Law, are, notwith-
"standing your present separation, in
"force

" force and practice in your Government,
" and that your articles of war are almoſt
" tranſcripts from ours.

" The maxims then, to which I have
" alluded will hold equally good in martial
" and other judicatures.

" I have only, Sir, to revert to the lead-
" ing propoſition, and affirm that the
" charges are proved in the fulleſt man-
" ner, even by the priſoner's witneſſes.
" It is not for me to ſuggeſt an opinion
" upon the nature of puniſhment. I
" ſcorn the idea of feeling joy from the
" moſt rigorous ſentence; and the moſt
" perfect acquittal would not harm me
" further, than that ſuch an example
" might continue the inſecurity of the
" troops. Inflexible and impartial juſtice,
" and rigid diſcipline, are the vital prin-
" ciples upon which a Republic riſes to
" maturity, and eſtabliſhes itſelf in reſpect
                              " and

" and fame——Should the Court, upon
" due reflection, find these principles re-
" concileable with lenity in the present
" case, and the great tribunal of the world
" be of a contrary judgment, this cause
" cannot be said to have miscarried.

" As to the displeasure which this pro-
" secution may bring upon me, I fear, in
" the present temper of this part of the
" country, it is not to be avoided. I
" stand in this circle, at best an unpopular,
" with the sanguine enemies of Britain,
" perhaps an obnoxious character. This
" situation, though disagreeable, does not
" make me miserable. I wrap myself in
" the integrity of my intentions, and can
" look round me with a smile. Implaca-
" ble hatred is a scarce weed in every soil,
" and soon is overcome and lost, under
" the fairer and more abundant growth of
" cultivated humanity.—To the multitude
" who only regard me with the transient
" anger

" anger that political opinions and the oc-
" currences of the time occasion, I retain
" not a thought of resentment, because I
" know the disposition and hour will
" come, when *steadiness of principle*, that
" favorite characteristic in America, will
" recommend me amongst my worst ene-
" mies: As Christians I trust they will
" forgive me; in spite of prejudice I know
" they will respect me.

" But from the present resentful senti-
" ments of this audience, should I carry
" my apprehension further, and suppose
" it possible that misapprehension or mis-
" representation of my conduct, should
" operate upon the supreme rulers of this
" country to treat me with severity, I hope
" I should still find myself prepared.---Let
" suspension be added to suspension, and
" health and fortune, and fame, and life,
" become successive forfeits in this lingering
" war—I shall lay at last down my devoted
" head

"head with this confolitary reflection,
"that I have done what I ought----that I
"have performed to the beft of my power
"my duty to my country, to the Britifh
"troops under my charge, and to my-
"felf----and above all, it will be confola-
"tion to reflect, that however mifinter-
"preted or abufed, I have acted in all
"inftances, and fpecifically in this trial,
"without a fpark of private malice to-
"wards any individual foever. With this
"declaration I opened, with the fame I
"conclude, and have only to affure the
"Court of my acknowledgements for the
"patience, the attention, and the civility
"which they have heard me."

Common juftice—the laws of Nature and of arms, were never more forcibly depicted, that in this flight of ingenuity and of eloquence, in which nothing appeared more confpicuous than truth, nor blazed higher than humanity—determined

prejudice

prejudice and enthufiaftic rage alone could withftand it—you might read conviction itfelf in every face, afhamed to be convicted—and fee, what will perhaps never be feen again, the blufh of confcioufnefs on the cheek of an American——for black as their hearts are, their countenance feldom betrays them.---Thefe are my fentiments, abftracted from party or intereft, God fend I may have reafon to change them.

Yours, &c.

LETTER LIII.

Cambridge, in New England,
March 20, 1778.

MY DEAR FRIEND,

BY this time you are become highly interested for the issue of this trial, and therefore I sit down to give you the Judge Advocate's reply, and the sentence of the Court. After the General had finished his speech, Mr. Tudor, the Judge Advocate, a little vain conceited fellow, in a pert flippant manner, addressed the Court as follows:

" Mr.

" *Mr. President, and Gentlemen of the
" Court.*

" It has at laſt become my duty to ſum up theſe proceedings, which by accidents and other unavoidable cauſes, have been drawn on to this period; they have excited much talk and public diſquiſition, but have acquired greater force from the abilities of the proſecutor, than from their real merits.

" Pains have been taken, and every alluring art has been uſed to perſuade the Court to conſider what may be the popular opinion in other countries; but, gentlemen, though it was neceſſary for the *public honor*, that Colonel Henley ſhould be removed from his command, that firſt a Court of Enquiry, and then a Court-martial ſhould be held, you will now regard the merits as they affect the Officer under trial, and the ſervice of the States alone.-----The Court ſits upon
" truth

" truth and honor, the ſtrongeſt ties upon
" ſoldiers; you will decide upon thoſe
" motives, and upon juſtice, and your pro-
" ceedings will ever remain a teſtimony
" againſt any men who would dare to ac-
" cuſe you of partiality.

" It is now my duty to ſtate the facts
" as they riſe from the evidence, ſtripped
" of all that meretricious colouring which
" uncommon ingenuity and refined elo-
" quence have thrown upon it. It is not
" my intention to catch the crowd by
" well turned periods; I am ſenſible of
" my deficiency.-----I am an American,
" warmly attached to my country, known
" to be a friend to the priſoner---yet, not-
" withſtanding thoſe reaſons may with the
" jealous ſubject me to cenſure, I ſhall
" endeavour to preſerve as impartial a line
" as poſſible----I am determined in this
" cauſe to be of no party.

" Inſinuations

"Infinuations of a general maffacre have been dreffed out in all the pomp which attic language could give, and wanted only truth to have made it felt as far as the public were concerned. It is unneceffary to fay more upon that fubject; I have endeavoured to reduce the other charges into method, and propofe to feparate them into five facts, in all of which Colonel Henley is confidered as a principal or an acceffary.

"The firft is as a principal, with refpect to ftabbing, wounding, or pricking (for it has been called by each of thefe terms) Corporal Reeves, of the ninth regiment.

"The next is to prove a Provincial Serjeant having ftabbed Thomas Trudgett, of the twenty-fourth regiment; Colonel Henley in this appears only an acceffary.

" The third is the ſtabbing of Wilſon,
" in which likewiſe he is conſidered as an
" acceſſary.

" The fourth fact alludes to the ſtab-
" bing Corporal Hadley, in which Colonel
" Henley is a principal.

" The laſt contains a general principle,
" not only of all the American officers
" being bloodily inclined towards the Bri-
" tiſh troops, but that Colonel Henley
" foſtered and encouraged principles of
" this bloody nature.

" The evidence, gentlemen, muſt be
" read, and I ſhall firſt read that of the
" proſecution, and then that in ſupport
" of the defence, fact by fact.

" The firſt fact is with reſpect to Colo-
" nel Henley's ſtabbing Reeves (*here be*
" *read the evidence on both ſides.*)——It
" may

" may be neceffary to mention a few cir-
" cumftances.

" It appears from the evidence of Major
" Sweafey, that Colonel Henley went to
" the barracks with the temper of a man
" going to gratify benevolent feelings.

" The prifoners were ordered out and
" paraded, and the Colonel addreffed them
" mildly.'

" The Court fits to judge of the credi-
" bility of the witneffes; there may be
" characters of fo fufpicious a nature that
" though they cannot be abfolutely ac-
" cufed of perjury, yet circumftances ap-
" pear ftrong againft them.

" The Court will be pleafed to recol-
" lect, that Buchanan was afterwards the
" means of getting Hadley ftabbed, and
" the Court will give what regard they
" chufe

"chuse to the credibility of his testimony:
"Upon the whole, it appears, that Reeves
"behaved with great insolence. It may
"be collected, that his looks and manners
"were more provoking than his words,
"which may frequently be the case, yet
"with all this provocation, there is no
"reason to suppose the Colonel even in-
"tended more than to frighten him to
"silence; the very act shews it, the
"bayonet was placed against his breast,
"not thrust with violence; this appears
"from the testimony of many witnesses,
"and the arguments to invalidate some
"of them are very uncommon, viz. that
"they have exactly agreed. I beg the
"Court to recollect with what an air of
"sincerity, as well as acuteness, one of
"the youths, in particular, gave his evi-
"dence: His ingenious manner must have
"made an impression.

"The

" The General has called upon me to
" explain, whether Colonel Henley's dif-
" mounting and taking a firelock was not
" malice *propense* in law? I think not, for
" the act that followed it seemed not the
" effect of any malicious intention.

" The next fact is the stabbing Trud-
" gett." *(Here he read the evidence on both
sides.)*

" A great deal of stress has been laid
" upon the doctrine of accomplice, and
" the General has argued with a know-
" ledge and ingenuity that would do credit
" to the ablest of my profession; but the
" doctrine does not apply, because there
" is no proof nor reason to suppose that
" the Colonel had given such orders, or
" used such influence as to excite men to
" acts of violence. His written orders
" indeed prove the direct contrary; and
" if a superior in command is responsible
" for

"for every action committed by his in-
"feriors, as well might we make the Ge-
"neral a party in the murder of Mifs
"Macrea (the cataftrophe of this young
"Lady I mentioned in a letter to you
during the campaign) "becaufe the In-
"dians who committed that murder, were
"under the General's orders; an act of
"which I believe he ftands acquitted in
"the opinion of every perfon."

I think you will coiticide in opinion, that the Judge Advocate plainly evinced his profeffion, as I think the comparifon can in no degree hold good: one was in time of hoftilities, where two parties are oppofing each other; the other at a time when a fet of men, unarmed, prifoners, are in a peaceable country, and amenable to the laws of the State for any crime they committed, therefore could only be meant as an obloquy againft the General.

"The

" The next fact, which is that of stab-
" bing Wilson, you will find depends
" much upon the rescue of Buchanan.
" The Court will judge whether this was
" a rescue or not; if it was one, I will
" maintain that Colonel Henley, exclusive
" of his military command, considered
" only as a private magistrate, in peace-
" able times, was justified by law and
" custom in putting to death any person
" who attempted to force a prisoner out
" of custody; and this leads to the con-
" sideration of the principal, and I must
" confess the most unaccountable trans-
" action, the stabbing of Hadley. *(Evi-*
dence on both sides read.)

" It must be acknowledged, that Co-
" lonel Henley acted in this affair with a
" degree of warmth which his best friends
" cannot defend, and it must rest with
" the Court to combine the various cir-
' cumstances of his situation, and to con-
                                    " sider

" sider the nature and extent of the pro-
" vocations he received. If they can sup-
" pose a man capable of deliberately and
" wantonly running an innocent man
" through the body, they will be bound
" by their oaths and their honor to inflict
" a proper punishment; on the other hand,
" if they think such repeated provocation,
" such insolence and insult, as were offered
" daily and hourly to the troops under his
" command, and particularly before his
" eyes, in the rescue of Buchanan, they will
" make due allowances for a high spirited
" officer, animated in his duty and by re-
" sentment for affronts offered to his
" country. As for the supposition that
" Colonel Henley fostered and encouraged
" principles of a bloody nature by his ge-
" neral conduct, it needs no other con-
" futation than the want of any proof on
" the other side, and his general character.
" My friend is known to be of a warm
" temper; it must be allowed, warmth has
                                    " carried

" carried him too far; but a more ge-
" nerous, honorable or humane man, does
" not live in the American, or any other
" army. The behaviour of the Britiſh
" troops in general, who, notwithſtanding
" their ſituation treated ours upon every
" occaſion with pride, contempt and out-
" rage, is notorious, and the inſtances
" were many which called upon an officer
" for inſtant and exemplary chaſtiſement.
" How little it was to be obtained by ap-
" plication to the Britiſh officers, appears
" by what paſſed with Colonel Lind, and
" by other parts of theſe proceedings."

Leaſt you might be led to imagine that the Britiſh officers were culpable, I ſhall quote part of Colonel Lind's evidence, to point out wherein the Judge Advocate had miſapplied the evidence. After proving the centry fired upon a woman, and with great difficulty got acceſs to the American officer that commanded, ſays Colonel Lind,

Lind, " I related to him what had paſſed between the woman and the centry, begging he would order him to be confined, that the affair might be enquired into, *he told me be could not* (theſe are the words the Judge Advocate has applied *vice verſa)* and that the centries had particular orders to fire upon all women, as well as ſoldiers, who attempted to paſs them. I then obſerved that it was a very extraordinary order, that I was ſure General Heath could never intend that women ſhould be fired upon, and that it muſt have been a miſtake; he replied, that it was not his particular affair, that the centry had his orders, and I might ſeek redreſs elſewhere; we then parted.——This is the whole evidence of Colonel Lind, therefore I leave you to judge how it can have the leaſt affinity to what the Judge Advocate has inſinuated, that no redreſs was to be had from the Britiſh officers : but to the concluſion of his ſpeech.

" I will

" I will trouble the Court no longer----
" it may perhaps appear that I have plead-
" ed for Colonel Henley more than I pro-
" pofed when I began: He is, I confefs,
" my friend; the man I efteem for the
" goodnefs of his heart, for his fpirit as
" an officer, and the attachment to the
" caufe of his country; and if I have
" erred in making myfelf more his coun-
" fel than counfel for the profecution, I
" have done fo, becaufe I thought a caufe
" fupported on one fide by fo able an ad-
" vocate as General Burgoyne, required
" every poffible fair affiftance on the
" other."

Throughout the whole of the Judge Advocate's fumming up the evidence, he has not taken the leaft notice of the Colonel's fpeech to Serjeant Fleming, which, in my opinion, points out his character very ftrongly; nor has he confuted the witneffes produced in fupport of the profecution,

fecution, but wishes to impress the Court that Colonel Henley is a good man, and to take his word for it, as he is his particular friend.

This trial, which commenced the 20th of January, and by adjournments, was protracted till the 10th of February, you must naturally imagine, raised our anxiety, as no doubt it does yours, for the sentence of the Court, when it was given to General Heath—but it was not given out 'till the 27th of February, thus you have it verbatim from our general orders.

Head Quarters, Boston, Feb. 27, 1788.

EXTRACT FROM GENERAL ORDERS.

" Colonel David Henley, late Com-
" manding Officer of the post at Cam-
" bridge, tried at the Special General
" Court Martial, whereof Brigadier Ge-
" neral Glover was President, accused by
" Lieutenant

" Lieutenant General Burgoyne, of a ge-
" neral tenor of language and conduct
" heinoufly criminal as an officer, and
" unbecoming as a man, of the moft
" indecent, violent, vindictive feverity
" againft unarmed men, and of an inten-
" tional murder.

" The Court, after mature confidera-
" tion, are of opinion, that the charge
" againft Colonel Henley is not fupport-
" ed, and that he be difcharged from his
" arreft.

" The General approves the opinion of
" the Court, thanks them for their un-
" wearied endeavors to inveftigate the
" truth, and orders Colonel Henley to
" reaffume his command at Cambridge
" immediately.

" The General thinks it to be his duty,
" on this occafion, to obferve, that al-
" though

"though the conduct of Lieutenant Ge-
"neral Burgoyne (as prosecutor against
"Colonel Henley) in the course of the
"foregoing trial, in his several speeches
"and pleas may be warranted by some
"like precedents in British Court-martials,
"yet as it is altogether novel in the pro-
"ceedings of any general Court-martial
"in the army of the United States of
"America, whose rules and articles of
"war direct, that the Judge Advocate
"General shall prosecute, in the name of
"the United States, and as different prac-
"tice tends to render Courts-martial both
"tedious and expensive, he does protest
"against this instance being drawn into
"precedent in future.

"Signed   J. KEITH, D. A. G."

In consequence of this acquittal, Colonel Henley reassumed his command the next day, but merely for form sake, as the next week Colonel Lee took the command, which

which he had when we firſt arrived. Affairs are much better regulated, every thing is now in perfect tranquillity, and a good underſtanding has taken place between our troops and the Americans.--- Colonel Lee has remedied one great evil, in which I cannot help thinking Colonel Henley was intereſted, which was compelling our ſoldiers to purchaſe all their proviſions at two ſtores in the barracks, and not permitting them to ſend to Cambridge, where they were much cheaper.— Paſſes have been granted for a Serjeant and ſo many men, to go out and purchaſe proviſions, by which means the ſtores cannot impoſe on the troops, and they now ſell their commodities at the market price. Having ſo long dwelt upon public affairs, you no doubt will be happy to hear ſomething relative to my own.

The reſolution of Congreſs in preventing our embarkation was a very ſevere trial

trial indeed, but we are now become more reconciled; and as Hope, that great support through life, never forsakes us, we are in expectation that at the end of the ensuing campaign. we may in all probability be regularly exchanged; for my own part, I have made up my mind;—and as I find Cambridge very expensive, on account of the great number of officers who reside there, I am going to remove my quarters to a farm house, near the town of Myftic, in order to live a little reasonable; we have had no pay since our arrival, but what has been in paper money, which lowers very fast, so that you are compelled to purchase such articles as you think you are in want of, otherwise your money will not be a third of the value it was at the time you received it. The exchange of hard money is now at the rate of forty and fifty paper dollars for a guinea. What muft you think of the depreciation in these few months,

months, fince we were made prifoners, when we could with difficulty get only nine. On account of unavoidable expences, and the depreciation of the paper currency, I have drawn on you for fifty pounds, which bill you will pleafe to honor, and place to the account of

Your's, &c.

LETTER LIV.

Mystic, in New England,
May 10, 1778.

MY DEAR FRIEND,

IT has ever been a maxim in all ages, and unhappily formed upon experience, that events are seldom answerable to expectations; when we form to ourselves a promising prospect, how mortifying is a disappointment—such is our present situation; for after a second application of General Burgoyne to Congress, to effect our liberty, in which state of suspence we have been for a length of time, he has at last received a positive denial

nial to his repeated folicitations. They have, however, on the 3d of laſt March, paſſed a refolve, that Lieutenant General Burgoyne, on account of his ill ſtate of health, may have leave to embark for England; and ſhortly after this intelligence, he left the army for that purpoſe This final refolution of Congrefs, makes our prefent fituation very trying; however, we are forced to be contented, for the greater power bears the fway all the world over.

From the converfation of a number of gentlemen of the firſt name and property, who were not quite fo violent in their meafure as a *Hancok* or an *Adams*; I have been thoroughly convinced, that none of them entertain the moſt diſtant thought of withdrawing from our Government at the commencement of hoſtilities, but now they have joined in that hereditary and fettled hatred which the New Englanders in general ever entertained againſt the conſtitution of our country, both in Church and State, ever exclaiming againſt tyranny and perſecution, have aſſumed a power unmaſked, and are cruel inſolent and perſecuting; excluſive of their daily impriſoning and harraſſing the poor Loyaliſts, I think the trial of Colonel Henley ſufficiently marks their character.

The Spring is now far advanced, and the country around has a charming appearance; our attention to the many novelties that preſent themſelves is taken off by the variety of birds, whoſe plumage is peculiarly beautiful, the moſt remarkable are the Fire-bird, Hanging-bird, Blue-bird and Humming-bird.

The Fire-bird is ſomewhat larger than a ſparrow, and its plumage is of a fine deep yellow, reſembling a flame color, from whence it derives its name.

The

The Hanging-bird is of about the same size, of a brilliant orange, with a few black feathers in the wing, which forms a pleasing contrast: It appears as if this bird was sensible what enemies men, as well as other animals, are to the young of the feathered creation, for they construct their nests upon the extremity of a large bough, not in the nature of other birds, but suspended at a considerable distance from the bough, resembling a hornet's nest; on one side there is a hole where the birds enter. It is somewhat remarkable that these nests, though suspended near two feet and a half from the branch of the tree, and that only by five or six small cords which these birds make from the loose hemp that they pick up, they are never blown down by the high winds. I was present at the taking of one of these nests, and it was with great difficulty it could be disengaged from the branch, without destroying the whole nest. The young ones are the most tractable of the feathered tribe, and in the hands of thofe who would beftow time and pains, they might be inftructed in a variety of little tricks and fancies.

An officer, who was ill and confined to his room, being a great bird-fancier, had a neft with thefe young ones brought him, which he amufed himfelf with, and finding them tractable, he fed them with flies, for which they would follow him all round the room: in a fhort time he had them in fuch command, that they would at his defire, retire to their neft, and come out again either fingly, or all three together: one he had fuch fway over, that he would take it into the garden, and let it fly into a tree, and the inftant he called it, the bird flew and perched on his fhoulder.

The Blue-bird is of the fize, and nearly as numerous as the fparrow; there is nothing remarkable about this bird but its plumage,

plumage, which is of the moſt beautiful mazarine, and when the rays of the Sun reflect on it, the color is greatly heightened.

The Humming-birds are in great plenty here, but not near ſo numerous, as I am informed, they are to the Southward.——— This bird being not only beautiful, but having many peculiarities, and being the leaſt of the feathered creation, not being much larger than an humble bee, you'll pardon my entering into a full detail of it.

The plumage of the cock is beautiful in the extreme, varying into an infinity of colour; in one light it is of a lively green, in another a beautiful blue, and in another a fine golden color: in ſhort, in every ray of light you can poſſibly turn it, you diſtinguiſh a different tint. This little creature ſubſiſts upon the juice of flowers, which it ſucks up with a long bill; it is
really

really diverting to see it putting its little bill into every flower in a circle; as soon as one is sucked, it flutters to the next; during the sucking the juice out of the flowers it never settles on them, but flutters continually like bees, and moves its wings so quick they appear hardly visible, and during this fluttering make a humming noise. This bird is not very shy, but if you attempt to seize it, flies off with the swiftness of an arrow. You would hardly conceive how predominant the passion of envy is amongst these little creatures; if several of them met on the same bed of flowers, they attack each other with such an impetuosity, that they seem as if they would pierce each other with their bills. In their combats they would often fly into a room if a window is open, fight a little, and flutter away again; they not only possess the passion of envy, but anger; for if they meet with a flower that is withered, or that is withering, and contains

tains no more juice, these little creatures, in a violent passion, pluck it off and throw it on the ground. I have seen in large gardens, where there has been many beds of flowers, the ground quite covered with the effects of their rage.

The Humming-bird being so exceeding small, and very difficult to catch, I was greatly at a loss to procure one to stuff and add to the collection I am making for you; sensible that firing at it with shot would shatter the little creature to atoms, I knew not what method to devise to obtain one, therefore consulted the inhabitants, who informed me, they never caught them unless they flew into a room when the window was open; for a week and upwards I sat in expectation that that would happen, during which time I employed my thoughts as to some other mode, when it occurred to me, if I loaded a pistol with powder, and
put

put some fine sand as a charge, I thought the great report would either stun them, or the grains of sand would beat them down: and after my patience was quite exhausted as to the other mode of catching them, I adopted my own, which I found succeeded to my wish; for seeing one alight upon a flower, I fired at it, and it fell with the flower, but was not killed, only stunned with the report; as shortly after I had taken it up, it was near escaping; what makes me imagine it was only stunned was, that the grains of sand had not hurt even its feathers; but to ascertain the matter, I procured several only by putting powder in the pistol, which fully proved it was the report that had effect on them.

It is looked upon as a great rarity indeed, if the nest of this little bird is found, and it is merely accidental, as they are only to be met with in swamps, when the
trees

trees are very thick of foliage. Having procured the bird, I was anxious to obtain a neft, as I no doubt imagined that it was equally as curious as the bird itfelf, but well knowing any fearch that I could make would be in vain, I told feveral Negroes, who where cutting wood in a fwamp, if they found a neft and fhewed it me I would give them a dollar; accordingly, one morning a negro came and informed me he had found one; I went with him into the middle of a large fwamp, and ftopping juft by where he had been cutting fome wood, he fays, " Maffa, Maffa, dere is de neft," which not being very eafily difcerned, he got a long pole and pointed to it, when even then I could not fee it, perceiving nothing but mofs; but taking away his pole haftily, he faid, " Maffa, keep your eye dere, and you will fee de old one;" and fhortly after the old one came and fettled on the neft, between the forks of a bough; I afcended the tree, and was then as much at a lofs to find it till the negro pointed to it, and I faw the old one on the neft: upon my approach fhe flew off, and kept hovering and humming about my head. In the neft there were two eggs; I cut off the branch the neft was on, and defcended the tree, but coming down the main ftem, I had the misfortune to drop one of the eggs out of the neft, as I was obliged to bring the branch it was on in my mouth, and although the negro and myfelf fearched for it near an hour, we could not find it; I cannot but fay I was heartily vexed, as the eggs are the greateft curiofity: it is rather fortunate I have one left to fend you, otherwife you would fcarcely credit it, when I tell you, that although the bird, which, as I before mentioned, is not much larger than an humble bee, the eggs are nearly as large as a wren's.

Upon

Upon an examination of the neſt, I was not ſurprized at my diſcerning it with difficulty from the other moſs that grew on the tree, for the outſide has a coating of green moſs, ſuch as is commonly on old pales, encloſures, and old trees; the neſt, as well as the bird, is the leaſt of all others; that which I have taken is round, and the inſide is of a brown and quite ſoft down, which ſeems to have been collected from the ſtems of the ſumach, which are covered with a ſoft wool of this color, and the plant grows in great abundance here; the inner diameter of the neſt is hardly a geometrical inch at the top, and the depth ſcarcely half an inch. I have taken peculiar care of it, as well as the neſt of the Hanging-bird, and ſhall ſend them by the firſt opportunity, and am ſure you will join with me in the adoration of that Being, who has endowed theſe creatures with ſuch natural inſtinct, to guard againſt the wiles of man and other enemies: but what creature

creature is there either offenfive, or inoffenfive, but fome of its fpecies has fallen a victim to the rapacious hand of man.

A few days fince, walking out with fome officers, we ftopped at a houfe to purchafe vegetables, whilft the other officers were bargaining with the woman of the houfe, I obferved an elderly woman fitting by the fire, who was continually eyeing us, and every now and then fhedding a tear. Juft as we were quitting the houfe fhe got up, and burfting into tears, faid, "Gentlemen, will you let a poor diftracted woman fpeak a word to you before you go?" We, as you muft naturally imagine, were all aftonifhed, and upon enquiring what fhe wanted, with the moft poignant grief and fobbing as if her heart was on the point of breaking, afked if any of us knew her fon, who was killed at the battle of Huberton, a Colonel Francis. Several of us
                                              informed

informed her, that we had seen him after he was dead. She then enquired about his pocket-book, and if any of his papers were safe, as some related to his estates, and if any of the soldiers had got his watch; if she could but obtain that in remembrance of her dear, dear son, she should be happy. Captain Ferguson, of our regiment, who was of the party, told her, as to the Colonel's papers and pocket-book, he was fearful they were either lost or destroyed; but pulling a watch from his fob, said, " There, good woman, if that can make " you happy, take it, and God bless you." We were all much surprized, as unacquainted, as he had made a purchase of it from a drum-boy. On seeing it, it is impossible to describe the joy and grief that was depicted in her countenance; I never in all my life, beheld such a strength of passion; she kissed it, looked unutterable gratitude at Captain Ferguson, then kissed it again; her feelings were inexpressible, she knew not how to express or shew them; she would repay his kindness by kindness, but could only sob her thanks; our feelings were lifted up to an inexpressible height; we promised to search after the papers, and I believe, at that moment, could have hazarded life itself to procure them.

You know, I ever had an aversion to tea, as being highly detrimental to the stomach, and always made use of some substitute, I have now adopted one, which the inhabitants make use of, ever since they made a virtue contrary to their inclinations, of not drinking tea at the time of the Boston Port Bill, which is the flowers that grow upon the sassafras tree; as to the efficacy of the root of this tree, in all scorbutic cases, it is well known, I therefore conceive the flowers must have more virtue; the flavor that they produce is extremely delicious, greatly resembling that of a peach:

the

the saffafras trees grow in abundance, they are scattered on the borders of the woods and near bushes and inclosures; and are generally one of the first trees that spring up on uncultivated ground; the cows are extremely greedy after the shoots of the tree, and search for them every where; if they are in an enclosure the cattle will knock down the fence to get at them; the women make use of the bark for dying worsted, which produces a beautiful orange that does not fade in the sun.

In the beginning of this letter I mentioned that General Burgoyne is sailed for England. No doubt, on his arrival, his enemies will be attacking him in all quarters, do not you be led away with the general voice and follow a misled faction, the General, in every situation of danger and difficulty, ever had the confidence of the army; even in the late recent

recent affair of Colonel Henley's, they were perfectly satisfied with his efforts and exertions to procure them redress; many ill-minded and malicious persons will assert that he has sought his own ease and comfort and forsaken his distressed army: In that respect I can with the utmost confidence assert, that neither officer or soldier expressed dissatisfaction at his return to England; so far from it, it was their wish he should go to Europe to justify his own and their conduct. He has shared at all times the dangers and afflictions in common with every soldier; they look on him as their friend, and would receive him in person, or any accounts of him with marks of affection; and wishing you may be impressed with those ideas, and hold it forth against all calumniators, I remain

Yours, &c.

LETTER LV.

Myſtic, in New England,
May 20th, 1778.

MY DEAR FRIEND,

THE intentions of Congreſs are very apparent as to our detention as priſoners, no doubt as hoſtages, in caſe of failure to the Southward the enſuing campaign, and apprehenſive that ſome diverſion may be made near Boſton; ſo that our ſoldiers might either be releaſed, or eſcape to any army that may make a landing. The Council of Boſton, under pretence that the troops would fare better, removed the firſt brigade of the Britiſh, consisting confifting of the artillery, advanced corps, and ninth regiment, on the 15th of laſt month from Profpect Hill, to a place called Rutland, fifty-five miles further up the country, at which place they are to ſtay till further orders from Congreſs; the reſt of the Britiſh troops are ſhortly to follow; as to the Germans, the Americans look upon them ſo tame and ſubmiſſive, that they are to remain at their old quarters, on Winter Hill.

By an officer who came from Rutland, we learn, that the firſt brigade arrived there the 17th, about two o'clock; the men were ſent to barracks that were picketed in with pickets, near twenty feet high, and had been treated with great feverity, very badly ſupplied with proviſions, and denied to go out for any thing amongſt the inhabitants. The officers with great difficulty obtained quarters in the neighbouring houſes, and thoſe at a
confiderable

considerable diftance from each other. It happened rather fortunately for the troops, that a veffel under a flag of truce arrived with fome neceffaries juft before they marched, otherwife the men would have been in a wretched ftate.

We do not fo readily procure neceffaries from the country people as we were accuftomed, having only Congrefs money to pay them for their commodities, for they entertain little opinion as to its value; and I am induced to think that the earneft civility and defire to oblige, which they firft fhewed us, proceeded from no other motive, than that they fhould receive hard money in payment for their goods.

The trees are now in full bloffom, and as every houfe has an orchard adjoining, the country looks quite beautiful; upon enquiry of the inhabitants, I find moft of
the

the European fruits have degenerated in
New England, except the apple, which it
is said, if it has not improved, it has
multiplied exceedingly. I am the more
induced to credit this, as the ufe of cyder
is more common here, than in any other
part of the world. Moſt of our roots and
garden-ſtuffs have had good fucceſs, but
the feeds, either for want of proper care,
or the methods of preferving them, do
not thrive fo well; wheat is apt to be
blighted, barley grows dry, and oats yield
more ſtraw than grain; but to fupply
thefe defects, the maize, or Indian corn,
thrives exceeding well, which is their grand
ſtaple commodity, that fupplies both
themſelves and cattle: as to Indian corn,
it is now fo generally known in England,
I ſhall not tire your patience with a long
defcription of it; but only obferve, that
were the heat more predominant in the
fummer months in England, I think it
might eafily be raifed; its grain is certainly
the

the heartiest, and most strengthening food for cattle and poultry, and gives their meat a firmness and exquisite flavor. I am averse to feeding horses with it, for it makes them so liable to founder. A few days ago I saw an instance of its pernicious effects at an ordinary, where a man, being in liquor, and had rode hard, and his horse exceedingly heated, would insist on its being fed——the poor creature eat his meal very heartily, and in about two hours after was deprived of the use of all his limbs, and lay on the ground trembling and shaking every nerve; the only remedy that could be applied, was to take off his shoes, and drag him into a wet swamp, and it was near four days before the creature could stand on its legs, and then it walked very crippled; it grieved me much as it was a very fine blood horse, that the owner had lately got from Virginia, which differ widely from the New England horses; for they, of all the various breeds

of

of that noble animal, certainly are the most peculiar and diabolical to ride; the horses in general have a pretty good head and neck, and from that to their rump, they fall off surprisingly; they are all, without an exception, what is termed amongst jockies, goose-rumped and cat-hamd; in a natural pace they will shuffle on for eight or nine miles an hour; it is not that easy kind of pacing that is taught ladies horses, but an unaccountable wriggling gait, that till you are accustomed to it, you are more fatigued in riding two miles, than a whole day's fox-chace; in short, you cannot possibly form a just idea of it, unless you were mounted on a New-England Rosinante, which title, they justly merit, for I assure you, they are very much *a la Quixote*; and to meet a New-Englander riding in the woods with his blazing iron (the term they give to a musket or gun) you might mistake him for the knight of the Woeful Countenance; their

horses

horses are of a very slender make, and not over fat, with a long switch tail and mane down to the horse's knees; for I should observe to you, they never cut either; then the master, with his long legs, bestrides it, which are in stirrups that the toe can but just reach; then his upright position, with his long lank visage, and on his head an old grizzly caxon and a large flapped hat, with his saddle-bags behind, and provision-bags before, and his blazing-iron on his shoulder; picture to yourself a man thus mounted, of such an *outré* appearance, and forbear to laugh if you can.

Exclusive of Indian corn, the inhabitants plant great quantities of squashes, which is a species of pumpions or melons; the seed of it, when imported from Europe, by the first settlers, has ever since been cultivated with assiduity, and found to thrive much better than in Europe; the fruit has an agreeable taste,

made

made use of at table as a vegetable, and dressed as turneps.

The soil of New-England is various, but I observed it was more prolific towards the Southward; there are excellent meadows in the low grounds, and good pasture almost every where; their best meadows will yield about a ton of hay by the acre; some will produce two, but that is what is termed timothy hay, which is rank and sour. The country, as I before observed, is not favorable to any grain except the Indian corn; the cattle in New-England are very numerous, and some of them very large; hogs are likewise in great abundance, and particularly excellent, being fattened upon the Indian corn, and some so large as to weigh twenty-five score.

We have of late been greatly amused in catching of ell-wives, or ale-wives, a species

cies of fish, greatly resembling a herring, both as to make and flavor, but somewhat fuller; they come up all the creeks and inlets from the sea at this season to spawn, floating in with the tide in large shoals, and proceeding as far as they can for fresh water; when the tide is going out they return, at which time they are caught by means of nets fastened round a hoop, and affixed to a long pole; the nets are very deep, and at one haul you may catch two or three dozen. It is part of the traffic of the inhabitants, who salt them down, and barrel them for the West-Indies.

I need not tell you of a restless disposition we English are of, and that we must be employed on something, situated as we are, without books, newspapers, or any other amusement: some officers, who came from the West of England, have instituted the diversion of fighting of cocks; for my own part, you know, I ever esteem-
ing

it a barbarous cuftom, and a difgrace to our nation, and cannot but fay I was a little pleafed at a reprimand that fome officers met with from an old woman, to whom they had applied for a couple of fine birds that were in the yard, fhe enquired if they were to fight, or to kill for eating; being told the former, fhe in a moft violent rage exclaimed, " I fwear " now you fhall have neither of them; I " fwear now I never faw any thing fo " bloodthirfty as you Britonions be; if " you can't be fighting and cutting other " people's throats, you muft be fetting two " harmlefs creatures to kill one another; " Go along, go; I have heard of your " cruel doings at Watertown (the place " where the cocks fought) cutting off the " feathers, and the poor creature's comb " and gills, and putting on iron things " upon their legs; go along, I fay." I could not help laughing to fee them decamp in hafte, as the old woman had worked herfelf into fuch a paffion, that

they

they expected she would have struck them with her crutch, which she lifted up to give the greater energy to her language. This is the only instance in my memory, that can reflect credit on American humanity.

New-England produces very good timber, the woods and swamps abounding with oak, elm, ash, cypress, pine, chesnut, walnut, cedar, astrin, beach, fir, saffafras, and sumach, with all other kind of trees that grow in England; the firs are of an extraordinary growth, for masts, yards and planks; the sumach is much used by the tanners and dyers, and the cedar produces sweet gums, besides being extremely useful in making shingles for coverings to their dwellings, as being the most durable, and least injured by the weather; but the treasure and glory of the woods are the monarch oak, the spruce, and fir trees, which are in such abundance, that the navy of England might be supplied with all sorts of naval stores at a cheaper rate than

than from the Baltic; and it is on this account that they build more ships in this province, than all the other parts of America; and they have the reputation of being very well built and ſtrong; to this ſtrength is chiefly imputed their being ſuch bad ſailing veſſels.

To Europeans, the noiſe of the frogs, of which there are vaſt numbers, and of various ſpecies, is at firſt very alarming, and till accuſtomed, you are at a loſs to make out from whence ſuch a hideous noiſe proceeds, there are thirty different voices among them, ſome of which reſemble the bellowing of a bull. In order that you may conceive how numerous they are all over the continent, as likewiſe how clamorous, I ſhall relate a circumſtance which has been told me, and vouched for an abſolute fact by the perſon who related it.

One

One Summer night, in the month of July, 1758, the town of Windham, which ſtands on the borders of Winnomantic River, in Connecticut, was greatly alarmed by a number of theſe reptiles which were marching, or rather hopping in a body, from an artificial pond, near three miles ſquare, that, by the exceeding heat of the weather was dried up. This pond was about five miles from Windham, in their way to the Winnomantic, were under the neceſſity of keeping the road that led through the town; they entered about midnight; the bull-frog, as being the moſt powerful, in the front, the reſt following; they were ſo exceedingly numerous, that they were ſome hours paſſing through, and for want of water unuſually clamorous. The inhabitants were greatly terrified, and fled from their beds naked, near half a mile, imagining it was the French and Indians; the men, after a little recollection, finding no enemy in purſuit, muſtered muftered courage to return; when they came near the town, they imagined they diftinctly heard the words *Wight, Helderkin, Dier, Tété*, which refembles the noife they make, and in their fright they thought the laft word meant *treaty*, when three of them, in their fhirts, approached to treat with the General of the French and Indians; but being dark, and no anfwer given, their terrors were greatly encreafed, and they were diftracted between hope and fear; at length day appearing, they were eafed from all their anxiety, by difcovering that this terrific enemy was an army of frogs, dying with thirft, going to the river for a little water. The people of Windham have ever fince been laughed at for their timidity by the New-Englanders; but I really believe, in a fimilar fituation, thefe Yankees would not have felt themfelves much bolder.

At

At this feafon of the year, every night you are furrounded with mufic, not the moft harmonic, from frogs, bull-frogs, hooping-owls, and the *whipper will*, a bird fo named by its nocturnal fong, being a conftant repetition of *whipper will*; it is alfo known by the name of the *Pope*, by reafon of its making a noife refembling that word, when it alights upon a tree or fence. I have endeavoured feveral times to fhoot one, but owing to its being dark, and their flying fo exceedingly fwift, I have never been able to kill. By the information I have gathered from the inhabitants, I find it is about the fize of a cuckow, with a fhort beak, long and narrow wings, a large head, and mouth enormous, what is remarkable, it is not a bird of prey; under the throat there is a kind of fkin which it can expand, and fill with air at pleafure, and that enables it to make the noife which refembles the word Pope. From this defcription, I conceive it to be a Mufquito hawk, abundance of which are to be feen in the day time; I accordingly fhot one, and found it exactly correfpond to the defcription of the other, only I could not perceive that loofe fkin under its throat; I rather think that circumftance is imaginary; and am apt to conclude, that the Mufquito hawk and whipper-will are the fame bird.

I am forry to inform you that the Americans are too fuccefsful in enticing our foldiers to defert; a few days fince the whole band of the fixty-fecond regiment, excepting the Mafter, deferted in a body, and are now playing to an American regiment in Bofton. The temptations held out to our foldiery are very great, and it muft be a Corporal Reeves, and fuch as poffefs his principles who can withftand them;

think

think how far it muft operate on a foldier's mind, that by defertion he fhall be free and protected, allowed to follow his trade, or if he enters their army, obtain a commiffion; there is now a Major Brown, who has fome poft in the fupplies of provifions, he was a private, and deferted from the forty-feventh regiment, at the battle of Lexington and Concord. The fellow, confcious of his bafenefs, when he meets an officer of that regiment, rides haftily away, but you muft allow it is rather grating to be in the power and under the command of fuch a villain. You will be pleafed with a noble and animated faying of a little drum-boy, not ten years old: this boy's father, who belonged to our regiment, fome time fince deferted into Bofton, and has been as nigh as he could venture with fafety to our barracks, to entice or feize his fon, and take him with him; but finding it in vain he fent an American to entreat

treat him to go to his father, when the little fellow replied, " No; tell my fa-
" ther, if he is such a rascal as to desert
" his King and country, his son won't;
" he has fed at their expence, and will die
" in their service." I remain

Your's, &c.

LETTER LVI.

Mystic, in New England,
Sept. 10, 1778,

MY DEAR FRIEND,

YOU must not be surprized if you hear of a massacre; bloody purposes are apparent since my last, three men have been fired at, one of whom was wounded, but the most melancholy catastrophe is the death of Lieutenant Brown, of the twenty-first regiment, who was shot dead in a chaise, as he was conducting two females from the barracks. The centinel who shot him was a little boy, scarce fourteen, who called out to him to stop, but

but the horses being headstrong, he could not, and putting his head out of the chaise to inform him so, the little rascal in an instant levelled his piece and shot him through the head. Had it not been for a few of our officers who happened to be on the spot, and the great discipline of our men, the boy would have fallen an instant sacrifice; as it was, notwithstanding the presence of our officers, the men could scarce be restrained from seizing the boy from the American guard. By this sad accident fell a brave young man, who had signalized himself during the campaign, and who, had he lived, would have been an ornament to his profession.

When the matter was reported to General Phillips, he instantly wrote the following letter to General Heath:

" Murder and Death has at length
" taken place; as to justice I do not ask
" it,

" it, every principle of it has long forsaken
" these provinces, I only request that an
" officer may be permitted to go to the
" Head Quarters of General Washington,
" to lay the affair before him."

To this letter the General received no
answer, but an order came to the Commanding Officer of the American troops,
to put General Phillips under an arrest,
and to confine him to his house and garden; he was accordingly laid under an
arrest, and his house and garden is surrounded by centinels.

A few days after the above melancholy
event, permission being obtained, the remains of poor Brown were interred in the
church at Cambridge; all the officers
at Cambridge and the environs attended, a most mournful sight! you can
easily paint to your imagination what our
feelings must have been at the time, for the
loss

loſs of a young man univerſally reſpected, eſteemed, beloved, and the reflection, we knew not how ſoon it might be our own fate; for in the hands of ſuch wretches, our lives are very precarious, and of little value.

I cannot paſs over the littleneſs of mind, and the pitiful reſentment of the Americans, in a very trifling circumſtance, during the time the ſervice was performing over the body, the Americans ſeized the opportunity of the church being open, which had been ſhut ſince the commencement of hoſtilities, to plunder, ranſack and deface every thing they could lay their hands on, deſtroying the pulpit, reading-deſk and communion-table, and aſcending the organ loft, deſtroyed the bellows and broke all the pipes of a very handſome inſtrument.

Although

Although, (as General Philips obferved in his letter, and which I am induced to believe, is the real fituation of affairs in thefe provinces) every principle of juftice had fled from them, ftill the Americans were not fo daring as to overlook fuch an atrocious crime without fome appeal to juftice, were it only to deceive the populace with an appearance of it, and therefore ordered a General Court-martial on the boy who fhot Lieutenant Brown, the judgment of which was fent by General Heath to General Phillips, that he might give it in orders to the Britifh troops, which was as follows: " The Ge-
" neral Court-martial that fat upon the
" trial of an American centinel, for fhoot-
" ing Lieutenant Brown, of the twenty-
" firft regiment, acquit the faid centinel,
" having done his duty as a good foldier."

Infults are not only fhewn to the officers and foldiers remaining at Cambridge, but

but if possible, they are treated worse at Rutland. As Mr. Bowen, the surgeon to the ninth regiment, Lieutenant Toriano, of the twentieth regiment, and Lieutenant Houghton, of the fifty-third regiment, were taking an evening's walk, they were met by an inhabitant, who, from his office of *Select Man* (these are a kind of overseers to their meeting-houses, who regulate the affairs of the parish, and report persons for non-attendance at worship, compelling those walking in the streets, or travellers, on a Sunday, to go to some place of worship; they are very consequential persons, and very officious) derived no small authority, and who had on every occasion distinguished himself for his insolence and persecution of the *prisoners of war*, as well as the unfortunate friends of Government, who had remained in that part of the country; this man of consequence charged those gentlemen with having trespassed on his property, and before they

they could explain that they had not been off what they confidered as the high road, he, in a moſt menacing manner, accompanied with many opprobious epithets, ſhook a whip over their heads. Mr. Bowen, who happened to be next the man on this occaſion, refented the infult with a blow, a conflict enfued, in which the countryman was worſted, though Mr. Bowen was feverely bruifed on the occaſion, the countryman prefuming, as well from his perfonal ſtrength as his authority.

Though this infult had been given thefe gentlemen in the fight of many people on the road, who alfo bore teftimony to Mr. Bowen's alone having ſtruck him, thefe three gentlemen (through the influence of this *Select Man)* were ſhortly after their return to their lodgings, taken by a party of the guards, conveyed to the guardhoufe, where they paſſed the night in the

common

common guard-room. The soldiers of the guard occupying the platform, these gentlemen were obliged to put up with the dirty floor; where they suffered every kind of indignity from the guard, who, not satisfied with making use of the most indecent language, would *spit* on them as they lay on the floor; in the morning they were removed to an adjoining barrack room, where they were very little better accommodated, and after seven or eight days confinement, they were given to understand, they were to be delivered up to the *civil* power.

The humanity of Major Carter, of the artillery, who was the senior officer of the Convention troops at Rutland (as well as considering it his duty to interfere) induced him from the first of the confinement of these gentlemen, to interest himself very warmly in their behalf, he had frequently remonstrated with the Commanding

manding Officer of the guard, at the cruelty and injuſtice of their conduct towards them, but not being able to obtain redreſs, demanded a paſs to ſend an officer to Cambridge, in order to repreſent the affair, through General Phillips, to the Commanding Officer at Boſton. Major Carter then informed theſe Gentlemen, that as he thought it neceſſary for the good of the troops in *general*, to make *their* treatment a *public concern*, it was *his* orders they ſhould wait the reſult of General Phillips's interference with the American General, and not to act for themſelves in the buſineſs on any account.

Before the return of the officer from General Phillips, theſe gentlemen were taken to a juſtice, who reſided ſome. diſtance from Rutland, before whom they were conducted with all the ceremony of criminals going to trial. The magiſtrate, who was an apothecary, poſſeſſed a
few

few *hard* words, and a moſt ſtarched puritanical air, and perhaps on this account, had been judged under the new government the only man of the neighbourhood capable of ſupporting the dignity of a country juſtice: he was ſurrounded with a numerous train of officers of the *police*, ſuch as *committee* and *ſelect* men, who, with a number of ſpectators, whom curioſity had brought together, to be preſent at the *trial* (as they expreſſed themſelves) made a very formidable groupe.

The gentlemen were no ſooner brought before this very awful *Court of Juſtice*, than Doctor Frienck (for ſo the Juſtice was called) who was placed in the moſt conſpicuous part of the room in an arm chair, with *infinite* ſolemnity, and all the importance of office (without even permitting the leaſt accuſation as to any offence committed by them) aſked them " whether they pleaded *guilty* or *not guilty* " of the crimes laid to their charge?"

On

On this occasion, I think it would have
been difficult for any indifferent person to
have restrained his risible faculties; nay,
the gentlemen themselves have declared it
was not without the utmost circumspec-
tion they could compose their muscles to
this curious demand of the Justice; one of
the gentlemen informed this worshipful
magistrate, " That they having suffered
" so many days confinement under the
" *military* guard very *unjustly*, as they con-
" ceived, and their commanding officer
" having thought it necessary to make the
" treatment they had met with a *public*
" concern, they looked up to *their General*
" for redress, consequently were not al-
" lowed to plead either one way or the
" other!"

The Justice, enraged at what he conceived a slight to his authority, without
hesitation committed them to *prison*, with
the additional charge of *contempt of Court*,

and the next morning they were conducted by a body of armed conftables to Worcefter, about ten miles diftance, and were lodged in the county jail, where, with two gentlemen, who were imprifoned as enemies to the *States*, they occupied a very confined dungeon, out of which a woman had, a very fhort time before, been taken to execution, for the murder of her hufband.

On their firft entrance into this moft gloomy ftate of fecurity, it may eafily be imagined, their feelings received no fmall fhock, and their fellow prifoners perceiving their diftrefs, one of them, who had been bred to the fea, by way of offering fome confolation in his own way, obferved, that he could only compare their fituation to that of fo many *young bears*, whofe misfortunes were all to come. The exceffive heat of the weather, with the confinement in this deteftable hole, which, when their mattraffes were laid on the
floor,

floor, compleatly filled it; and from whence, on no occasion, or the pressing calls of nature, they were allowed to retire, must, in a very short time, have rendered their existence burthensome, if not deprived them of it, had they not found means of softening the heart of a Mulatto woman, who served them with provisions through a hole, and who, by the force of bribes and fair promises, was prevailed upon to open the door upon these occasions for fresh air.

During their confinement, no attention was wanting on the part of their brother officers, to alleviate the horrors of their wretched situation, who gave them hopes of soon being relieved, through the interposition of *their* General. But at the expiration of *three* days, they received a message by an officer from Major Carter, at Rutland, expressing his extreme concern that *he* should in any measure be accessary to their being sent to prison, at the same time lamenting that his representation of their very unjust and cruel usage had produced no other effect than a letter from General Phillips, part of which the Major had transcribed for their perusal, which reprobated in the strongest terms, the imprudence of those gentlemen, in paying attention to the insolence or abuse of the people of the country, the General observing, " that they should listen to the abuse " of the Americans, as to the mere *cack-* " *ling of geese*;" and concluded with saying, " He should not concern himself with " a *boxing-match*."——Here I cannot but censure the conduct of General Phillips, for if he had his reasons for not making an application to General Heath, he should not have retorted so severely on the gentlemen, especially when it is considered two of them were innocent of the crime alledged; at the same time, the General might have recollected his own warmth of

temper

temper was, at that very moment, the occasion of his confinement to his house and garden.

In consequence of Major Carter's message, these unfortunate gentlemen (two of whom, as I have just observed, had not even been guilty of the crime imputed to them, who had always found some consolation in reflecting, that they were *then* suffering in conformity to the *will* of *their* Commanding Officer, and as they were given to understand, for the *public good*, and that through the interposition and zeal of *their General*, they should obtain justice, and be set at liberty, found themselves reduced to the necessity of shifting for themselves.

On consulting a lawyer (the assistance of whom is seldom wanting in *any* country for certain *considerations*) the learned limb of the law, after examining their commitment,

ment, and satisfying himself, with respect to the state of their finances, gave them to understand, that he should be able to prove a *flaw* in it—for *it* specified a crime against the *States*, when it was evident the *breach of peace* that they were charged with, could only *affect* the State of *Massachusets* (the State they were then in) but added, to bring their cause forward for the consideration of the Court during the assizes, that were *then* sitting, the *fees* would be considerable.--- His terms, though exorbitant, were readily acceded to by these gentlemen, and by that means they were enabled to relieve themselves from the horrors of a dungeon, on quitting which, it was their observation, that they had little more reason to *extol the humanity* of their *own General*, than they had the justice of the Americans.

Having often made several remarks, as to the footing military discipline is upon, I think

I think, by the prosecution of these gentlemen, you will see upon what grounds of justice and equity their civil laws are founded, and even supposing they gain their independency, what anarchy and confusion must ensue, for want of rulers with good hearts, to enforce the laws of equity and justice. The mist that is before the eyes of Americans must shortly pass away, when they will clearly see how easily they have given up the sweet content and happiness they possessed, and the innumerable privileges and liberties they enjoyed when under our Government.--- Deluded people, when it is too late, you will see your error! I speak not partially nor vaguely, but am confident there is not one, let him be ever so bigotted to Independency, can lay his hand upon his breast and say, that he experiences that ease and happiness he ever was accustomed to, and when he looks forward, in all human probability, neither he nor his generation

generation ever will---Many, I am certain, are now open to conviction, and would wiſh to retract, but having engaged, they are aſhamed; and rather than abandon a principle that they haſtily adopted, prefer ſacrificing their lives and fortunes: Difference of opinion ever will prevail, but it is the very height, nay, the very principle of madneſs, not to be open to conviction. In hopes that they ſoon may, and a permanent union formed between the Mother-country and her colonies, I remain,

Yours, &c.

LET-

LETTER LVII.

Myſtic, in New England,
Nov. 6th, 1778.

MY DEAR FRIEND,

I Cannot impute any blame to you, but no letter has reached me for an age. Your friendſhip for me is ſo ſincere, that agreeable to my firſt requeſt on communicating our literary correſpondence, you no doubt have anſwered all my letters; all muſt be laid to my preſent ſituation, and the want of friends at New-York, to ſend them to me. Many officers have received letters; and by our friend, Captain B——, who has a ſhort epiſtle from you, I have

I have the happiness to hear you enjoy a perfect state of health, and that you altogether reside at the old family mansion, in Norfolk. I do not claim your promise of answering this, but wait till the next, as it is very uncertain where any letter will find me, for the Congress have passed a resolve, to march the Convention army from the State of Massachusets to Charlottesville, in the province of Virginia, where barracks are erected, and where the troops can be more readily supplied with provisions.

When this resolve of Congress was made known, every one was struck with amazement; but upon reflection, it certainly is obvious, that the views of Congress, by marching the men eight hundred miles in the depth of winter, would be the means of their deserting in numbers, rather than endure such fatigue. General Washington has had the humanity to order

der waggons for the women and children; what adds to the diftreffes of the foldiers, is their being fo badly cloathed, having only the jackets that were made from their coats in the winter, whilft in Canada; and what is ftill more mortifying, a cartel fhip arrived but two days fince from New-York, with cloathing for the army: however, the men are to be fupplied with fhoes, fhirts, ftockings and cloth leggings, and the reft is to go round to James River, in Virginia. General Phillips will afk no favor of General Heath, otherwife, I think, he could not be fo divefted of humanity, as not to defer the march for a week, during which time the men might be cloathed; all is now hurry and confufion, as the firft divifion march the 10th inftant; the army is to follow in divifions, the fame as they did from Saratoga to Cambridge.

We

We are in great diftrefs for want of money too, to undertake this march, none has arrived from New-York, and to add to our confolation, the Commander in Chief has written to General Phillips, that it is his Majefty's pleafure, no more hard money fhould be fent to the Convention army; this is, no doubt, with a view that fo much coin as is neceffary for the payment of our army fhould not be in circulation among the Americans, and be an inducement to detain us longer; the motive certainly is very good, but what is to become of poor fubalterns, who, as it is, can fcarcely fubfift on their pay? No matter for that, you'll fay, " private intereft muft " give way for the public good." Therefore we muft have recourfe to the only method of removing the evil, by drawing bills on the Paymafter; but you are not aware of the fad effects attending it, it muft inevitably ruin one half of the officers, for it is with great difficulty you can

get

can get a bill difcounted, and that only in paper money, which depreciates fo exceedingly faft, that it foon lofes a third of its value: only imagine, fince our arrival it is fo depreciated, that we get fixty and feventy dollars for a guinea; but in difcounting a bill you can with difficulty get forty; what with difcount and depreciation, what a lofs there muft be upon every bill that is drawn. It may certainly be judicious in politics, to withhold the pay from the troops, but at the fame time it muft be highly injurious to fortunes of individuals, for I can affert it as a fact, that for every bill of ten pounds, you do not in reallity, get more than fix guineas and a half, and fo in proportion.

The inhabitants of Maffachufetts would certainly keep up the credit of the Congrefs money, and make it fomewhat more valuable, but the people from the Southward, from the Carolinas and Virginia, who

who in the courfe of their large dealings, are compelled to take the money in payment, fenfible of the uncertainty of its value, wifh to realize it into folid coin; therefore think little of the journey, from thofe diftant provinces to Bofton, to exchange with our army; they are fenfible of the rifk they run, and are very cautious. But as the people to the Southward poffefs more liberal fentiments, and know the principles of Britifh officers, they, as we walk by, will enter into converfation, and frankly afk if you want any paper dollars? They are rather cautious as to the Germans, for two German officers not being able to get fo much from a man as they wanted, they informed againft him, and he was fent to prifon in Bofton. Thefe traders of paper money are very uncertain, fometimes there will be a fcarcity of them for fome days, at other times there will be a dozen or two at a time; we then ftick out for our exchange; one day guineas rofe
from

from twenty-five and twenty-six dollars, up to thirty-six, and I should observe to you, that when once they rise, they never fall.

A few days since there was a meeting of the Commanding Officers of the several corps, at General Phillips's, to consult upon some method of procuring money for the different regiments; various were the modes proposed, and the Paymaster-General consulted; but they could not agree upon any, when a Commanding Officer observed to General Phillips, that it was impossible the troops could march without money, and he was certain the officers of his regiment had not twenty paper dollars among them. General Phillips, with a warmth that spoke his good intentions, replied " Good God, Sir, what would you " have me to do, I cannot make money; " I wish to God you could slit me into " paper dollars, I would chearfully sub- " mit for the good of the troops?" At last
it

it was resolved, that the Paymaster-General was to use his best endeavours, in which he succeeded, and the next day procured a considerable sum, which was immediately distributed to the different regiments. It is sufficient to enable the troops to march, and the Paymaster is to go to New-York, in hopes the Commander in Chief will issue some money upon this emergency.

It fell to the lot of an officer who is quartered with me, to go express with the money to the different regiments at Rutland, and you would have laughed at his distress, in what manner to deposit the paper dollars, for he was not without his apprehensions of being way-laid, and it was then nearly dark. He had scarcely two hundred pounds sterling, but that sum in paper dollars, makes a great bulk; at last, he thought the safest mode would be, to sew it in the lining, accordingly
ordering

ordering his servant, he ripped open his coat, sewed in the dollars by large parcels—and thus accoutred he set off, and was a welcome visitor at Rutland—had not this seasonable relief arrived, the confusion would have been very great, as many officers, rather than march without, had got themselves arrested, and were going to jail.

Were it not for the distresses of the soldiers, I cannot, for my own part, but say, this march was rather agreeable, for it enables me to see the southern part of America, which I must confess, I have a strong inclination for, having heard very great accounts of those Provinces, and how much superior they are in every respect to this; and it is no unpleasing reflection, after the cruelties and barbarities the troops have experienced since our arrival, that we are quitting such an inhospitable country; but in the most

Vol. II. S flourishing

flourishing times, I find this province was never remarkable for its courtesy to strangers.

Being at present much taken up in preparing for this long march, I hope you'll excuse the shortness of this epistle, at the same time assuring you, that you shall hear from me by every opportunity that occurs.

Your's, &c.

LETTER LVIII.

*Sherwood's Ferry, upon the Banks of the
Delaware, Dec. 10, 1778.*

MY DEAR FRIEND,

ON my leaving New-England, I joined the regiment, juft as they had croffed the Connecticut River, at Endfield; but in my way to this place, I and another officer, who accompanied me, had a very narrow efcape of being fent to prifon, for in travelling at night we miftook our road, and got into the town of Springfield, which was out of the route laid down for us, and is unfortunately the great arfenal of all military ftores for the State of Maf-fachufetts sachusets; happily for us, the landlord of the house we put up at was a friend to Government, who concealed us, and we were glad to get away before day-break, not but it could be clearly proved it was merely accidental: But these Americans will not hearken to reason, and no doubt they would have found people ready enough to swear, that we went there either as spies, or to destroy their stores.

At a small town we passed through in Connecticut called Sharon, there is an exceeding curious mill, invented by one Joel Harvey, and for which he received a present of twenty pounds from the Society of Arts and Sciences. By the turning of one wheel the whole is set in motion; there are two apartments where the wheat is ground; two others where it is bolted, in a fifth threshed, and in a sixth winnowed; in another apartment, hemp and flax are beaten; and in an adjoining apartment it

is

is dreſſed; what adds greatly to the ingenuity of this conſtruction is, that either branch may be diſcontinued without impeding the reſt.

Moſt of the places you paſs through in Connecticut are called townſhips (as the townſhip of Endfield, Suffield, &c.) which are not regular towns as in England, but a number of houſes diſperſed over a large tract of ground, belonging to one corpotion, that ſends members to the General Aſſembly of the States. About the centre of theſe townſhips ſtands the meeting-houſe, or church, with a few ſurrounding houſes; ſometimes the church ſtands ſingly. It is no little mortification, when fatigued, after a long day's journey, on enquiring how far it is to ſuch a town, to be informed you are there at preſent; but on enquiring for the church, or any particular tavern, you are informed it is ſeven or eight miles further.

I could

I could not help remarking, that the houses are all after the same plan, and what was rather singular, most of them were only one half finished, the other half having only the rough timbers that support the building; upon enquiry I found, that when a man builds a house, he leaves it in this state till his son marries, when he fits it up for his family, and the father and son live under one roof, as though they were two distinct houses; but as the houses are entirely compleat on the outside, and the windows all glazed, they have the appearance of being finished, but on entering a house, you cannot at first help lamenting that the owner was unable to complete it.

Just before we crossed the North River, we came to the town of Fish Kill, which has not more than fifty houses, in the space of near three miles, but this place has been the principal depot of Washington's ton's army, where there are magazines, hofpitals, workfhops, &c. which form a town of themfelves; they are erected near a wood, at the foot of a mountain, where there are a great number of huts, which have been the winter quarters of the American army, and to which they are fhortly expected to return for the enfuing winter; they are a miferable fhelter from the fevere weather in this country, and I fhould imagine, muft render their troops very fickly, for thefe huts confift only of little walls made with uneven ftones, and the intervals filled up with mud and ftraw, a few planks forming the roof; there is a chimney at one end, at the fide of which is the door. Near the magazines are fome well-conftructed barracks, with a prifon, furrounded with lofty pallifadoes. In this prifon were a number of unfortunate friends to Government, who were feized in their plantations, for refufing to take the oath of allegiance to the United States,

and

and who were confined till a sloop was ready to take them to New-York; for the Americans are so oppressive, they will not let any one remain neuter; and they compel every inhabitant, either to take the oath, or quit the country. When we crossed the river, there were two large sloops going to New-York, crouded with people of this description, many of whom, the boatmen informed us, had left beautiful houses, with extensive, and well cultivated plantations.

General Washington was not without his apprehensions, that Sir Henry Clinton would make some efforts to retake us, either by an expedition up the North River, or in our march through the Jerseys, and therefore took every precaution to frustrate any plan that might be concerted, for upon the arrival of our army at Fish Kill, General Washington moved his army into the middle of the Jerseys, and
detached

detached a considerable body of troops to escort us, so very apprehensive was he of a rescue, that to each brigade of ours they had a brigade of armed men, who marched the men in close columns. As to the officers they paid little attention, as we had signed a very strict parole, previous to our leaving New-England. Now we have passed the Delaware, the Pensylvania Militia are to guard us, and the brigades that escorted us through New-York and the Jerseys, return to Washington's army.

In a former letter I delivered my sentiments on our having possession of the North River, and on crossing it, they were fully confirmed; for the Americans judging it was the plan of the campaign, 1777, to make ourselves masters of the North River, and thus to separate the Eastern from the Western States, after the taking of Forts Montgomery and Clinton, and our troops proceeding so far as Œsopus, and then returning

turning to New-York, they immediately began to fortify West Point, which is not at present compleated, but when it is, will be impregnable, and effectually prevent any fleets passing; it being a point of land that projects, and makes a winding in the river, and at the same time narrows it, so as to have the whole command at that place. No doubt the Americans made choice of this post, as the most important to fortify, and Fish Kill as a place the best calculated for a depot of provisions and other stores, as being situated on the high road from Connecticut, and near the North River. It is by this important post of West Point, that the Americans are enabled to keep possession of the North River, and a communication between the Northern and Southern Provinces; and I do once more assert, not only upon my own opinion, but of the Americans themselves, that had we kept possession of the North River, the war would have been

by

by this time, nearly terminated in favor of Great-Britain.

As we paſſed through the Jerſeys, I was much delighted with the falls that are on the Paſiac River, being totally different from thoſe of Montmorency, and others I had ſeen. The river is near forty yards wide, and runs with a ſwift, but ſmooth current, till coming to a deep chaſm, that croſſes the channel, it falls in one entire ſheet near ſeventy feet perpendicular; one end of the chaſm or cleft of the rock is cloſed up, and at the other, the water ruſhes out with an incredible rapidity, in an acute angle, and is received into a large baſon, from whence it winds through ſeveral rocks, and then ſpreads in a conſiderable channel. The ſpray formed a beautiful rainbow, which rendered the ſcene ſuch as left the imagination nothing to add to its grandeur. This extraordinary phenomenon, no doubt,

muſt

muſt have been the production of an earthquake. The inhabitants who reſide near it, have a ſtory handed down to them of two Indians, who venturing too near the falls in a canoe, were carried down the precipice and daſhed to pieces. What conſiderably heightened the ſcene is, another fall, about thirty or forty yards from the great one, where the water moſt beautifully glides down ſome ledges of the rock, that are two or three feet perpendicular.

I was much ſtruck at the grandeur of the North River, from the majeſtic appearance of the high lands that are on one ſide of it, and the beautiful meadows interſperſed with farm houſes on the other. What greatly adds to its beauty is the width, being near a mile and a half acroſs; although pleaſed with the river and the ſurrounding objects, ſtill this idea would preſent itſelf, that the water I was then
failing

failing on, might in a few hours, be at New-York where every one is continually wishing to approach. You must pardon these melancholy reflections, they are the effusions of nature, and will burst forth---but to return to my description of the river: It is navigable from New-York to Albany, for large sloops, from whence there is a communication by the Mohawk and other rivers (except a few carrying places) into the most interior parts of America, through the country of the Six Nations, as far as Lake Ontario; then by a continuation of the Hudson, or North River, for they are the same, there is communication with the River St. Lawrence, through the Lakes George, Champlain, and the river Sorel, This river merits the greatest attention, and had not the present contest arose, some spirited gentlemen had it in contemplation, by means of locks and canals, to have opened a passage for small sloops. No doubt, a century hence, there will

will be water carriage for schooners and sloops from Quebec to New-York, which must greatly add to the wealth and commerce of America.

The small part of New-York we passed through, seems to be well cultivated; it affords grain of all sorts; there are abundance of cattle, hogs and poultry. As to the Jerseys, they marched us so much in the back settlements, that I had not an opportunity of seeing those parts, which were, before the war, deemed the garden of America.

We passed through a little town called Hopel, before we crossed the North River, which is chiefly inhabited by the Dutch. At a house where we were quartered, the people behaved extremely civil and attentive, and upon leaving them, would scarce permit us to pay for what we had: from which circumstance we concluded they
were

were friends to Government, and some officers opening their heart, spoke very freely about the Congress, Washington, &c. observing how great a shame it was, that we should be put to such expence, and that Congress ought to pay for us, the man went out of the room in a moment, and just as we were mounting our horses, brought us an enormous bill, exorbitant in every article, which he insisted upon being paid, and upon our urging that we had paid him what he had demanded, he replied, " Yes, gentlemen, so you have, " but then I thought Congress were to de- " fray all your expences; now I know you " are to pay me, I can't take a farthing " less than this bill," which we were compelled to discharge; however, it served as a lesson in future, to be cautious before whom we railed against Congress.

The Paymaster, as we expected, joined us in the Jerseys, which has enabled us to proceed

proceed on our march, and by whom we have received accounts, that Sir Henry Clinton purpofes to make an exchange of prifoners this winter; a partial exchange, as to officers has taken place, and many have quitted us; this partiality has given much offence, as it is but juftice, when a number are to be exchanged, they fhould draw lots.

Hitherto the weather has been remarkably temperate and fine, which is extremely fortunate for the men, as they have moftly flept in the woods; but fince we came into a more populous country, they have flept in barns. When we left New-England the frofts were very fevere, here we have not any, being fo much to the fouthward, and in a manner, the further we proceed we fall in with the clofe of the Autumn.

One morning, as we renewed our march, the weather being remarkably fine, fome

officers

officers were extolling the beauty of the morning, an old woman who was in the croud, and overheard him, in the moſt violent rage exclaimed, "Well, for my "part, I believe God Almighty has turned "*Tory*, to give theſe Britainers ſuch fine "weather for their march."

At a houſe where I ſlept in the Jerſeys, the owner, who was a friend to Government, had left an exceeding fine plantation, near Trenton, and retired to this place till the termination of the war, made heavy complaints of the troops plundering both friends and foes. He obſerved, as to the British ſoldiers, they only pilfered poultry and pigs, but the Heſſians entered houſes, broke open drawers, taking away plate, cloaths, and other valuables; but to point out to you what an idea they muſt have of plundering ſomething, he related that he ſaw ſome Germans enter a houſe which was abandoned by the owner,

in which they had left an eight day clock, and a few tables and chairs, that he shortly after observed one of the Germans come out of the house with the works of the clock, pendulum, and all the leaden weights; this enormous weight, in addition to his knapsack and accoutrements, the fellow had near twenty miles to carry to New-York, where the most he could possibly get for it, would be three or four dollars. After he had related this story, he observed, that the desolation of the Jerseys, which included friends, and moderate persons, as well as enemies, had done great injury to our cause, as it had united the latter more firmly, and detached numbers of the former---exaggerated accounts of all the enormities that had been committed were published in all their prints, which determined those who were wavering, and imbittered the minds of every class throughout the colonies, and he concluded with a sigh, observing, that the reſentment,

sentiment, occasioned by the depredations carried on through the Jerseys, had left few, or scarce any friends to Britain in the province.

The inhabitants of New-York, as well as the Jerseys, are chiefly the posterity of the first settlers in those provinces, who were Dutch, and they seem to retain their principles, industry, frugality, and an assiduous perseverance in the means of thriving. Before the war they must have been in an affluent and happy state, especially their farmers, but now they sow and plant, and know not who will reap the fruits of their labor, for their grain and other produce are taken for the use of the continental army, and in lieu certificates are given to be paid at the Treasury at Philadelphia; to many of them, especially those they imagine are inimical to their cause, they have barely left sufficient for the support of their families and the stock on the farms for the enfuing Winter. Oh deluded Americans, you muſt be independent, and thefe are the bleſſed fruits of thofe principles!

I was much delighted at meeting a bird lately, peculiar to America, termed the Mocking-bird, which derives its name from imitating the note of every bird they hear; its plumage is very fimple and not fhewy, it is a Summer bird, very difficult to bring up, and has a very melodious voice, which, in my opinion, would far exceed the Bullfinch, if the fame pains were taken with it, from its amazing readinefs in catching every note it hears. This one I faw imitated a cock in fuch a manner, that you could hardly believe but that there was a cock crowing in the room. The inhabitants fay this bird is fo very fhy, that if any perfon difcovers its neft, which is moftly built in bufhes, and looks at its eggs, it will never return again to the neft. When a neft of young ones are taken, and put into a cage, they take great care to hang it where the mother cannot get at it, for if fhe can, fhe will feed them three or four days; and finding fhe cannot releafe them flies away, after which, the young ones fhortly die, as in general they cannot eat what is given them? but the inhabitants attribute their death to the mother, who, they fay, the laft time fhe feeds them, contrives to give them poifon, in order to releafe them from captivity.---If that really is the cafe, it fhews how repugnant it is to the principles of nature, to confine any thing, and that fhe calls aloud to partake of the bleffings of liberty, but at prefent it reminds me of my own fituation, I muft therefore drop the fubject.

Your's, &c.

LETTER LIX.

Lancaster, in Penfylvania,
Dec. 16th, 1778.

MY DEAR FRIEND,

WE halt a day or two at this town, and I cannot so well employ my leisure time as to give you a description of our march from the Delaware: we crossed the river in scowls, which are flat bottom boats, large enough to contain a waggon and horses; they are a safe conveyance, and mostly used to cross the rivers in this country, they are rowed with oars upon large rivers; but over a creek, which is about three miles from this town, called Coneftoga, they pull them acrofs by means of ropes faftened to either fhore.

After you get over the Delaware, a new country prefents itfelf, extremely well cultivated and inhabited; the roads are lined with farm houfes, fome of which are near the road, and fome at a little diftance, and the fpace between the road and houfes is taken up with fields and meadows; fome of them are built of ftone, two ftories high, and covered with cedar fhingles, but moft of them are wooden, with the crevices ftopped with clay; the ovens are commonly built a little diftance from the houfe, and under a roof to fecure them againft the weather.

The farmers in Penfylvania, and in the Jerfeys, pay more attention to the conftruction of their barns than their dwelling-houfes. The building is nearly as large

large as a common country church, the roof very lofty, and covered with fhingles, declining on both fides, but not very fteep, the walls are about thirty feet; in the middle is the threfhing-floor, and above it a loft for the corn unthrefhed; on one fide is a ftable, and on the other a cow-houfe, and the fmall cattle have their particular ftables and ftyes; and at the gable end of this building there are great gates, fo that a horfe and cart can go ftrait through: thus is the threfhing-floor, ftable, hay-loft, cowhoufe, coach-houfe, &c. all under one roof.

The Penfylvanians are an induftrious and hardy people, they are moft of them fubftantial, but cannot be confidered rich, it being rarely the cafe with landed people. However, they are well lodged, fed, and clad, and the latter at an eafy rate, as the inferior people manufacture moft of their own apparel, both linnens and woollens,

and

d are more induſtrious of themſelves, ving but few blacks among them.

They have a curious method to prevent eir geeſe from creeping through broken :loſures, by means of four little ſticks, out a foot in length, which are faſtened ɔfsways about their necks. You cannot ιagine how extremely aukward they apar, though it is diverting enough to ſee em walk with this ornament; their mode eventing horſes from leaping over their :loſures is equally as curious, they faſten und the horſe's neck a piece of wood, at e lower end of which is a hook, which, tching in the railing, ſtops the horſe juſt he is riſing to leap over; ſome indeed, ſten the fore and hind foot together, ιich makes them walk ſlow; both theſe ethods are extremely dangerous to the ırſes.

In

In New England they have a very few hives of bees, but in this province, almoſt every farm houſe has ſeven or eight; it is ſomewhat remarkable they ſhould be more predominant here, as all the bees upon the Continent were originally brought from England to Boſton, about one hundred years ago; the bee is not natural to America, for the firſt planters never obſerved a ſingle one in the immenſe tract of woods they cleared, and what I think ſtands forth a moſt indubitable proof that it is not the Indians, as they have a word in their language for all animals, natives of the country, have no word for a bee, and therefore they call them by the name of the *Englishman's Fly*. On the high road from Philadelphia to this town are mileſtones, which are the firſt I obſerved put up in this country, as to the other parts, the inhabitants only compute the diſtance at gueſs. It was no little mortification that we were debarred

ſeeing

ing one of the firſt cities of America
(Philadelphia) we paſſed within twelve
miles of it, and ſeveral of us made application to the Commanding Officer who
eſcorted us, to grant permiſſion for us to
go into the city, aſſuring him we would
upon our honour join the troops at night.
He was a good-natured man, and nearly
complying with our requeſt, but on a ſud-
den ſaid, he really could not, as Congreſs
would be mightily diſpleaſed at it; however, we conſole ourſelves, that on our exchange, we may have an opportunity of
ſeeing it.

In the greateſt part of our march the
inhabitants were making of cyder, for in
almoſt every farm there is a preſs, though
made in a different manner; ſome make
uſe of a wheel made of thick oak plank,
which turns upon a wooden axis, by means
of a horſe drawing it, and ſome have ſtone
wheels, but they are moſtly of the former.

In

In travelling through Penfylvania, you meet with people of almoft every different perfuafion of religion that exifts; in fhort, the diverfity of religions, nations, and languages here is aftonifhing, at the fame time, the harmony they live in no lefs edifying, notwithftanding every one, who wifhes well to religion, is hurt to fee the diverfity that prevails, and would, by the moft foothing means, endeavour to prevent it; yet, when the misfortune once takes place, and there is no longer an union of fentiments, it is neverthelefs glorious to preferve an union of affections, and certainly it muft be highly pleafing to fee men live, though of fo many different perfuafions, yet, to the fame Chriftian principles, and though not of the fame religion, ftill to the great end of all, the profperity and welfare of mankind. Among the numerous fects of religion with which this province abounds, for there are Churchmen, Quakers, Calvinifts, s, Lutherans, Catholics, Methodists, nists, Moravians, Independants, Anaptists, there is a sect which, perhaps, never heard of, called the Dumplers; sect took its origin from a German, o, weary of the world, retired to a very itary place, about fifty miles from Philelphia, in order to give up his whole e to contemplation; several of his counmen came to visit him in his retreat, d by his pious, simple, and peaceable nners, many were induced to settle near n, and, in a short time adopting his des, they formed a little colony, which y named Euphrates, in allusion to that er upon whose borders the Hebrews re accustomed to sing psalms.

Their little city is built in the form of triangle, and bordered with mulberry d apple-trees, very regularly planted. the center of the town is a large chard, and between the orchard and the
ranges

ranges of trees that are planted round the borders, are their houses, which are built of wood, and three stories high, in these every Dumpler is left to enjoy his meditations without disturbance; these contemplative men, in the whole, do not amount to more than five hundred; their territory is nearly three hundred acres in extent, on one side is a river, on another a piece of stagnated water, and on the other two are mountains covered with trees.

They have women of their community, who live separate from the men; they seldom see each other but at places of worship, and never have meetings of any kind but for public business; their whole life is spent in labor, prayer, and sleep; twice every day and night they are summoned from their cells to attend divine service; as to their religion, in some measure, it resembles the Quakers, for every individual, if he thinks himself inspired, has a right to preach.---The subjects they chiefly difcourfe upon are humility, temperance, charity, and other Chriftian virtues; never violating that day held facred amongft all perfuafions; they admit of a Hell and a Paradife, but deny the eternity of future punifhments. As to the doctrine of original fin, they hold it as impious blafphemy, together with every tenet that is fevere to man, deeming it injurious to divinity.---As they allow no merit to any but voluntary works, baptifm is only adminiftered to the adult; neverthelefs, they think it fo effentially neceffary to falvation, as to imagine the fouls of Chriftians are employed in the other world, in the converfion of thofe who have not died under the light of the Gofpel.

Religion among the Dumplers, has the fame effect philofophy had upon the Stoics, rendering them infenfible to every kind

kind of infult; they are more paffive and difinterefted than the Quakers, for they will fuffer themfelves to be cheated, robbed, and abufed, without the leaft idea of retaliation, or even a complaint.

Their drefs is very fimple and plain, confifting of a long white gown, from whence hangs a hood to ferve the purpofes of a hat, a coarfe fhirt, thick fhoes, and very wide breeches, fomething refembling thofe the Turks wear. The men wear their beards to a great length, fome I faw were down to the waift; at the firft fight of them, I could not help comparing them to our old ancient bards, the Druids, from their reverential appearance; the women are drefied fimilar to the men, excepting the breeches.

Their life is very abftemious, and eating no meats, not that they deem it unlawful, but more conformable to the fpirit of Chriftianity,

Chriſtianity, which they argue has an averſion to blood, and upon thoſe grounds they ſubſiſt only on vegetables, and the produce of the earth.

They follow with great chearfulneſs their various branches of buſineſs, in ſome one of which, every individual partakes, and the produce of their labor is depoſited in one common ſtock, to ſupply the neceſſities of every individual, and by this union of induſtry, they have not only eſtabliſhed agriculture and manufactures, ſufficient to ſupport this little ſociety, but ſuperfluities for the purpoſes of exchange for European commodities.

Though the two ſexes live ſeparate, they do not renounce matrimony, but thoſe who are diſpoſed to it leave the city and ſettle in the country, on a tract of land which the Dumplers have purchaſed for that purpose, the couple are supported at the public expences, which they repay by the produce of their labor, and their children are sent to Germany for education. Without this wise policy, the Dumplers would be little better than Monks, and in process of time annihilated.

Although there are so many sects, and such a difference of religious opinions in this province, it is surprizing the harmony which subsists among them; they consider themselves as children of the same father, and live like brethren, because they have the liberty of thinking like men, to this pleasing harmony, in a great measure, is to be attributed the rapid and flourishing state of Pensylvania, above all the other provinces. Would to Heaven that harmony was equally as prevalant all over the globe; if it was, I think you'll acquiesce
with

with me in opinion, that it would be for the general welfare of mankind.

An officer who is exchanged, and going to New-York, having sent for my letters, I must hastily conclude, assuring you, I am

Yours, &c.

LETTER LX.

Lancaster, in Penſylvania,
Dec. 17, 1778.

MY DEAR FRIEND,

IN our way hither, we croſſed the Skuylkill, over the bridge built by General Waſhington's army, when they were encamped at Valley-Forge. I imagine it was the intention of the Americans, that this bridge ſhould remain as a triumphal memento, for in the center of every arch is engraved in the wood, the names of the principal Generals in their country; and in the middle arch was General Waſhington's, with the date of the year: this

bridge

bridge was built to preserve a communication, and to favor a retreat, in cafe they were compelled to quit their encampment.

Our troops flept in the huts at Valley-Forge, which had been conftructed by the Americans; and as we waited till late the next day for the delivery of provifions before we marched, I had a full opportunity to reconnoitre the whole camp: on the eaft and fouth fide were entrenchments, with a ditch fix feet wide and three deep, the mound not four feet high, very narrow, and eafily to have been beat down with cannon; two redoubts were alfo begun, but not compleated, the Skuylkill was on the left, and as I before obferved, with a bridge acrofs; the rear was moftly covered by an impaffable precipice formed by Valley Creek, having only a narrow paffage near the Skuylkill: this camp was by no means difficult of accefs, for the right

right was attainable, and in one part of the front the afcent was fcarcely to be perceived, the defences were exceedingly weak, and this is the only inftance I ever faw of the Americans having fuch flight works, thefe being fuch as a fix-pounder could eafily have battered down; the ditches were not more than three feet deep, and fo narrow, that a drum-boy might with eafe leap over.

A Loyalift, at whofe houfe I was quartered, at Valley Forge, and who refided there at the time Wafhington's army was encamped, told me, that when General Wafhington chofe that fpot for his Winter quarters, his men were obliged to build them huts with round logs, fill the interftices with clay, and cover them with loofe ftraw and dirt, very uncomfortable, as the fhelter was not fecure from the weather, where the men fuffered exceedingly from the inclemency of the
feafon,

season, the camp disorder raged among them, the greater part of them were in a manner naked at that severe season of the year; many without shoes and stockings, and very few, except the Virginia troops, with the necessary cloathing: his army was wasting away by sickness, that raged with extreme mortality in all his different hospitals, which are no less than eleven, and without the essential medicines to relieve them; his army was likewise diminished by constant desertions in companies, from ten to fifty at a time, that at one period, it was reduced to four thousand men, and those with propriety could not be called effective. The horses from being constantly exposed to showers of rain and falls of snow, both day and night, were in such a condition, that many of them died, and the rest were so emaciated, as to be unfit for labor; had he been attacked and repulsed, he must have left behind all his artillery, for want of horſes to convey it; in addition to all theſe diſtreſſes, Waſhington had not in his camp, at any one time, a week's proviſion for man and horſe, and ſometimes he was totally deſtitute.

The Loyaliſts greatly cenſure General Howe, in ſuffering Waſhington to continue in this weak and dangerous ſtate from December till May, and equally aſtoniſhed what could be the motive he did not attack, ſurround, or take by ſiege, the whole army, when the ſeverity of the weather was gone—they expected that in the months of March, April, and May, they ſhould hear of the camp being ſtormed or beſieged. Certainly the ſituation of it favored either, for on the left was the Skuylkill that was impaſſable, but over the bridge, on the rear, lay Valley Creek, with the precipice and narrow paſs; on the right, and in the front, it could be approached on equal terms; by posting two thousand men on a commanding ground, near the bridge on the North side of the Skuylkill, it would have rendered the escape of the enemy on the left impossible. Two thousand posted on a like ground opposite the narrow pass, effectually prevented a retreat by the rear, and five or six thousand men placed on the right and in the front of his camp, would have deprived them of flight on those sides; the positions were such, that if any corps were attacked, they could instantly have been supported; under all these favorable circumstances, success was to be little doubted; but it should seem that General Howe was exactly in the same situation as General Burgoyne, respecting intelligence, obtaining none he could place a perfect reliance on. In fact, the Americans have a most decided superiority over us this war in that respect, our post and situations, nay, even secret marches, with their

their intentions, are made known to General Washington by the inumerable spies and secret enemies who come into our camp and lines, under the specious character of Loyalists; it is quite the reverse with him, every man who enters his camp is known to some one or other, as his army is composed of troops from every province.

[The Loyalists in Pensylvenia generally accuse General Howe with ungrateful conduct, in abandoning Philadelphia, after all the assistance they had given him, and not having, during the Winter, endeavored to dislodged General Washington at Valley Forge, suffering the enemy to harrass and distress the loyal inhabitants on every side of the British lines, destroying their mills, seizing their grain, horses and cattle, imprisoning, whipping, branding and killing the unhappy people, devoted to the cause of their Sovereign, who, at every risque, rifque were daily fupplying the army, navy, and Loyal inhabitants within the lines, with every neceffary, and luxury the country afforded.

Indeed, the Loyalifts of Penfylvania are greatly to be pitied, for they have been much perfecuted fince our troops evacuted Philadelphia, their loyalty is greatly abated, as they conceive themfelves made a facrifice of by the conduct of General Howe; and are fo exceeding incenfed, and violent againft him, they do not hefitate to fay, that in eafe and comfort, in the city of Philadelphia, he cared little for military fame or glory; that he neglected his duty to his King and country, that he neglected the intereft and fafety of the country he was fent to protect, and that his whole conduct was founded on private intereft and ambition; you fhall not know my fentiments 'till we meet.

At

At a poor farm houſe I was quartered at, the night before we came into this town, I was much ſurprized when it grew dark, to ſee the landlady bring in a couple of green wax-candles, which at firſt we really took them to be; but lo! they were made from the berries of a tree, which is called the tallow ſhrub, as they produce a kind of wax or tallow; this plant grows in England, and known by the name of the candleberry tree. The method of making the fat from theſe berries, is by gathering them late in the Autumn, then they are put into a pot of boiling water; of courſe the fat melts out, and floats on the ſurface, which is ſkimmed off, and this proceſs is continued, 'till there is no fat left when congealed, it has a green dirty color, but after refined, becomes perfectly tranſparent; with this they manufacture their candles; they were formerly much uſed, but before the war, they could procure tallow in great abundance, and there fore used it in preference, as the time for gathering the berries and preparing them, scarcely repays the trouble. Now the poor inhabitants are obliged to have recourse to them, as no tallow is imported, and all the cattle is taken for the supply of the army. There are many qualities appertaining to the candles made from their berries; they do not easily bend or melt in Summer, as common candles, they burn better and slower, and when extinguished, do not smoak, but rather evaporate with an agreeable odour.

The town of Lancaster is the largest inland town in America, it contains at least ten thousand inhabitants, chiefly Germans and Irish, there are some few good houses, and exclusive of those, it appears neither handsome, nor agreeable; however the markets are plentifully supplied with all sorts of provision, and the cyder is very excellent,

cellent, the neareſt to Engliſh of any I met with in America.

Moſt of the houſes before the door have an elevation, to which you aſcend by ſteps from the ſtreet, reſembling a ſmall balcony with benches on both ſides, where the inhabitants ſit and enjoy the freſh air, and view the people paſſing; moſt of them have ſtoves ſimilar to thoſe of the Canadians.

This town, before the commencement of theſe unhappy troubles, carried on a conſiderable trade with Philadelphia, and the frontier ſettlements; now it has ſcarcely ſufficient to ſupply the inhabitants, and the neighbouring farms; it is really a diſtreſſing circumſtance, to ſee ſuch a populous, and no doubt, flouriſhing town once a ſcene of buſtling induſtry, now in a ſtate of ſupineneſs, the ſhopkeepers lolling and ſmoaking at their doors

thei

their shops which were overflowing with sorts of commodities, scarcely contain more than Shakespere's Apothecary's " a " beggarly account of empty boxes," unless indeed, some French frippery, which the inhabitants will not purchase; the only little sign of trade that I could perceive, was among sadlers and gunsmiths, who were making materials for the Continental army:——This unhappy war has thrown the Americans into such a state, that it will be a century before they can recover from it.

The town of Lancaster has no building of any consequence, except the Lutheran church, which, is only built of brick, the inside has a most magnificent appearance; the large galleries on each side, the spacious organ-loft, supported by Corinthian pillars, are exceedingly beautiful, and there are pillars of the Ionic order, from the galleries to the roof. The altar-
piece

piece is very elegantly ornamented; th
whole of the church, as well as the or
gan, painted white with gilt decorations
which has a very neat appearance; i
greatly reminded me of the chapel a
Greenwich Hofpital; the organ is reckon
ed the largeft and beft in America, it wa
built by a German, who refides abou
feventeen miles from Lancafter, he mad
every individual part of it with his ow
hands; it was near feven years in com
pleating; the organ has not only ever
pipe and ftop that is in moft others, bu
it has many other pipes to fwell the bafs
which are of an amazing circumference
and thefe are played upon by the feet
there being a row of wooden keys that th
performer treads on. I do not recollec
ever feeing an organ of this conftruction
except thofe of the Savoy Chapel and St
Paul's; in the latter they are fhut up as th
vibration of found was found too power
ful for the dome; but then they had onl
fou

four or five of thefe wooden keys, whereas this organ has a dozen: the man who fhewed the inftrument played on it, and the effect of thefe keys was aftonifhing, it abfolutely made the very building fhake. It is the largeft, and I think the fineft I ever faw, without exception; and when you examine it, you wonder it did not take up the man's whole life in conftructing; to eftimate its goodnefs and value, I fhall only tell you it coft two thoufand five hundred pounds fterling; to you who are fo mufical, what a treat would it be to be here a few hours only, unlefs indeed, you would think a few more not thrown away entirely, when allotted to

Yours, &c.

LETTER LXI.

Frederick-Town, in Marylan[d]
Dec. 25th, 1778.

MY DEAR FRIEND,

AFTER we left Lancaster, we cross[ed] the Susquehannah, which, though large, broad, and beautiful river, is e[x]tremely dangerous, on account of the r[a]pidity of the current, and innumerab[le] small rocks that just make their appearan[ce] above the surface; in crossing it we we[re] not without our fears, for a scowl, belon[g]ing to the second brigade, in which Lo[rd] Torphinchin, and a number of office[rs] and soldiers of the twenty-first regime[nt] was near being loft by ftriking on one of thefe rocks; this river falls into the Chefapeak and forms the head of that vaft water, which, though one of the largeft and moft beautiful rivers in America, is the leaft ufeful, as it is not navigable above twelve or fifteen miles at the fartheft, for fhips of any burthen, and above that fcarcely fo for canoes; the utility of this river would be great, if the navigation, even for canoes was practicable, as the fource of the eaft branch of this river is in the Mohawk country, and from thence to the mouth in the Chefapeak, is near feven hundred miles.

After we croffed the Sufquehannah, we arrived at York-town, which was fome time the feat of Congrefs; this is reckoned the fecond inland town in America, it is not near fo large as Lancafter, but much pleafanter, being fituated on Codorow-creek, a pretty ftream which falls into the Sequehannah;

hannah; this town contains between two and three thousand inhabitants, chiefly Irish, intermixed with a few Germans; here was formerly more trade than in Lancaster, and notwithstanding the troubles, it has still more the appearance of it; as we came into the town at four o'clock in the afternoon, and marched the next morning, you may easily imagine I had but little time to make any very particular observations; but in walking about, I saw the Court-house and a few churches, which are very neat brick buildings, and I remarked the houses were much better built, and with more regularity than at Lancaster; of the two though York is considerably less than the other, I should give it the preference for a place of residence.

As I observed in a former letter, it was with a view and hope that the men would desert, that the Congress marched us a
th

this inclement season; numbers have answered their wishes, especially the Germans, who seeing in what a comfortable manner their countrymen live, left us in great numbers, as we marched through New-York, the Jerseys and Pensylvania; among the number of deserters is my servant, who, as we left Lancaster, ran from me with my horse, portmanteau, and every thing he could take with him. I did not miss him till night, as I concluded he was with the baggage waggons; the next morning I obtained permission from the officer that escorted us, to return back in pursuit of him, as I had reasons to suppose he was going back to New-England; in the afternoon, on the other side of Lancaster, I met the first brigade of the Germans, who were marching into the town. Being acquainted with Colonel Mingen, who commanded, he enquired if I had orders for him, but telling him the purport of my return, he informed me that he had

met my servant that morning, just as they
were going to march; he enquired of him
how I did, and the reason of his returning
when the fellow said " I was very well
" and that I desired my compliments to
" him, if he should meet him, and that
" he was returning for a pair of saddle
" bags that he left behind on the road.
After this I thought any pursuit in vain
therefore returned back to the regiment
who, by this time, had arrived in this
town.

We have been greatly perplexed in our
march through the different provinces, b
the dollars being of such various value; i
some it is only six shillings, in other
seven, seven and sixpence, and eight shi
lings. The provinces entertain little op
nion as to the value of their neighbour
money, as it will not pass in the nex
province; the New-York money will no
pass in the Jerseys, nor that of the Jerse

in Penſylvania, and ſo on. The Congreſs money is taken throughout the whole of them, but there are ſome provinces which deem their own money of more real value than that of Congreſs, and take it in preference, not that they dare refuſe the other, as it would be deemed high treaſon.

Till our arrival at this place, we have had the moſt delightful weather imaginable, but yeſterday morning there came on a moſt violent ſnow ſtorm, and which laſted the whole day; it was as ſevere as any I ever ſaw in Canada; the ſnow is up to one's knees, which has rendered the Potowmack ſo dangerous, that we are waiting here till it either freezes over, or becomes paſſable, the firſt brigade are fortunate, for by this time, they are arrived at Charlotteſville.

Frederick Town is a fine large town, and has a very noble appearance, as the

houses are mostly formed of brick an
stone, there being very few timber build
ings in it; it contains near two thousan
inhabitants, chiefly Germans, quite in
land, the nearest port being George Town
which is fifty miles distant, the only rive
which is the Potowmack, is eight mile
from the town.

About four miles before you enter i
you cross the Monoccacy Creek, which
without a guide to shew the ford,
stranger must inevitably be carried dow
the stream; this ford is in the form of
crescent, and made with large loose stone
that a horse is in continual danger of fall
ing; the water, in general, is up to th
skirts of the saddle, and after the least fa
of rain, it is impassable for some hours
there is a ferry-boat, but it is so badl
attended, and in such a shattered state
that you are afraid to venture in it.

I am quartered at the houfe of a Mr. McMurdo, who is the Commiflary of Provifions in this town, and, although ftrongly attached to the caufe of the Americans, poffeffes very philanthropic ideas, his treatment and polite behaviour to the officers quartered at his houfe, truly mark the gentleman and man of the world.---His attention is fuch, that although for this day, which is as much a day of feftival as in England, he has been engaged for fome time paft among his friends and relations, he would ftay at home, and entertain us with an excellent Chriftmas dinner, not even forgetting plumb-pudding. If the Americans in general poffeffed fuch liberal fentiments, it would prevent the many horrid barbarities and perfecutions which arife in confequence of this unnatural war, and which have branded the name of America with an odium, that no time can obliterate, no merit expunge.

I now experience what has been often told me, that the further I went to the southward, I should find the inhabitants possess more liberality and hospitality I remain

Your's, &c.

LETTER LXII.

Jones's Plantation, near Charlottesville, in Virginia, Jan. 20, 1779.

MY DEAR FRIEND,

AFTER we left Frederick Town, we crossed the Potowmack River with imminent danger, as the current was very rapid, large floats of ice swimming down it, though the river was only half a mile wide, the scowl that I crossed over in had several narrow escapes; at one time it was quite fastened in the ice, but by great exertions of the men in breaking it, we made good our landing on the opposite shore, near a mile lower than the Ferry.

The difficulty of crossing was only a fore-runner of the hardships and fatigues we were to experience on our entering Virginia; for on our march to this place, the men experienced such distresses, as were severe in the extreme; the roads were exceedingly bad from the late fall of snow, which was encrusted, but not sufficiently to bear the weight of a man, so we were continually sinking us up to our knees, and cutting our shins and ancles, and, perhaps, after a march of sixteen or eighteen miles in this maner, at night the privates had to sleep in woods; after their arrival at the place of destination, the officers had to ride five or six miles to find a hovel to rest in.

But on our arrival at Charlottesville, no pen can describe the scene of misery and confusion that ensued; the officers of the first and second brigade were in the town, and our arrival added to their distress;

this

this famous place we had heard so much of, consisted only of a Court-house, one tavern, and about a dozen houses; all of which were crowded with officers, those of our brigade therefore, were obliged to ride about the country, and entreat the inhabitants to take us in.

As to the men, the situation was truly horrible, after the hard shifts they had experienced in their march from the Potowmack, they were, instead of comfortable barracks, conducted into a wood, where a few log huts were just begun to be built, the most part not covered over, and all of them full of snow; these the men were obliged to clear out, and cover over to secure themselves from the inclemency of the weather as quick as they could, and in the course of two or three days rendered them a habitable, but by no means a comfortable retirement; what added greatly to the distresses of the men,
was

was the want of provisions, as none had as yet arrived for the troops, and for six days they subsisted on the meal of Indian corn made into cakes. The person who had the management of every thing, informed us that we were not expected till Spring.

Never was a country so destitute of every comfort, provisions were not to be purchased for ten days; the officers subsisted upon salt pork, and Indian corn made into cakes, not a drop of any kind of spirit, what little there had been, was already consumed by the first and second brigade; many officers, to comfort themselves, put red pepper into water, to drink by way of cordial.

Upon a representation of our situation by Brigadier General Hamilton, to Colonel Bland, who commanded the American troops, he promised to render the situa tion of the men as comfortable as poffible, and with all expedition. As to the officers, upon figning a parole, they might go to Richmond and other adjacent towns, to procure themfelves quarters, accordingly a parole was figned, which allowed a circuit of near one hundred miles. And after the officers had drawn lots, as three were to remain in the barracks with the men, or at Charlottifville, the principal part of them fet off for Richmond, many of them are at plantations, twenty or thirty miles from the barracks. I am quartered with Major Mafter and four other officers of our regiment, at this plantation, about twenty miles from the barracks; the owner has given up his houfe, and gone to refide at his overfeer's, and for the ufe of his houfe, we pay him two guineas a week.

On the arrival of the troops at Charlottefville, the officers, what with vexation,
and

and to keep out the cold, drank rather freely of an abominable liquor, called peach brandy, which, if drank to excefs, the fumes raife an abfolute delirium, and in their cups, feveral were guilty of deeds that would admit of no apology, the inhabitants muft have actually thought us mad, for in the courfe of three or four days, there were no lefs that fix or feven duels fought.

Colonel Bland, who commands the American troops, was formerly a phyfician, at a place called Peterfburg, on the James River, but on the commencement of the war, as being fome way related to Bland, who wrote a military treatife, he felt a martial fpirit arife in him, therefore quitted the Æfculapian art, and at his own expence raifed a regiment of light horfe. As to thofe troops of his regiment with Wafhington's army, I cannot fay any thing, but the two that th

Colonel has with him here, for the purposes of expresses and attendance, are the most curious figures you ever saw; some, like Prince Prettyman, with one boot, others less fortunate, without any; some hoseless, with their feet peeping out of their shoes; others with breeches that put decency to the blush; some in short jackets, some in long coats, but all have fine dragoon caps, and long swords slung round them, some with holsters, some without, but gadamercy pistols, for they have not a brace and a half among them, but they are tolerably well mounted, and that is the only thing you can advance in their favor; the Colonel is so fond of his Dragoons, that he reviews and manœuvres them every morning, and whenever he rides out, has two with drawn swords before, and two behind; it is really laughable to see him thus attended with his ragged regiment, which looks, to borrow Shakespeare's idea, as if the gibbets had been robbed to make it up---then the Colonel himself, notwithstanding his martial spirit

spirit, has all the grave deportment, as he was going to a confultation.

The houfe that we refide in is fituat[ed] upon an eminence, commanding a profp[ect] of near thirty miles around it, and t[he] face of the country appears an immer[se] foreft, interfperfed with various plant[a]tions, four or five miles diftant from ea[ch] other; on thefe there is a dwelling-hou[se] in the center, with kitchens, fmoke-hou[se] and out-houfes detached, and from t[he] various buildings, each plantation has t[he] appearance of a fmall village; at fo[me] little diftance from the houfes, [are] peach and apple orchards, &c. and fc[at]tered over the plantations are the negr[o] huts and tobacco-houfes, which are la[rge,] built of wood, for the cure of that arti[cle.]

The houfes are moft of them buil[t of] wood, the roof being covered with fhing[les] and not always lathed and plaftered wi[th]in, only thofe of the better fort that
finif[h]

finifhed in that manner, and painted on the outfide; the chimneys are often of brick, but the generality of them are wood, coated in the infide with clay; the windows of the better fort are glazed, the reft have only wooden fhutters.

The fences and enclofures in this province are different from the others, for thofe to the northward are made either of ftone or rails let into pofts, about a foot afunder; here they are compofed of what is termed *fence rails*, which are made out of trees cut or fawed into lengths of about twelve feet, that are mauld or fplit into rails from four to fix inches diameter.

When they form an inclofure, thefe rails are laid fo, that they crofs each other obliquely at each end, and are laid zig zag to the amount of ten or eleven rails in height, then ftakes are put againft each corner, double acrofs, with the lower ends drove a little into the ground,

and above these stakes is placed a rail o
double the size of the others, which i
termed the rider, which, in a manner
locks up the whole, and keeps the fenc
firm and steady.

These enclosures are generally seven o
eight feet high, they are not very strong
but convenient, as they can be removed t
any other place, where they may be mor
necessary; from a mode of constructing
these enclosures in a zig zag form, th
New-Englanders have a saying, when
man is in liquor, *he is making Virgini
fences.*

Their manner of clearing the land i
by cutting a circle round the tree throug
the bark quite to the wood, before the sa
rises, which kills it; they then clear th
small brush-wood and cultivate the groun
leaving the trees to rot standing, whic
happens in a very few years; and aft
receivir

receiving the circular wound, they never more bear leaves; a large field in this state has a very singular, striking, and dreadful appearance, it should seem dangerous to walk in them, for the trees are of a prodigious magnitude and height, from which are impending in awful ruins vast limbs, and branches of an enormous size, which are continually breaking off, and frequently whole trees are falling to the ground with a most horrible crash, the sound of which is greatly encreased and protracted by the surrounding echoes: yet I am informed, notwithstanding the danger, few accidents happen from them, except to cattle.

Upon our informing the Commissary of Provisions where we were quartered, he gave us an order upon a Colonel Cole, who resides about four miles distant, to supply us, he being appointed to collect for the use of the Congress in this district,

who, upon application, sent us about
month's provision of flour and salt por[k]
for ourselves and servants. As the car[t]
with the provisions came through th[e]
plantation, I was much surprized to se[e]
all the cattle, horses, sheep, and hogs fol[-]
lowing it, nor could the driver keep the[m]
off, till he came to the house. I foun[d]
this was to lick the barrels which con[-]
tained the salt meat.

The inhabitants throughout America
whose habitations are at any great dis[-]
tance from the sea or salt-water, giv[e]
their cattle and horses salt once or twice [a]
week, with which they are satisfied, bu[t]
here they were so distracted after it, as t[o]
lick the earth where there has been any po[rt]
liquor in which salt meat has been boile[d]
till they have licked up all the saline parti[-]
cles, and if a horse that has been rode har[d]
and in a sweat, is turned out with other[s]

they each inſtantly ſurround and lick him.

Nature ſeems to have prompted theſe animals by inſtinct, as if ſenſible theſe ſaline particles were abſolutely neceſſary to correct the acidity ariſing from a ſuperabundant accumulation in the ſtomach of the vegetable juices; the inhabitants therefore not only give them ſalt as medicinal, and to promote their encreaſe of fleſh, but to render them gentle and tame, and to allure them to viſit their plantations; otherwiſe, as they are not deficient in provender in Winter, they would run wild and roam beyond the reach of their owners, in theſe immenſe woods; yet notwithſtanding this precaution, great numbers do run at large entirely wild, and have no proprietors, but thoſe on whoſe lands they are found.

Moſt perſons who are in poſſeſſion c
any conſiderable plantation, have what i
called a right in the woods, by which the
are entitled to a certain proportion of th
ewe cattle that run wild, which they ca
diſpoſe of, or transfer as affixed property
there is no other criterion to aſcertain ther
but by branding, or putting ſome mar
on them; each perſon differs in this, an
they are recorded in the county court, ſuc
property is further ſecured by an act (
the aſſembly, which made it felony, t
alter or deface the marks.

Moſt of the planters conſign the care (
their plantations and negroes to an ove
ſeer, even the man whoſe houſe we ren
has his overſeer, though he could wit
eaſe ſuperintend it himſelf; but if the
poſſeſs a few negroes, they think it b
neath their dignity, added to which, the
are ſo abominably lazy. I'll give yc

a sketch of this man's general way of living.

He rises about eight o'clock, drinks what he calls a julep, which is a large glass of rum, sweetened with sugar, and then walks, or more generally rides round his plantation, views his stock, inspects his crops, and returns about ten o'clock to breakfast on cold meat, or ham, fried hommony, toast and cyder; tea and coffee is seldom tasted, but by the women. He then saunters about the house, sometimes amusing himself with the little negroes who are playing round the door, or else scraping on a fiddle; about twelve or one he drinks toddy, to create him an appetite for his dinner, which he sits down to at two o'clock; after he has dined, he generally lays down on the bed, and rises about five, then perhaps sips some tea with his wife, but commonly drinks toddy 'till bed time; during all this he is
neither

neither drunk nor fober, but in a ftate of ftupefaction; this is his ufual mode of living, which he feldom varies, and only quits his plantation to attend the Court-Houfe on court days, or to fome horfe race or cock fight; at which times he gets fo egregioufly drunk, that his wife fends a couple of negroes to conduct him fafe home.

Thus the whole management of the plantation is left to the overfeer, who as an encouragement to make the moft of the crops, has a certain portion as his wages, but not having any intereft in the negroes, any further than their labour, he drives and whips them about, and works them beyond their ftrength, and fometimes till they expire; he feels no lofs in their death, he knows the plantation muft be fupplied, and his humanity is eftimated by his intereft, which rifes always above freezing point.

It is the poor negroes who alone work hard, and I am forry to fay, fare hard. Incredible is the fatigue which the poor wretches undergo, and that nature fhould be able to fupport it; there certainly muft be fomething in their conftitutions, as well as their color, different from us, that enables them to endure it.

They are called up at day break, and feldom allowed to fwallow a mouthful of homminy, or hoe cake, but are drawn out into the field immediately, where they continue at hard labour, without intermiffion, till noon, when they go to their dinners, and are feldom allowed an hour for that purpofe; their meals confift of homminy and falt, and if their mafter is a man of humanity, touched by the finer feelings of love and fenfibility, he allows them twice a week a little fat fkimmed milk, rufty bacon, or falt herring, to relifh this miferable and fcanty fare. The man

man at this plantation, in lieu of thefe, grants his negroes an acre of ground, and all Saturday afternoon to raife grain and poultry for themfelves. After they have dined, they return to labor in the field, until dufk in the evening; here one naturally imagines the daily labor of thefe poor creatures was over, not fo, they repair to the tobacco houfes, where each has a tafk of ftripping allotted which takes them up fome hours, or elfe they have fuch a quantity of Indian corn to hufk, and if they neglect it, are tied up in the morning, and receive a number of lafhes from thofe unfeeling monfters, the overfeers, whofe mafters fuffer them to exercife their brutal authority without conftraint. Thus by their night tafk, it is late in the evening before thefe poor creatures return to their fecond fcanty meal, and the time taken up at it encroaches upon their hours of fleep which for refrefhment of food and fleep together can never be reckoned to exceed eight.

When they lay themselves down to rest, their comforts are equally miserable and limited, for they sleep on a bench, or on the ground, with an old scanty blanket, which serves them at once for bed and covering, their cloathing is not less wretched, consisting of a shirt and trowsers of coarse, thin, hard, hempen stuff, in the Summer, with an addition of a very coarse woollen jacket, breeches and shoes in Winter. But since the war, their masters, for they cannot get the cloathing as usual, suffer them to go in rags, and many in a state of nudity.

The female slaves share labor and repose just in the same manner, except a few who are term'd house negroes, and are employed in household drudgery.

These

These poor creatures are all submissio[n]
to injuries and insults, and are obliged t[o]
be passive, nor dare they resist or defen[d]
themselves if attacked, without the smalle[st]
provocation, by a white person, as the la[w]
directs the negroe's arm to be cut off wh[en]
raises it against a white person, should
be only in defence against wanton ba[r]
barity and outrage.

Notwithstanding this humiliating sta[te]
and rigid treatment to which this wretch[ed]
race are subject, they are devoid of ca[re]
and appear jovial, contented and happ[y.]
It is a fortunate circumstance that th[ey]
possess, and are blessed with such an ea[sy]
satisfied disposition, otherwise they m[ust]
inevitably sink under such a complicati[on]
of misery and wretchedness; what is s[in]
gularly remarkable, they always carry o[n]
a piece of fire, and kindle one near th[eir]
work, let the weather be ever so hot a[nd]
sultry.

As I have several times mentioned homminy and hoe-cake, it may not be amifs to explain them: the former is made of Indian corn, which is coarfely broke, and boiled with a few French beans, till it is almoft a pulp. Hoe-cake is Indian corn ground into meal, kneaded into a dough, and baked before a fire, but as the negroes bake theirs on the hoes that they work with, they have the appellation of hoe-cakes. Thefe are in common ufe among the inhabitants, I cannot fay they are palateable, for as to flavor, one made of fawduft would be equally good, and not unlike it in appearance, but they are certainly a very ftrong and hearty food.

Having given you a pretty good fketch of thefe back-fettlers, in my next I fhall be able to afford you fome account of the country, and the lives and manners of the people in the lower parts of this province,

for

for in a few days I am going to Richmo
to purchafe fome liquors and neceffari
to render our fituation a little comfo
able, in this dreary region of woods a
wretchednefs. I remain

Yours, &c.

LE

LETTER LXIII.

Richmond, in Virginia,
Feb. 12 1779.

MY DEAR FRIEND,

A FEW days after my laft letter, with your friend Johnfon of our regiment, I fet off for this place, and an uncomfortable journey we had, as the feafon was unfavorable, and rendered travelling very dangerous, on account of the fnow then on the ground, and the continued falls of fleet, till our arrival at this place.

The country is fo much covered with woods, that you travel a long time without

out seeing an habitation, (the first
met with, was near eighteen miles fro
Charlottesville) you can scarcely concei
the difficulty in finding the proper road
as they are hardly to be guessed at by tho
who have often used to travel in America
when one is bad, they make another in
different direction, added to which, tl
planters, *sans ceremonie* turn a road to fu
their own convenience, and render it mo
commodious to their plantation, if pe
chance you meet an inhabitant and e
quire your way, his directions are,
possible, more perplexing than the roa
themselves, for he tells you to keep t
right hand path, then you'll come to
old field, you are to cross that, and tl
you'll come to the fence of such a o
plantation, then keep that fence, ;
you'll come to a road that has three fo
(which is their manner of describing
partings in the roads) keep the right h
fork for about half a mile, and then yc

come to a creek, after you crofs that creek, you muft turn to the left, and then you'll come to a tobacco houfe; after you have paffed that; you'll come to another road that forks, keep the right hand fork, and then you'll come to Mr. fuch a ones ordinary, and he will direct you. Thus you fee it requires the moft retentive memory to be able to proceed at all, if unaccuftomed to the roads.

We adopted a fingular mode, which proved fortunate. One day after travelling a ftraight road for near fifteen miles at the leaft, as we calculated by our watches, during the whole way, we neither met or overtook a living creature, and were greatly a lofs, as totally uncertain of being in the right road. Our perplexities greatly increafed by the roads dividing; unacquainted with the country, or in what direction the place we wifhed to reach, lay. We continued for a length

of time undetermined which road to take
at laſt my companion propoſed we ſhould
toſs up a dollar, and if heads, to take the
right hand, if tails, the left; it chanced
to come up heads, and we took the right
hand road accordingly, when after tra
velling about four miles, we came to the
ordinary where we baited, the landlord of
which informed us that had we taken
the other road, we ſhould have gone
near ſixteen miles further without ſeeing
an houſe.

Having ſeveral times mentioned an ordi
nary, it may not be amiſs to acquaint you
that out of the principal towns, all taverns
and public houſes are, in Virginia, called
ordinaries, and 'faith not improperly in
general; they conſiſt of a little houſe pla
ced in a ſolitary ſituation, in the middle
of the woods, and the uſual mode of de
cribing the roads, is from ſuch an ordina

to such a one, so many miles; the entertainment you meet with is very poor indeed, seldom able to procure any other fare than eggs and bacon, with Indian hoe cake, and at many of them not even that; the only liquors are peach brandy and whiskey. For this miserable fare they are not remiss in making pretty exorbitant charges; but I am not surprized that accommodation for travellers is so bad, as I am informed, before the war, the hospitality of the country was such, that travellers always stopt at a plantation when they wanted to refresh themselves and their horses, where they always met with the most courteous treatment, and were supplied with every thing gratuitously; and if any neighbouring planters heard of any gentleman being at one of these ordinaries, they would send a negroe with an invitation to their own house.

On our journey to this place we over took a flock of wild turkeys; a couple o spaniels we had with us purfued them and it is incredible how fwift they run, a neither of us, though we galloped ou horfes, could overtake them, althougł they run near two hundred yards before they took flight; they appeared confider ably larger than ours, and I am told fometimes weigh thirty or forty pound each. Juft before we came to Goochlan Court houfe, we faw the manner by whicl the inhabitants catch them; they make log fence of about twelve feet fquare, fe curing the top with heavy logs, but befor they cover it over dig a paffage fron the center, to the outfide of the fenc which is covered over fo as to admit ligh and round about the entrance, an through this paffage they ftrew India corn, as well as a quantity for them feed on when in the trap, the birds feeir
tł

the corn in the infide, keep walking round to gather it, till they meet that which is laid to conduct them into the paffage, which having confumed, they keep eating on till they get into the trap, and thefe foolifh birds, when they wifh to get out, inftead of returning the way they came in, keep continually flying up, by which means one or two out of the flock, in the morning are found dead, and they frequently catch a flock of ten or a dozen at a time in this manner.

At Weftham, about feven miles, the falls of James River commence, which continue to about half a mile below this place, where the tide comes up. The grand ftaple commodity of this province is tobacco, carried down the river from the back fettlements to Weftham, upon canoes lafhed together, and then it is brought by land carriage to this place, as the falls prevent any communication by water,

through the distance of seven miles; an
during the courfe of that part of the rive
the water rushes down in vast torrent
raging with great impetuofity, and dash
ing from rock to rock with a most tre
mendous noife, which may be heard fo
many miles.

At this place the land suddenly rifes in
to hills of a great height, abounding with
prodigious rocks, large stones and trees
and as the summit of many of thef
hills hang over the falling torrent o
James river, they command most roman
tic profpects.

A little below Richmond, the tide flow
up to the rocks of the fall, and ther
James River is half a mile wide, at whic
place there are ferry-boats.

At the foot of the falls there are thre
towns; Richmond, which is the largeft

separated by a creek named Shockoes, from the town of Shockoes, that joins it; these are on the North side of the river, and on the South side stands Chesterfield, but from its situation, more generally known by the name of Rocks Bridge; small sloops come up to the falls, and two miles lower, large ships come up to load.

I am informed, above the falls, the river, after heavy rains, swells to a great height, and overflows all the low ground for several miles; and at the falls, where the river is confined by the mountains that abruptly arise on each side, the noise, force, and impetuosity of the torrent, are most dreadfully tremendous and awful.

Many gentlemen around Richmond, though strongly attached to the American cause, have shewn the liberality and hospitality so peculiar to this province, in their
particular

particular attention and civilities to o
officers, who are quartered here, and
the adjacent country; among thofe w
are moſt diſtinguiſhed in this line, are C
lonel Randolph, of Tuckahoe; Colo
Good, of Cheſterfield; Colonel Cary,
Warwick, &c. &c. The illiberal part
their countrymen charge them with bei
partial to Great-Britain, but theſe
gentlemen of fixed principles, of affluer
and authority, and therefore deſpiſe
popular clamour.

There happened the moſt remarka
phenomenon a few nights ago, that
imagined might be peculiar to this clima
but at which we found the inhabitants
ceedingly alarmed and terrified; it wa
moſt terrible ſtorm of thunder and ligl
ning; the day had been as piercingly ke
and penetrating as any we had felt tl
Winter, and in the evening the ſto
came on; the eruſcations and flaſhes
lightni

lightning inceſſantly followed each other in quick and rapid tranſitions, and the thunder was a conſtant ſucceſſion of loud contending peals; this ſtorm laſted near two hours; at its commencement, the air felt warm, which encreaſed ſo faſt, that at one time it was intenſely hot; but as the ſtorm decreaſed, ſo the heat left us, and the next morning was a ſharp froſt.

As I was walking with ſome officers, I was ſhewn a gentleman of the town, a Mr. Fanchée, a ſurgeon and apothecary, who had the misfortune to have one of his eyes gouged out, it was happily in time replaced, and there were hopes that he would recover the uſe of it. I ſhall relate the way the accident happened, to ſhew the ferociouſneſs of the lower claſs in this country; this gentlemen was at play in the billiard-room, where there were a number of gentlemen, and ſeveral of our officers: a low fellow, who pretends to gentility

gentility came in, and in the courfe [of]
play, fome words arofe, in which he fi[rst]
wantonly abufed, and afterward wo[uld]
infift on fighting Mr. Fauchée, defiring [at]
the fame time, to know upon what ter[ms]
he would fight, as the lower fort ha[ve]
various modes; Mr. Fauchée declin[ed]
any, faying, that he was totally ignora[nt]
as to boxing, but the other calling him[felf]
a gentleman, he would meet him in a ge[n]
tleman-like manner; he had fcarcely [ut]
tered thefe words, before the other flew [at]
him, and in an inftant turned his eye o[ut]
of the focket, and while it hung upon [his]
cheek, the fellow was barbarous enou[gh]
to endeavor to pluck it entirely out, b[ut]
was prevented. You can eafily imagi[ne]
what the officers who were prefent, m[uft]
have felt, as fpectators of fuch a fcen[e,]
who were obliged to fuffer fuch a wret[ch]
to go off with impunity, their hands b[e]
ing reftrained, by their parole, from a[ny]
interference.

This moſt barbarous cuſtom, which a ſavage would bluſh at being accuſed of, is peculiar to the lower claſs of people in this province; at one time it was ſo prevalent, that the Governor and Aſſembly were obliged to paſs a law which made it criminal, and that law is now in force, but the rabble are ſuch a lawleſs ſet, eſpecially thoſe in the back woods, that they are little reſtrained by any laws the State can paſs, and in the back ſettlement, this ſavage cuſtom prevails.——I have ſeen a fellow, reckoned a great adept in gouging, who conſtantly kept the nails of both his thumbs and ſecond fingers very long and pointed; nay, to prevent their breaking or ſplitting, in the execution of his diabolical intentions, he hardened them every evening in a candle.

It is an univerſal opinion, that death is preferable to loſs of ſight, and as every occaſion of quarrelling with the officers is
greedily

greedily fought after, we feldom go
without our fide arms. What pity it
that a country where the fuperior clafs
of fuch an hofpitable and friendly difp
tion, fhould be rendered almoft unfaf
live in by the barbarity of the peo
That I was but out of it, and once m
in Old England, is the conftant prayer

Yours, &c.

LETTER LXIV.

Richmond, in Virginia,
Feb. 18th, 1779.

MY DEAR FRIEND,

I HAVE been detained at this place beyond my original intention by the hospitality of the neighbouring gentlemen, who would not let me leave them without visiting the whole circle; among the number was Colonel Carey, who resides at Warwick, where he has a most superb house, near which are some curious mills and iron-works, whose building cost some thousands of pounds; they have not only been of great emolument to himself, but
very

very beneficial to the public. His house is situated on the border of James River, and on the opposite shore is another of a Major Randolph; it may not be unnecessary to observe, that the Randolphs are descended from one of the first settlers in this province of that name, and are so numerous, that they are obliged, like the clans of Scotland, to be distinguished by their places of residence.

Petersburgh being but a few miles from Colonel Carey's, and several of us, one evening, expressing a desire to see that town, but lamenting it was out of our parole. He, the next morning after breakfast, said, " Come, gentlemen, we'll mount " out horses, and take a ride before din- " ner, to Petersburgh," we expressed how happy it would make us to accompany him, but were restrained by our parole, when he replied, " not so, gentlemen," and produced a letter from the American Commanding

manding Officer, granting us permiſſion; this little circumſtance I mention, to ſhew that his hoſpitality is accompanied with true politeneſs and attention.

The town of Peterſburgh is ſituated on the borders of the Apamatock River, and on the oppoſite ſhore are a few houſes, which is a kind of ſuburb, independant of Peterſburg, called Pocahunta----the principal trade of Peterſburg ariſes from the exporting of tobacco, depoſited in warehouſes and magazines, but before it is lodged in theſe warehouſes, it is examined, to confirm it in a proper ſtate for exportation by inſpectors, who prove the quality of the tobacco; and if found good, they give the planter a receipt for ſuch a quantity, and theſe receipts paſs current as caſh: Thus any one depoſiting tobacco in theſe warehouſes, and obtaining a receipt, may go to Williamſburg, or any other city in the province, and purchaſe any kind

kind of commodities, paying with receipts, which circulate through a multitude of hands before they come to the merchant who purchafes the tobacco for exportation; thus this valuable commodity is equally Bank ftock, and current coin; and the inhabitants, in defcribing the prices of their different purchafes, inftead of faying " I gave fo many pounds for fuch an ar-" ticle;" " I gave fo many hogfheads of " tobacco."

The Apamatocks River is nearly as wide as the Thames, and runs into the James River, about twelve miles from the falls, which are a little above Peterfburgh, and juft below the falls, there is a large wooden bridge, at the town of Pocahunta, up to which floops, fchooners, and fmall veffels continually fail.

The town of Pocahunta is named after the daughter of a famous Indian Chief, or

Emperor

Emperor Powhatan (which is the Indian name of the James River) who gave all the land round this place to his daughter as a marriage portion.

At Peterſburgh reſides a Mrs. Bowling, who has conſiderable warehouſes, beſides a very extenſive plantation and eſtates, whoſe ſon has married a very agreeable young lady, lineally deſcended from Pocahunta. After Colonel Carey had given us the brief hiſtory of Pocahunta, relating to her friendſhip for the Engliſh, in their firſt ſettlement in this province, and her marrying an Engliſhman, with whom ſhe went to Europe, he related the following anecdote of a great man of her own nation, that ſhe had in her ſuite, when ſhe left Virginia:

" This man had orders from Powhatan
" to count the people of England, and give
" him an account of their numbers. As

"the Indians have no letters or figures
"among them, he, at his going afhore,
"provided a ftick, in which he was to
"make a notch for every perfon he faw;
"but he, as you may fuppofe, foon grew
"weary, and threw away his ftick: Upon
"his return, the King afked him how
"many people there were?" "*He defired
"him to count the ftars in the fky, the leaves
"upon the trees, and the fand on the fea
"fhore, for fo many people he faid were in
"England.*" At this conclufion, Colone[l]
Carey archly remarked, "Don't you thin[k]
"you cou'd make that reply to your King
"if he afked you how many people yo[u]
"faw in America?"

The tobacco warehoufes at Peterfbur[g]
as well as at Richmond, are crowded wit[h]
that commodity, as they cannot find pu[r]
chafers, and the planters will not expo[se]
it themfelves, on account of our numero[us]
privateers; fome few merchants have ve[n]
tur[ed]

tured small sloops to the Bermuda islands, and have been successful; it is only these who have any commodities in their stores, the rest being shut up; and I cannot help making the same reflection, at seeing such towns as Petersburgh and Richmond in the same state as that of Lancaster, all trade being at a stand in these places, where no doubt, before the war, it must have been very considerable, these two towns having formerly supplied the back settlers with all manner of stores for their plantations. Except in the principal cities, such as Boston, New-York, and Philadelphia, the towns have not various branches of manufactures, such as linen-drapers, mercers, grocers, hosiers, haberdashers, stationers, &c. but are all comprized under the name of merchant and store-keeper; and what are called shops in England, are here denominated stores, which furnish every article in life, not only necessary but ornamental, and even

even jewellery; exclusive of the great stores in the capital towns, there are smaller ones scattered all over the country.

I spent a few days at Colonel Randolph's, at Tuckahoe, at whose house the usual hospitality of the country prevailed; it is built on a rising ground, having a most beautiful and commanding prospect of James River; on one side is Tuckahoe, which being the Indian name of that creek, he named his plantation Tuckahoe after it; his house seems to be built solely to answer the purposes of hospitality, which being constructed in a different manner than in most other countries; I shall describe it to you: It is in the form of an H, and has the appearance of two houses, joined by a large saloon; each wing has two stories, and four large rooms on a floor; in one the family reside, and the other is reserved solely for visitors; the saloon that unites them, is of a considerable magnitude, and on each side are doors; the ceiling is lofty, and to these they principally retire in the Summer, being but little incommoded by the sun, and by the doors of each of the houses, and those of the saloon being open, there is a constant circulation of air; they are furnished with four sophas, two on each side, besides chairs, and in the center there is generally a chandelier; these saloons answer the two purposes of a cool retreat from the scorching and sultry heat of the climate, and of an occasional ball-room. The outhouses are detached at some distance, that the house may be open to the air on all sides.

Colonel Randolph possesses that fondness for horses, which I observed was peculiar to the Virginians of all stations, sparing no trouble, pains, or expence, in importing the best stock, and improving the breed; and it was with no little pleasure

he shewed us a fine one, named Shake
speare, which he imported just as the wa
commenced. There was a stable built pur
posely for this horse, in which was a rece
for a bed for the negroe who looked afte
it, that he might be with it at night
This horse is of a handsome dapple
grey, about sixteen hands and a half high
with a most beautiful head and neck; a
to any other points about him, it is impossible to tell, for the creature was so
amazingly pampered and fat, and being
of the race breed, his legs were so smal
and slim, that they appeared unable t
support the weight of his body, exactl
like the horses one sees painted in old pic
tures; the best idea you can possibly forn
of his size, is by telling you, that fron
his withers to his tail, there was such
groove of fat, that you might pour wate
upon his withers, and it would run in
straight line down his tail; the horse i
obliged to be kept in high condition, t
enabl

enable him to receive the numerous visitors attending on him in the Spring.

In the course of a few days I shall return to Charlottesville, at which I am by no means displeased, for notwithstanding the hospitality and great attention shewn me, I do not feel myself *comme il faut*, feeling that uneasy sensation, which the English in general possess, and which may be ridiculous perhaps, but it is constitutional, arising from a consciousness of its being out of my power to make a return for the civilities shewn me. I cannot but in justice say, that in all the gentlemens houses I have visited, they never started, for would suffer any conversation on politics; sometimes, when alone with the ladies, they would indulge and rally us a little, at our being prisoners, but all with great good humour; the only unpleasant circumstance of the kind that I recollect was at Tuckahoe, where an officer

cer suffered his vexation to overcome that gratitude he was bound to shew for the hospitality he met with.

 Colonel Randolph every year made a present of two hogsheads of tobacco to his daughter as a venture, to purchase dresses and ornaments, and the ships had always been so unfortunate as to be captured. As several officers were sitting with the ladies, the conversation ran upon politics, when Miss Randolph innocently asked, " How " we came to be taken prisoners?" the officer with some warmth replied, " Just " as your tobacco was, by a superior " force." I need not tell you the distress and confusion of the young lady, as well as of the officer himself, who immediately became conscious of what he had said, and for his ill-timed violence, he forfeited all claim to the hospitality of Tuckahoe.

Yours, &c.
LET.

LETTER LXV.

Jones's Plantation, near Charlottesville,
in Virginia, April 10, 1779.

MY DEAR FRIEND,

DURING my journey to Richmond, General Phillips and General Reidesel arrived at Charlottesville, and the day after their arrival, went to the barracks; they were greatly incensed at the treatment the army met with, at present the soldiers are more comfortably lodged, but had General Phillips seen them in the state they were in on the first arrival of the troops, I think his warmth of temper and regard for them, would have laid him under the same re-
striction

striction as at Boston. The men have been exceedingly ill supplied with provisions in general, having meat only twice or thrice a week, and for some weeks none what they get is scarcely wholesome, this is at present what the poor fellows term a fast, they not having any meat serve them since the twenty-fifth of last month. General Phillips has greatly exerted himself since his arrival, and there are hopes that in future, the troops will be more regularly supplied.

Congress certainly are to be acquitted of all this bad management, as they have been misguided and duped by one of their own members, a Colonel Harvey, who is a delegate for this Province.

When they passed the resolve to detain us prisoners, contrary to the articles of convention, the state of Massachusetts deemed it oppressive, that it should be obliged to support our army, as they had cheerfully supplied their own troops with more in quota than the other Provinces, and that as they had already supplied our army for near a twelvemonth, it would be but equitable for the southern Provinces to partake of the burthen; they accordingly instructed their delegates to apply to Congress for that purpose. When the motion was made, the petition of the State of Massachusets appeared founded upon equity, and it was then considered to what Province we should be removed to, the Jerseys and New-York Provinces were improper, as being the seat of war, as to Pensylvania, that Province had been so ravaged by the two armies, that they deemed it incapable of furnishing provision to supply their own with the quota allotted them. As to Maryland, it was so small a Province, it did not admit of any consideration, and Virginia was deemed the Province best calculated,

from

from its extenfivenefs, as well as its ferti
lity; and that by ftationing the army ii
the back fettlements, it removed all fear
of any attempts of a refcue, by a part o
the army from New York.

When Virginia was fixed upon, thi
Colonel Harvey propofed to Congrefs, t
remove the convention army to a tract o
land that belonged to him about fix mile
from Charlottefville, about four from
the blue mountains, and near two hun
dred miles from the fea coaft, that if Con
grefs approved of that fituation, he woul
engage to build barracks and lay in pro
vifions by the enfuing Spring. This pro
pofal meeting with approbation, wa
paffed into a refolve about the latter en
of laft June.

Colonel Harvey immediately reforted t
Virginia, and fet all his negroes and
number of the inhabitants to built the
barrack

barracks, and to collect provisions; after having planned every thing, he left the completion of it to the management of his brother, and returned to Congress. His brother not possessing so much activity and not being, perhaps, so much interested in the business, did not pay proper attention to it, which was the cause why the barracks were not finished, and affairs being in such a state of confusion on our arrival. When Colonel Harvey left Virginia, he fully imagined that every necessary comfort and supply of provisions would be ready for the reception of the troops, at Christmas; being fully sensible that the log-huts would be erected long before that time, and as to provisions, he had left such directions as, if obeyed, could not fail; it is just to observe, that Congress consulted Colonel Harvey previous to their passing their resolves, and sending their orders of our removal out of the Massachusets State.

The

The houfe and plantation where Gen
ral Phillips refides is called *Blenheim*; t
houfe was erected fhortly after that m
morable battle in Germany, by a M
Carter, who was Secretary to the colon
and was his favorite feat of refidence:
ftands on a lofty eminence, commandir
a very extenfive profpect, and is bui
after the manner of that I have defcril
ed to you in my laft. The prefent pr
prietor, Colonel Carter, poffeffes a mo
affluent fortune, and has a variety of feat
in fituations far furpaffing this of Bler
heim, which he fuffers to go to ruin; ar
when General Phillips took it, this charn
ing manfion was crouded with negroc
fent from various other plantations,
clear a fpot of ground a few miles of
The tract of land Colonel Carter poffefl
in this province is immenfe, and his fto
of negroes the moft numerous, he bei
poffeffed of one thoufand five hundred
his different plantations.

T

The firft night after our leaving Richmond, I flept at an elegant villa, called Belvidera, which formerly belonged to a Colonel Bird, who diftinguifhed himfelf greatly in the laft war, in that fad difafter of General Braddock's. He poffeffed a moft affluent fortune, and was proprietor of all the lands round the falls for many miles, as well as the greateft part of the lands round the town of Richmond. His great abilities and perfonal accomplifhments, were univerfally efteemed, but being infatuated with play, his affairs, at his death, were in a deranged ftate. The widow whom he left with eight children, has, by prudent management, preferved out of the wreck of his princely fortune, a beautiful houfe, at a place called Weftover, upon James River, fome perfonal property, a few plantations, and a number of flaves. The grounds around the houfe at Weftover, are laid out in a moft beautiful manner and with

great tafte, and from the rive
delightful.

From my obfervations and re
my late journey, it appeared to
before the war, the fpirit of eq
levelling principal was not fo pre
Virginia, as in the other provir
that the different claffes of peop
former fupported a greater d
than thofe of the latter; but
war, that principle feems to ha
great ground in Virginia; an ir
it I faw at Colonel Randolph's, a
hoe, where three country peafa
came upon bufinefs, entered
where the Colonel and his comp
fitting, took themfelves chairs,
the fire, began fpitting, pulling
country boots all over mud,
opened their bufinefs, which w
about fome continental flour
ground at the Colonel's mill

they were gone, some one observed what great liberties they took; he replied, it was unavoidable, the spirit of independency was converted into equality, and every one who bore arms, esteemed himself upon a footing with his neighbour, and concluded with saying, " No doubt, " each of these men conceives himself, in " every respect, my equal."

There were, and still are, three degrees of ranks among the inhabitants, exclusive of negroes; but I am afraid the advantage of distinction will never exist again in this country, in the same manner it did before the commencement of hostilities.

The first class consists of gentlemen of the best families and fortunes, which are more respectable and numerous here, than in any other province; for the most part they have had liberal educations, possess a thorough knowledge of the world, with great eafe and freedom in their manners and converfation, many of them keep their carriages, have handfome fervices of plate, and without exception, keep their ftuds, as well as fets of handfome carriage horfes.

The fecond clafs confifts of fuch a ftrange mixture of characters, and of fuch various defcriptions of occupations, being nearly half the inhabitants, that it is difficult to afcertain their exact criterion and leading feature. They are however, hofpitable, generous, and friendly; but for want of a proper knowledge of the world, and a good education, as well as from their continual intercourfe with their flaves, over whom they are accuftomed to tyrannize, with all their good qualities, they are rude, ferocious, and haughty, much attached to gaming and diffipation, particularly horfe-racing and cock-fighting;

ing; in fhort, they form a moft unaccountable combination of qualities and principles directly oppofite and contradictory; many of them having them ftrangely blended with the beft and worft of principles, the moft valuable and moft worthlefs, many poffeffing elegant accomplifhments and favage brutality, and notwithftanding all this inconfiftency of character, numbers are valuable members of the community, and very few deficient in intellectual faculties.

The third clafs, which, in general, compofes the greateft part of mankind, are fewer in Virginia, in proportion to the inhabitants, than perhaps in any other country in the world; yet even thofe who are rude, illiberal, and noify, with a turbulent difpofition, are generous, kind, and hofpitable. We are induced to imagine there is fomething peculiar in the climate

climate of Virginia, that should render a classes of so hospitable a disposition.

The lower people possess that impertnent curiosity, so very disagreeable and troublesome to strangers, but in no degree equal to the inhabitants of New England, they are averse to labor, much addicted to liquor, and when intoxicated extremely savage and revengeful; nay, at such times, revenge insults of long date even after they have been amicably adjusted; for the insult arising in their mind and the new friendship totally forgotten, they seek their object with keen attention and satiate their passion with savage barbarity.

Their amusements are the same with those of the middling sort, with the addition of boxing matches, in which they display such barbarity, as fully marks the innate ferocious difpofition. An Englifh boxing match, though a difgrace to a polifhed nation, is humanity itfelf, compared with the Virginian mode of fighting; for, previous to the combatants falling too, they enter into an agreement, whether all advantages are allowable, which are biting, gouging, and (if I may fo term it) Abelarding each other. If thefe three preliminaries are agreed upon, they inftantly fall to, and, after fome little ftruggling, feize upon their adverfaries with their teeth. What is very remarkable, and fhews what coolnefs there muft be in thefe difputes, and that they are not wholly the effect of anger is, that whatever terms are fpecified, if only one or two out of the three conditions, let the conflict be ever fo fevere, they never infringe on any other.

Vegetables not being over abundant in thefe back woods at any time, and there being

a great deficiency of them in the Spring
year, the we adopt the cuftom of the inh[a]
bitants who gather the leaves of the pok[e]
plant, juft as they fhoot above ground an[d]
are tender and foft; it is no bad fubftitu[te]
for fpinnage, and greatly refembles it i[n]
flavor, yet great care muft be taken in g[a]
thering of it, that it is neither too ol[d]
nor the ftalk grown, for in that cafe,
in breaking off the upper fprouts, yo[u]
leave any part that is woody, the conf[e]
quence of eating it is inevitable death, [as]
it purges the body to excefs. Notwith[-]
ftanding this plant has this perniciou[s]
quality, the children eat the berries of [it]
in the Autumn, without any ill conf[e]
quence attending it. The juice of t[he]
berries produces a moft beautiful crimfo[n]
color, the fineft in the world, but no m[e]
thod has yet been found to fix it, as cloth
and woollens dyed with it fade very foo[n]
Many perfons of great ingenuity and ch[y]

mical knowledge have endeavored, at fixing of this color, which is sought after with as much eagerness as the philosopher's stone, and no doubt would be equally as beneficial, if attained.

Yours, &c.

LETTER LXVI.

Jones's Plantation, near Charlottesville, in Virginia, May 12, 1779.

MY DEAR FRIEND,

A FEW days ago the flag of truce with cloathing for the army arrived at Richmond, and among the great number of letters delivered out, I had a great mortification, as well as disappointment not to receive a single one, surely my friends must imagine, at such a distance in these endless woods, that it is next to an impossibility a letter can reach me; it certainly would afford me great pleasure to hear that they were alive and

As to the rest, I would dispense with. I write continually from time to time; nevertheless, from the uncertainty of conveyance, the same accusation may hold good against me.

Your old friend Clark, of Boston, who is our Commissary of Provisions, lately arrived from New-York, I spent a few days with him at his quarters; exclusive of the great fund of information and amusement, which I derived from a number of English news-papers and magazines he brought with him, I was informed of the transactions that happen upon this continent, among the rest, with a full account of the retreat of our army from Philadelphia to New-York.

You may recollect, in a former letter, I mentioned, that a good retreat was looked on as the *chef d'œuvre* of a commander, and in this retreat, I think Sir Henry Clinton has

has clearly evinced it, and demonstrated
that he is equally as judicious and able a
he is brave, in surmounting the innumer
able difficulties and dangers he had to en
counter: His way lay entirely through a
enemy's country, univerfally hoftile, an
where he could expect no afliftance; there
fore, previous to his fetting out on thi
dangerous retreat, he took the precautio
of providing for all exigencies, and a larg
quantity of provifions was a neceffary
though not a fmall incumbrance, as we
as the baggage of the army which ac
companied it, forming a line of marc
of near twelve miles in extent; efpeciall
when it is confidered this army had to pa
through a country interfected with hill
woods, rivers, defiles, and difficult pafles
from thefe caufes, the march of the arm
being flow, afforded the Americans tim
to affemble, which they readily did to har
rafs it, and in a fhort time Wafhingto

had collected a sufficient force to render its movements extremely dangerous.

When Sir Henry Clinton observed the Americans were meditating an attack, he naturally concluded, it was with a view to cut off the baggage and rear of the army, which, from its extent, he was fearful might be easily accomplished. He told Clark to in form General Phillips, among other descriptions of the battle, that the day before he sat upon a stone for near an hour viewing the baggage as it passed along, and debating in his own mind, whether he should not give instant orders to destroy it. At length, as he concluded it would be a matter of great exultation with the Americans, and a disgrace to the British army, he determined to preserve it at all events; therefore, on the day of the action at Monmouth, he sent forward the baggage, early in the morning,

ing, under the care of General Kny
haufen, in order that it might proce
without moleftation.

The various movements, and po
tions of both armies in that engageme
and the iffue of it, as you muft have fe
it in Sir Henry Clinton's official accou
I fhall pafs it over, only giving you tl
opinion of that battle, which he fent
Clark to General Phillips---after havi
given a particular defcription of it,
Henry Clinton drew fome rough fketcl
of the various grounds and pofitions tak
during the action. At length, recolle
ing himfelf, he faid, " Clark, you mi
" not take thefe, for if the America
" find them on you, they'll certainly ha
" you; therefore, only tell General Ph
" lips, '*that on that day I fought up
"* velvet*,' he will fully underftand me."

A very singular circumstance took place in that battle, which fully marks the coolness and deliberation, though in the heat of action, of Sir Henry Clinton: As he was reconnoitring, with two of his Aid de Camps, at the short turning of two roads, they met with an American officer, exceedingly well mounted upon a black horse, who, upon discerning them, made a stop, and looked as if he wished to advance to speak to them, when one of Sir Henry Clinton's Aid de Camps fired a pistol at him, and he instantly rode off. Sir Henry was much displeased at his Aid de Camp, and censured him for being so hasty, adding, he was confident that the man wished to speak to him, and perhaps, might have given intelligence that would have been very essential, remarking, that when he was in Germany last war, and reconnoitring with Prince Ferdinand, a man rode up in a similar
manner,

manner, and gave such inttelligence a decided the fate of the day.

The weather becomes very unpleasant being for the most part of the day intensely hot; notwithstanding, the poor negroes are exposed to the heat all day long, hoeing tobacco, even at noon, when the rays of the sun are scorching; yet, with all this heat, they scarcely perspire; there certainly must be some natural endowments, through which these poor creatures are able to withstand this excessive heat it cannot be their color, for we well know that black attracts the rays of the sun more than any other, and therefore imagine it must proceed from the oily substance continually oozing out of the pores for I remarked, even in the coldest weather, their skins always appear glossy and certain it is, they are considerably smoother than ours, which must proceed from the causes I have assigned.

observe

observed, from the negro to the mulatto, and they have their various tinges; they all perspired in proportion, the further they remove from the black, and white people considerably more than any.

Having mentioned that there are mulattoes of various tinges, it may not be amiss to inform you from whence it arises, and no doubt, but you will be surprized, when I tell you it is by the planters having intercourse with their negroes, the issue of which being a mulatto, and having a connection with that shade becomes lighter; as an instance, I remarked at Colonel Cole's, of whom I have made mention; there were mulattoes of all tinges, from the first remove, to one almost white; there were some of them young women, who were really beautiful, being extremely well made, and with pretty delicate features; all of which I was informed, were the Colonel's own. I could

could not help reflecting, that if a m[an] had an intercourse with his flaves, [it] was fhameful in the extreme, to make [his] own offspring fo; for thefe mulatt[oes] work equally the fame as thofe who co[me] from Africa: To be fure, you may fa[y] it is a pleafant method to procure flav[es] at a cheap rate. I imagine there cou[ld] not be lefs than twenty or thirty m[u]lattoes of this defcription, at Colon[el] Coles's, notwithftanding he has a ve[ry] agreeable and beautiful wife, by who[m] he has had eight children.

You know as to the principal emplo[y]ment of the poor negroes, I fhall n[ow] give you a defcription of the method [to] cultivate and cure the grand ftaple co[m]modity of this province, tobacco.

This plant is a native of America, a[nd] of very ancient ufe, though it was neit[her] fo generally cultivated, nor fo well mar[nu]factur[ed] factured, as it has since the province has been settled with Europeans; for the Indians made use of it, by gathering the leaves as it grew spontaneously: The plant, at its proper height, is nearly as tall as a middle sized man, the stalk is strait, hairy, and exceeding clammy; the leaves grow alternately of a faded yellowish green, and towards the lower part of the plant of great magnitude.

The seeds of tobacco are first sown in beds, from whence they are transplanted the first rainy weather into a ground disposed into little hillocks, something similar to our hop gardens; in about a month's time from their transplanting, they grow about a foot high, they then top them and prune off the suckers and lower leaves, and then, with the greatest attention, are cleaned twice a week from weeds and worms, by which you will perceive what immense labor there must be on a large plantation,

plantation, where they grow nothing [
tobacco. In about fix weeks after be
topped and pruned, the plant attains
full growth, and then begins to t
brownifh, and thefe marks are the c
terion by which they judge the toba
to be ripe.

The plants are thus cut down as faft
they ripen and are heaped up; and
much as is gathered in a day lies in t
ftate a night to fweat; the next day i
carried to the tobacco-houfe, which i
conftructed, as to admit of as much
as is requifite, and at the fame time ke
ing out the rain; the plants are t
hung feparately to dry for four or
weeks, and the firft moift weather a
they are taken down, for unlefs the pl
were damped, they would crumble to c
they are then laid upon fticks, and co
ed up clofe to fweat for a week or
longer; then the negroes ftrip and
t

them, the top being the beft, and the bottom the worft tobacco; they then put the leaves into hogfheads, or form them into rolls; wet feafons muft be carefully laid hold on for this laft procefs, otherwife the tobacco will not be fufficiently pliable. The cultivation of this plant may appear extremely fimple, but it is impoffible to defcribe to you the immenfe labor, care and fatigue there is attending it, from the firft fetting the feeds to the packing it in hogfheads, and the great anxiety the perfon who fuperintends it has for through the whole procefs it requires the utmoft fkill and judgment.

Travelling in this country is extremely dangerous, efpecially if it is the leaft windy, from the number of rotten pines continually blowing down; after a ftorm, it is no uncommon thing to turn into the woods fix or feven times in the fpace of a mile, to pafs the trees that have been

been blown into and choak up the ro[ad]
even in calm weather it is not altoget[her]
fafe, for there are old rotten pines, div[est]
ed of all their branches, which totter w[ith]
the leaft breeze. An accident happe[ned]
a few days fince, by the falling of one [of]
thefe trees, in which Madame de Reide[fel]
with two of her children, had a very n[ar]
row efcape: as fhe was going to the b[ar]
racks in her poft-chaife, when the c[ar]
riage had paffed a wooden bridge (wh[ich]
are of themfelves very terrific, being o[nly]
fo many rough logs laid acrofs bea[ms]
without any fafe-guard on each fide) [an]
old rotten pine fell directly between [the]
horfes and the chaife, but providenti[ally]
did no other damage, than crufhing [the]
two fore-wheels to pieces and laming [one]
of the horfes.

Not being overftocked with frefh pr[ovi]
fions, I accompanied feveral other offi[cers]
to the woods, to procure a few rabb[its]

if the dogs once get scent of them they are soon taken, for they do not burrow as ours do in England, but run up hollow trees, which they will climb to a considerable height, but from which place of refuge they are taken by putting up a hickory sapling, split at the end and twisted in their skins. As we were employed in catching these rabbits, the dogs kept an incessant barking at the branch of a tree, and when we came up to them, we found an opossum, suspended at the extremity of the branch by its tail, which this creature always does when pursued; we sent a servant up the tree, who shook him off, and he fell among the dogs, from whom he did not make the least attempt to escape, but appeared as if dead. It was taken and carried home, all which time it shewed no other signs of life than gently breathing; it was put in a court-yard, where it could not escape, and we watched it for near half an hour, during which it

never moved, but lay as dead; at laſt,
gently raiſed its head, looking all aroun
and not perceiving any danger, imm
diately ran off. We opened the door a
let out the dogs, who purſuing it, t
creature lay down as before, without ſhev
ing any ſigns of life, nor would th
meddle with it, but were returning bacl
we went out and ſet the dogs at it, a
notwithſtanding two ſpirited ſpaniels wo
ried and ſhook, nay, even ſnapped its ve
bones, which we could diſtinctly hea
the creature never ſhewed any ſympton
of life. After the dogs had worried it, a
broke almoſt every bone in its body, whic
perhaps you will ſay, did not reflect mu
credit to our humanity, a heavy ſto
was dropt on its head, to end its torture
and even then, at parting with li
it ſcarcely ſtruggled; but this mode
feigning death, is what preſerves th
creature from the mountain cat, and oth
carniverous animals.

A few days ago, I went with several officers to fee a a diverfion peculiar to this country, termed quarter-racing, which is a match between two horfes, to run a quarter of a mile in a ftraight direction, and near moft of the ordinaries, there is a piece of ground cleared in the woods for that purpofe, where there are two paths about fix or eight yards afunder, which the horfes run in, this diverfion is a great favorite of the middling and lower claffes, and they have a breed of horfes to perform it with aftonifhing velocity, beating every other for that diftance with the greateft eafe. I think I can, without the leaft exaggeration, affert, that even the famous Eclipfe could not excel them in fpeed, for our horfes are fome time before they are able to get into full fpeed, and thefe are trained to fet out in that manner the moment of ftarting. It is the moft ridiculous amufement imagineable, for if you happen to be looking another

ther way, the race is terminated befo
you can turn your head; notwithftandi
which, very confiderable fums are bett
at thefe matches. We ftayed and faw
veral; and then returned, as we were gi
en to underftand, that after the rac
were finifhed, the day was conclud
with feveral of thofe horrid boxin
matches I defcribed to you in my la
and that two or three daring fellows h
faid they would feek a quarrel with t
Britifh officers; therefore we left the
buck-fkins to fight by themfelves, a-pr
pos, it may not be amifs to explain th
epithet which was given to the Virgir
ans, by the New Englanders, (in reta
ation for their calling them Yankees)
allufion to their anceftors, being hunte
and felling buck, or rather deer-fki
for there are no roe-bucks in Virginia.

Thefe races are only among the fettl
in the interior parts of this Province,
th

they are much laughed at and ridiculed by the people in the lower parts, about Richmond and other great towns; at Williamſburg, is a very excellent courſe for two, three, or four mile heats, where there are races every Spring and Fall; they run for purſes are generally raiſed by ſubſcription, and the horſe that wins two four-mile heats, out of three, is entitled to the prize, which is one hundred pounds the firſt day's running, and fifty pounds every other day, and theſe races commonly laſt a week; at which very capital horſes are ſtarted, that would make no contemptable figure at Newmarket.

There are two ſorts of inſects extremely troubleſome, which are the wood-tick, and the ſeed-tick; the former are about the ſize, and greatly reſemble a bug, reſorting moſtly upon trees and ruſhes, from which, if they fall upon you,
they

they fix their probofcis into the pores
the fkin, and fuck the blood till they
of an enormous fize, and then drop
they are exceedingly troublefome to
cattle; the latter derive their name fr
not being much larger than fmall fe
thefe are chiefly upon the long grafs,
if they get on you, being fo fmall, tl
enter the pores of the fkin, which occaf
a violent irritation, and if rubbed, is
tended with very dangerous confequen
as it inevitably brings on an inflamn
tion, and fometimes a mortification;
only mode of preventing any of thefe co
fequences, is to fumigate the parts affe&
with tobacco, which penetrating the por
deftroys the infects.

There is a fhrub peculiar to this pr
vince, that bears a fmall flower, which t
inhabitants term the bubby flower, it
fembles that which grows on clover gra
and has peculiar qualities, for it retains
gratef

grateful and odoriferous perfume for a length of time after being gathered, and as it withers, encreafes; the name given to the flower arifes from a cuftom that the women have of putting this flower down their bofoms, letting it remain there till it has loft all its grateful perfume,

Having fome bufinefs with Colonel Bland, of whom I made mention in a former letter, I went to his houfe juft as he had mounted horfe, but he, with the politenefs which, but in juftice to him, I muft fay, he fhews to the Britifh officers, difmounted, and invited me in, and after communicating my bufinefs, upon my taking leave of him, notwithftanding his politenefs and attention, I could not help fmiling at the pompofity, and the great importance he affumes, to make himfelf appear to us confequential; for to convince us that he was converfant with the French language, having mounted his

horfe

horſe without his ſword, he called to
negro, he had purchaſed from one
the French Weſt-Indian iſlands, to bri
it him, which the fellow did without t
ſcabbard; when the Colonel, in great a
ger, ſaid to him, *Donney moi, donney m*
and after great heſitation, *donney moi m*
ſcabbard.

We have been of late greatly perple
ed with the paper money, not on
by that iſſued from Congreſs, but th
iſſued by theſe States, they both havi
been counterfeited; the former, thoug
not altogether, is in part refuſed in cor
ſequence of it, and the latter is entire
ſtopt, and new impreſſions are iſſue
which the Governor and Aſſembly cor
ceive will not eaſily be counterfeited, as
is made upon paper difficult to be ol
tained in theſe parts, nor have they a
rived to ſuch perfectien of making pap
as to manufacture it; indeed, througho
Ameri

America they are greatly deficient in this art, as moſt of their news-papers are printed upon blue, or elſe coarſe white paper, ſimilar to that uſed by ſhopkeepers, but the paper of this new emiſſion, is the ſilver paper uſed by hatters, great quantities of which were found in a veſſel that was captured, and was ſeized on by the Governor for this purpoſe: excluſive of the great loſſes that we conſtantly experience with paper money in general, we have ſuffered much by this new emiſſion, as likewiſe by the great depreciation of the Congreſs money, as the exchange at preſent is after the rate of five hundred paper dollars for one guinea.

The depreciation of Congreſs money ariſes from the vaſt quantity of the counterfeit, which any perſon who hazards the riſk, may have gratis, at New-York, to circulate throughout the province, and to point out to you what confuſion there
muſt

muſt be at the concluſion of this unhap
conteſt, on whichever ſide it may terr
nate, when I inform you, that there
many perſons now in actual poſſeſſion
plantations, which they purchaſed w
the counterfeit money they brought fr
New-York. As I have repeatedly m
tioned in ſeveral of my letters, various
cumſtances concerning paper money, a
thinking they may not be unacceptable,
have encloſed a few dollars in this letter

Yours, &c.

L E

AMERICAN DOLLARS.

REVERSE.

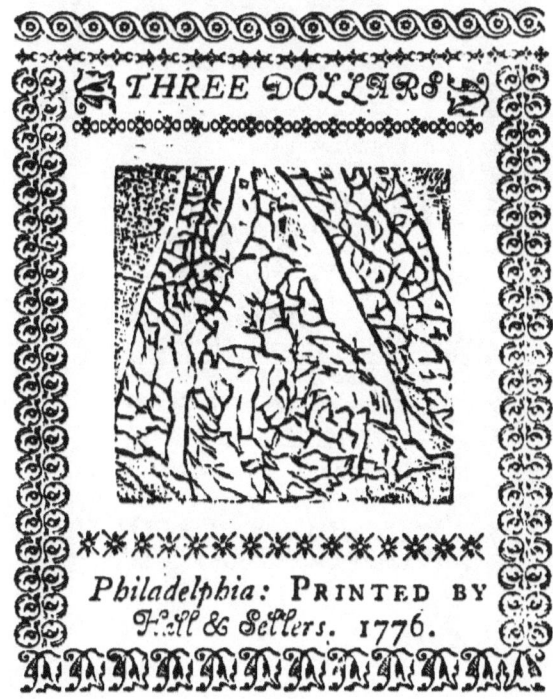

AMERICAN DOLLARS.

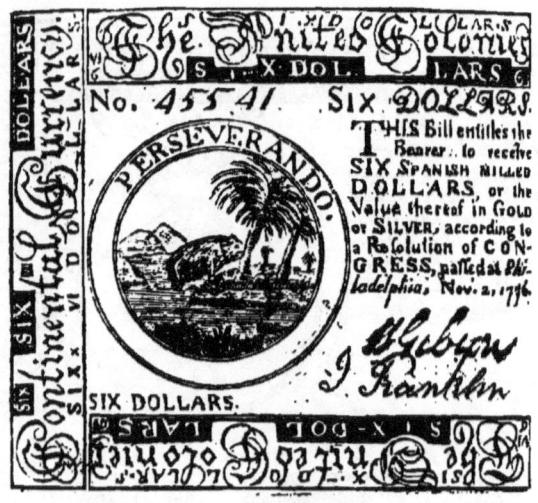

REVERSE.

AMERICAN DOLLARS.

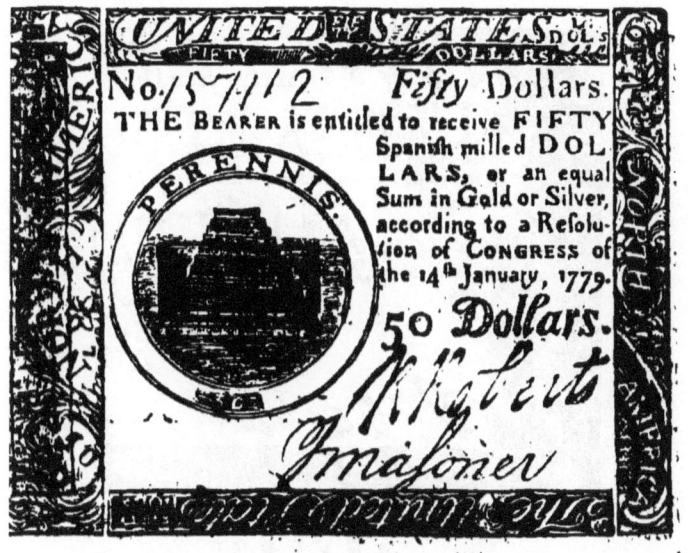

REVERSE.

AMERICAN DOLLARS.

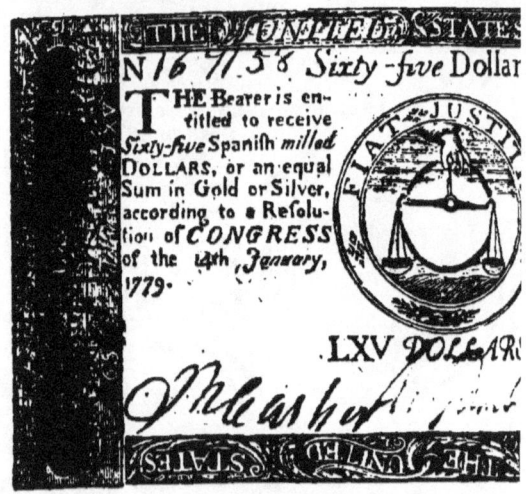

REVERSE.

LETTER LXVII.

Richmond, in Virginia,
July 14, 1779.

MY DEAR FRIEND,

YOU will naturally conclude, at receiving another letter from this place, that the kind reception I met with when laſt here, induced me to pay a ſecond viſit; but however pleaſant ſuch a journey would be, my preſent one is not only very diſagreeable to myſelf, but has proved extremely ſo to others; my buſineſs being to communicate General Phillips's orders, that none of the officers are

to reside at a greater distance from
barracks than twenty miles.

On my way to this place I stopt
slept at Tuckahoe, where I met with C
nel Mead, Colonel Laurens, and ano
officer of General Washington's suite
More than once did I express a wish
General himself had been of the party
have seen and conversed with a charac
of whom, in all my travels through
various provinces, I never heard any
speak disrespectfully, as an individual,
whose public character has been the
miration and astonishment of all Euro

The conversation, in general, tu
ing upon horses, Colonel Mead was p
ing his as being remarkably high spir
which prevented its falling into the h
of a party of our light dragoons, as
negro, who had the care of it, was l
ing after forage, who was surprized,

sued, and nearly surrounded by the party, in a field, enclosed with a prodigious fence, near nine feet high; the poor negro, fearful of himself, and dreading his master's displeasure, in case he lost the horse, run him at the fence, which he leaped over, and rode off into the woods, to the astonishment of the dragoons; the Colonel attributed the safety of his person to the swiftness of this horse at the battle of Monmouth, having been fired at and pursued by some British officers as he was reconnoitring. Upon the Colonel's mentioning this circumstance, it occurred to me, he must have been the person that Sir Henry Clinton's Aid de Camp had fired at; and requesting to know the particular color of his horse, he informed me it was black, which convinced me it was him; when I related the circumstance of his meeting Sir Henry Clinton, he replied, he recollected in the course of that day, to have met several British officers, and one

of them wore a ſtar. Upon my menti[on]
ing the obſervation Sir Henry Clinton h[ad]
made to his Aid de Camp, the Colo[nel]
laughed, and replied, " Had he known [I]
" had been the Commander in Chief, [I]
" ſhould have made a deſperate effort [to]
" have taken him priſoner."

At Goochland Court-houſe, I was i[n]
formed in what a ſpirited manner Colo[nel]
Randolph had reſented the illiberality [of]
ſome of his neighbours, who had i[n]
ſinuated and threatened to ſet fire to ſo[me]
valuable mills, on account of his hoſ[pi]
tality to the Britiſh officers: At the n[ext]
court day, after he had heard of this [re]
port, he in a very animated ſpeech ſtat[ed]
that no one had a right to ſcrutinize i[nto]
his private concerns, that his public c[ha]
racter was well known, and that no [one]
could with more zeal and perſeverer[ce]
ſupport the cauſe of the America[ns]
than he had done, and concluded w[ith]

offering a reward of five hundred pounds for the difcovery of thofe who had made ufe of thofe threats. Since this tranfaction, the Colonel has paid more attention to the officers, acting truly confiftent with the principles of independence, and to fhame his countrymen for their want of liberality.

I was detained near two days in my journey to this place, on account of the overflowing of the river, at what is termed the Point of Forks, where James River divides, and was rather furprized at this fudden rifing of the water, as it had not rained for feveral days, but on enquiry found, that any fall of rain, unlefs extremely violent, never encreafed the water till fome time after, during which it collects from the mountains, and rufhes in amazing torrents; the waters were fo encreafed, that they had overflowed the banks of the river for many miles, and as it

comes

comes down with great impetuofity fr
the mountains, it wafhes away the ea
which being of a red caft, appears lil
torrent of blood. Since the waters h
abated, there has been caught a great nu
ber of fturgeons and rock-fifh, at the f
of this place: Indeed fifh is at this fea
in great plenty, efpecially eels, which
of a great fize, and caught in wei
numbers of which are upon James Riv
above the falls, and indeed upon moft
the rivers and creeks; thefe weirs
conftructed of ftones laid acrofs the ri
of the ufual height of the current, a
brought to a point in the center, wh
is placed a wicker bafket, or a wooden b
in which they catch great quantities
fifh.

I think nothing more fully evinces
real diftreffes of the inhabitants in gene
throughout America, and how great
fpirit of perfecution and oppreffion rei
through

throughout all the provinces, as the amazing emigrations to a new settlement, at a place called Kentucky, where the soil is extremely fruitful, and where there are abundance of buffaloes, the country around, for a great number of miles, is an extensive plain, with very few trees growing on it. New discoveries are continually making, as to the vast extent of the continent of America, and in some future day it may be learnt, what the boundaries are to the westward. This new settlement is near a thousand miles from this place, nevertheless, those travelling to it, though to so great a distance, and perhaps have left comfortable houses and plantations, which have been the labor of their whole lives to clear and bring to perfection, appear chearful and happy, pleased with the idea, that they will be free from the tyranny and oppression of the Congress, and its upstart dependants. Their mode of travelling greatly resembles that

of the patriarchs of old, for they t
with them their horses, oxen, sheep, a
other cattle; as likewise all kinds of po
try. On my journey to this place, I {
a family setting off for this new sett
ment, leaving behind them a neat ha
tation, which appeared surrounded w
every requisite to make it at once
mansion of content and happiness.
to the manner of quitting it, that
vorite poet, Dr. Goldsmith, has m
charmingly described it in the follow
lines:

" Good Heavens! What sorrows gloom'd that parting
" That called them from their native walks away;
" When the poor exiles, every pleasure past,
" Hung round the bowers and fondly looked their last

Nor can I more forcibly describe
family's setting out on their journey, t
he has done----where he says,

" The good old sire, the first prepared to go
" To new-found worlds, and wept for other's woe ;

" But for himself in confcious virtue brave,
" He only wifh'd for worlds beyond the grave ;
" His lovely daughter, lovelier in her tears,
" The fond companion of his helplefs years ;
" Silent went next, negleƈtful of her charms,
" And left a lover's for a father's arms ;
" With tender plaints, the mother fpoke her woes,
" And bleft the cot where ev'ry pleafure rofe ;
" And kift her thoughtlefs babes with many a tear,
" And clafpt them clofe in forrow doubly dear,
" Whilft her fond hufband ftrove to lend relief,
" In all the filent manlinefs of grief".

The heat of the weather is at prefent very intenfe, and renders travelling unpleafant, efpecially on horfe-back, the rays of the fun are fo very powerful in the middle of the day, that neither yourfelf nor your horfe are able to withftand it, and you can only travel in the mornings and evenings. The inhabitants jog on in a vehicle called a fulky, a kind of one horfe chaife, but conftruƈted juft large enough to contain one perfon; they fay thefe are not fo fatiguing to the horfe as

a per-

a perſon's riding on its back. In trav
ling on horſe-back, you muſt either w:
or gallop your horſe, as the motion
trotting is too fatiguing for yourſelf a
the beaſt.

At every plantation you paſs by, t
peach trees preſent their fruit, to allay t
parching thirſt the heat occaſions; a
it is deemed no treſpaſs to ſtop and ɪ
freſh yourſelf and your horſe with then
if the owner of the plantation perceiv
you gathering, he will come and dire
you to the tree that bears the beſt fru
for the peaches of this country are of v
rious ſorts; and though they are in ſu
abundance, that they feed the hogs wi
them, yet there are very few except
gentleman's gardens, which have th
flavor and juice of thoſe that grow
England.

Havi

Having seen the procefs of making peach brandy, I no longer am furprized at this fpirit having fuch pernicious effects when drank to excefs, and how unwholefome it muft be taken in ever fo fmall quantities; for after gathering the fruit, it is put in large vats, where it remains till it is in fuch a ftate of putrefaction, as to be extremely offenfive to approach it, in this ftate the peaches are preffed and the liquor that comes from them is diftilled; from whence the cuftom arofe to let the peaches be in fuch a putrified ftate, I never could learn; for upon afking feveral of the inhabitants if they bruifed the peaches as foon as gathered, and preffed the liquor from them, whether the flavor and ftrength of fpirit would not be fuperior, the only anfwer I could obtain was, that they believed it might, but the other was the ufual mode.

The

The town of Richmond, as well as
plantations around for some miles,
been in imminent danger, as the w(
have been on fire, which for some t
past has raged with great fury, and
element seemed to threaten universal
truction; but providentially, befor(
had done any material damage, there
a very heavy rain, which neverthelefs,
not altogether extinguished it, as i
daily breaking out in places, but not
violent but it can be easily prevented fr
spreading.

During the Summer months, t
fires are very frequeut, and at Charlot
ville I have seen the mountains on a b
for three or four miles in length,
are occasioned by the carelessness of w
goners, who, when night approac
after they have unharnessed the horses,
them, pannelled them, and tying a
round their necks, turned them loof(

the woods to graze, make a large fire to warm them when they sleep, which on purfuing their journey the next morning, they neglect to extinguish, this communicating to the dry leaves which lay on the ground, spreads rapidly and caufes thefe dreadful and dangerous conflagrations.

To-morrow I leave this place, to return Charlottefville, when I fhall embrace the next favorable opportunity to write, this I fend by the flag of truce that is returning to New-York, and in hopes it may fafely reach you, I remain,

Yours, &c.

LETTER LXVIII.

Jones's Plantation; near Charlotte
in Virginia, Aug. 4, 1779.

MY DEAR FRIEND,

ON my return from Richmond witnessed the mode that renders Virginian rifle-men so expert in the u[se of] arms---as great numbers were assemb[led] shooting at marks, and which I un[der]stand, long before the commencemen[t of] the war, was the constant diversion in [that] country; so certain are they of hitt[ing] that they are not fearful of holding [a] board at arm's length; nay, some a[re so] little apprehensive of danger, that t[hey] will place it between their legs for another to fire at.

There is an insect, termed the fire-fly, which in itself is a great curiosity, being really a perfect phosphorus: for a considerable portion of its life, most of the interior parts of its body being at times luminous, and from whence it emits rays of light for a great part of the night, by means of two glandular spots, that are placed between the head and shoulders; nevertheless, though these luminous rays issue naturally from the insect, while awake it seems to possess power of interrupting them at will, and then these spots are opake; though, as I observed most of the internal parts of these insects emit a light, yet the thickness of its cover prevents it appearing through any other place but those constituted by nature for the purpose; yet, on extending the rings that cover the different parts of the body a
little

little afunder, you may obferve the fa
light to iffue.

By the light of one of thefe infects,
held between the fingers, and moved g
dually with the luminous fpots over
chryftal of a watch, you can with e
tell the hour; and ten or twelve of th
put into a clear phial, will give fuffici
light to read or write by very diftinctly.

Thefe infects make their appearance
the evening, and are to be feen for a co
fiderable part of the night; they are
tremely unpleafant to travellers at a l
hour, being at times fo numerous, as
perfectly dazzle the eye, and by their
fcure intervals and fudden glare, the fi
is diverted from every object of dan
that at night prefents itfelf; an infta
of which lately happened, that had n
been fatal to an officer, who, loft in
bye paths in the woods, by the reafon

thefe infects, did not perceive a tree that was not entirely blown down, but refted on another, againft which he came with fuch violence as to be ftunned, and on regaining his fenfes, found that in falling from his horfe, he had broke one of his legs, and he remained in that ftate till the next morning, when he was found by a negro, who conducted him home.

You may recollect, in a former letter, I mentioned what a lawlefs fet the lower clafs were, and of their ferocious difpofition; an inftance has recently occurred, wherein the moft wanton cruelties were intended to be put in execution againft an officer of the artillery, who, in the moft miraculous manner, made his efcape from thefe brutal favages, as they were conducting him to the place where they intended to perpetrate their horrid purpofe.

The officer was quartered at the plan[tation] of one Watson, a wretch who [is] reckoned an adept in gouging, and w[ho] prepares his nails for that purpose, [he] has an agreeable, but by no means pretty woman, for his wife, and on a[c]count of the common civilities in fupp[ly]ing the officer with poultry, milk, &[c.] which he regularly paid for; this ignor[ant] fellow pretended to be jealous, and co[m]municating his fentiments to fome nei[gh]bours of a fimilar difpofition to his ov[vn] they concerted a fcheme to be revenge[d on] the officer.

Accordingly, a few days after, t[hey] broke into his chamber at the dea[d of] night, but the noife awaking him, [he] had juft time to feize his fword, [with] which he defended himfelf for fome t[ime,] till it broke, when he was overpow[ered] by his landlord and three other ruff[ians,] who made him put on his clo[aths] and after tying his hands behind him, led him into the yard, and placing him on his own horse, they set out with him armed with muskets, to proceed to another of these desperadoes, who resided about two miles distant, to consult on the mode of revenge---only conceive what must have been the situation of his mind when in their way to this neighbours house, these fellows were consulting whether they should cut his throat and secrete the body, or castrate him and roll him down a steep rock.

Arriving at the plantation, they took him off the horse and conducted him into the house, the owner of which declined any concern in the transaction, and dissuaded the others from it, but they were steady to their bloody purposes; the ruffians then desired some peach brandy toddy, which they drank till intoxicated, all this time consulting what they should

do with the officer. The villain Watſ
who particularly ſuppoſed himſelf to
aggrieved, and was the firſt inſtigator
this baſe plot, occaſionally preſented
piece, and threatened immediate vengear
At length the dawn of day appearing,
wretches as if conſcious of their iniquit
proceeding, remarked it would ſoon
light, and reſolving to put the laſt
their threats in execution, they quit
the houſe, mounting the officer on
horſe, and proceeded to the ſpot where tl
were to perpetrate it, which was at
foot of a mountain, near a very ſt
precipice.

The ſituation of the officer was tı
dreadful, for however reſigned he mi
be to meet his fate, the manner of it
moſt lamentable; in the hands of Ameri
deſperadoes, who are worſe than ſava
revengeful and drunk, alternately preſ
ing their muſquets and vowing inſ
death.

W

When they had proceeded with him near three miles, it was quite day light, they then judged it neceffary to haften their pace, fearful of meeting any one, and by now and then making the horfe trot, it loofened the cord with which the officer's hands were tied; perceiving this, and after fome little ftruggle, finding he could releafe his hands, he very prudently waited an opportunity till he came to fome road he was acquainted with. After they had proceeded about half a mile further, very near the place they were to conduct him to, he difcerned a bye path which led to the barracks, inftantly difengaged his hands, feized the bridle and fpeaking to his horfe, which had been an old quarter-racer, it fet off full fpeed. Thefe wretches all dicharged their pieces at him, but owing to the thicknefs of the wood and their intoxication, he efcaped, and arrived fafe at the barracks.

This

This matter was reprefented to the [Go]vernor of the province, by the General [at] the fame time defcribing the inhabita[nts] and their place of refidence; the an[swer] from the Governor was, that he was [ex]tremely concerned at it, but at prefent [the] civil power was of little ufe, the offi[cers] not daring to make ufe of their autho[rity] among thefe back-woods men, as it [en]dangered their lives; and he had onl[y to] recommend the officer to be on his gu[ard] and not quit the barracks, and tha[t at] night, for his perfonal fafety, he wrote to the Commanding Officer of [the] continental troops, to place a ferje[ant's] guard at his houfe: yet, notwithftan[ding] the wretches are acquainted with this cur...ftance, they have had the aud[acity] to hover about the barracks, in orde[r to] feize him; but it having been intim[ated] to them, that the American Comman[ding] Officer had orders to apprehend them, send them down to the Governor at Williamsburgh, they have defisted in their attempts. I think there needs not a more convincing proof to shew the anarchy and confusion at present existing in America, and that all pretensions to civil government are ideal, I assure you, my dear friend, Congress, aided by the military, is the only ruling power at present; they are despotic, and their orders enforced by the military with as arbitrary a sway as that with which the King of Prussia governs his dominions.

The shrub which supplies our manufactures with cotton, is much cultivated in this Province, and the inhabitants of the lower sort, through the scarceness and difficulty of procuring clothing for themselves and their negroes, pay greater attention to it at present than tobacco, this plant is of a quick luxuriant growth, and
rises

rifes from five to six feet in height, ⟨
perfing a number of branches as it fho⟨
it requires a dry foil, and thrives beſt
grounds already tilled, for though
plant flourifhes more in frefh lands,
from its luxuriance, it produces m
wood than fruit, it is planted in regu
walks, and at a moderate diftance fr
each other, for the branches to fpre
when it is grown to the height of five
fix inches, the ftems are pulled up exc
two or three of the ftouteft, which
cropped twice before the end of Augu
this precaution is abfolutely neceffary
the wood bears no fruit till after the
cond cropping; and if by neglect
plant is fuffered to exceed four feet h
in its growth, the crop will be greatly
ferior in quality and quantity, and
fruit difficult to gather.

The fruit that the cotton fhrub be
proceeds from a flower which blows

the extremity of its branches, the piftil of which turns to a fhell of the fize of a pigeon's egg, and when the cotton contained in it is ripe, it burfts and expofes the feeds wrapt up in the native flocks to the fun; when the greateft part of them are thus opened, the negroes gather them, and the feeds which are naturally mixed with the cotton are cleaned by means of a machine called a gen, which is made of two fmooth rollers placed clofe and parallel to each other in a frame, and move in contrary directions by means of different wheels at the oppofite fide of the machine, which are put in motion by the foot, the cotton being put to thefe rollers, while they move round, it readily paffes between them, bearing the feed which are too large for the interfpace behind. What paffes in this operation is afterwards hand picked to clear it from the fmall dirt that

comes

comes with the cotton through
machine, and then it becomes fit
ufe.

The carding and fpinning of cotto
the chief employment of the female
groes, for fince the inhabitants have
deprived of our Englifh cottons, they
nufacture a fort themfelves, little inf
to that made at Manchefter, and al
all the families in this Province,
male and female, are cloathed with
own manufacture, the fuperior claf
an example to their inferiors, who
compelled by neceffity.

The weather being fo extremely
woollen cloaths are infufferable, th
fore from neceflity, and as is the cu
of the country, the officers wear co
habiliments; the cotton of which

is made I obtained from my landlord, and saw the whole procefs of its growth and manufacture, from the feed being sown, till it came out of the loom.

I remain,

Yours, &c.

LETTER LXIX.

Jones's Plantation, near Charlottesville, in Virginia, Dec. 12, 1779.

'MY DEAR FRIEND,

CONSIDERING the innumerable difficulties and inconveniences which the colonies have laboured under in maintaining their independency, and their successes appear astonishing, such as could only be effected by that unanimity which universally prevails among the leading and conspicuous characters in each state ; and it is no less surprizing that in their strenuous support of public measures, the internal arrangement of their affairs should be neglected, and by such neglect hazard a general confusion. In this state, at present, their internal concerns, merchandizes of all kinds, and the common and necessary articles of life are at such enormous prices, that few can procure them, and for want of them all classes are highly distressed; Congress have adopted various measures to remedy these evils, but their endeavours have been frustrated by a few monopolizing wretches at Philadelphia and other great cities: to this is owing much of the public distress, which becomes a scource of hindrance and discouragement in the prosecution of the various designs and undertakings of Congress.

But of all the arduous and trying situations they have had to encounter, none has proved more difficult than the present, which they are using their utmost endeavours to overcome, and if not effected,
they

they muft bid farewel to all hopes of gaining independency, and this is the depreciation of their paper money. From th firft emiffion of bills at the commencement of the war to the prefent period they have, by the neceffity of the times iffued near forty millions fterling of continental dollars, and what contributes ftill more to the depreciation, is the immenfe fums of counterfeit money iffued from New-York, and other places in our poffeffion.

Therefore Congrefs wifely forefeeing the indifpenfible neceffity of removing all doubts and diftrefs, that the united ftates were unable to redeem their bills, and that raifing more money by a new emiffion would encreafe the paper in circulation and be the caufe of ftill more decreafing its value, have diftributed throughout the the colonies their refolve, in order to remove thofe apprehenfions that were daily

gaining

gaining ground, in which after stating the great depreciation of their currency, by the means of selfish men, who disregarded the great object they were then, and had for several years been struggling to obtain, and the enormous sums of counterfeit money their enemies had caused to be put in circulation with that of Congress, they had thought proper to declare, that after such a date, no currency should pass, but that issued from that time; and sensible that as many persons might lose considerable sums by reason of counterfeit money, whatever sums of any sort were brought to the treasury at Philadelphia, they should receive one dollar of the new emission, for every forty dollars. And the more fully to establish the credit and value of the new currency, the Congress pledged their public faith, to pay its value in gold or silver specie.

This

This has had the desired effect of Congress, that of solely keeping up the spirit of the people; for it must be obvious to every one, that it is impossible to fulfi their engagements, and to go to Philadelphia, to procure specie for a single dollar would perhaps only be insulted and laughed at. That this opinion prevails the present depreciation is a convincing proof; for we obtain forty-five dollars of this emission for one in specie.

Among the various fruits upon this continent, there is one that seems peculia to this province, named the persimmon and which, until meliorated by severa sharp frosts, is not eatable, or scarcely t be tasted. Many of us were deceived b this fruit, when ripe and hanging on th trees, it having the appearance of a Orlean plumb; but which we found pos sessed of such powerful astringent qualitie as to contract the mouth to such a degree
tha

that it was feveral hours before we regained the fenfe of tafte; of this fruit the inhabitants, in fome parts, brew a liquor called perfimmon beer.

Animals reforting to the words are extremely fond of its flavor, particularly the bears, who come from a great diftance in queft of it, efpecially on the approach of winter, at which time the inhabitants chace and moftly kill them, as they are unable to regain the mountains before the dogs overtake them. If they reach the mountains, the purfuit after them is attended with danger, on account of the vaft number of carniverous animals reforting there in abundance. An accident was near happening to an officer who, with fome others, and a few 'inhabitants, were in purfuit of a bear at the foot of the mountains; at the very inftant, a ferocious animal, which I defcribed in a former letter, called the mountain cat,

was going to spring upon him. One o
the inhabitants obferving it, with his rifl
shot him through the head, and it fel
dead to the ground.

There is in this province, what I neve
recollected to have feen in any other, a larg
ravenous kind of bird that feeds on car
rion, nearly as big as an eagle, called ;
turkey-buftard, from having red gills, re
fembling thofe of a turkey, whence it de
rives its name. It feems to be a fpecie
of the kite, hovering on the wing lik
that bird, and being carniverous. The in
habitants kill them for the fake of thei
feet, which diffolved into an oil, is efteem
ed very falutary in the fciatica, old ache
and pains.

You would fcarcely credit, from the la
borious and harraffing life the negroe
lead in this country, that the paffions o
love and jealoufy fhould act very powe

fully on them, naturally concluding, that their whole ideas would concenter in one, that of rendering their miferable fitu-tion a ftate of comfort, yet fo forcibly do thofe paffions operate on their minds, they are continually poifoning each other, thro' difappointment, or jealoufy: what is remarkable, they can adminifter the poifon that it fhall affect the life for a longer or a fhorter period, agreeable to their ideas of revenge on the object. The owner of our plantation has had feveral female negroes poifoned, fome of whom have lingered out a life for fix or eight months after, and others again, only a week or a fortnight. There was one remarkably ftout wench, who expired on the eighth day after being poifoned; the decay of nature was remarkably vifible from the fecond day, and fhe only complained of a violent pain in her head, and a conftant ficknefs at the ftomach; when medical affiftance was called in, it was pronounced impoffible to counteract

teract the poison, unless what the poiso
consisted of, could be known whic
though in frequent use amongst th
negroes, had never yet been discovered.

Although we have been now near
twelvemonth in this province, the soldier
fare little better than on their first arrival
for the greatest part of the summer the
have been thirty and forty days, at differen
periods, without any other provisio
delivered to them than the meal of India
corn. Great quantities of salt provision
have arrived at the barracks, but owing t
some defect in airing, and the heat of th
climate, are in a state of putrefaction
some person advised the American Com
missary to bury the meat in the earth fo
a few days, and it would regain its purity
which, when dug up, and although swarm
ing with vermin, he insisted was exceed
ingly good, only a little tainted with th
weather, which the utmost care could no
prevent

prevent, and served it out to the soldiers as so many days ratio of meat. All complaints by General Phillips to the Governor of the Province were of little avail, he receiving for answer, that it was the concern of Congress, and what did not affect the government of his state. There are hopes, however, that the disputes of the soldiers will be remedied, as both General Phillips and General Reidesel, who were a short time since exchanged, and gone to New York, purposed, in their way to that city, to obtain an audience with General Washington, and lay those grievances before him; if that was impracticable, it was the intention of the Generals to lay the situation of the troops before Sir Henry Clinton, and through him to seek redress, by an application to General Washington. As to redress from the Americans, little is to be expected, though their Commander in Chief possesses humanity that reflects the highest honour on him; he has not been

been able, notwithstanding so much love
and esteemed, to diffuse that benevolenc
and god-like virtue, among those who lool
up to him for protection. The only hop
we can any way rely on is, that Sir Henr
Clinton will, in compassion to the suffer
ings of the troops, use every exertion in hi
power to effect a general exchange thi
winter. Should that take place, I ma
venture to affirm, that he will no
have braver troops in his army; for th
soldiers, from the cruelty and ill usage the
have continually experienced, since the
became prisoners, will fight to despera
tion.

Great numbers have deserted, with
view to get to New-York, rather than en
dure such distress, they certainly had n
other inducement, as many of them com
municated to their officers their intentions
previous to their desertion, requesting
certificate, that on that day there was du

to them so much pay and so many years clothing, which we could refuse no more than we could their desertion, but to be candid, rather than be witness of the hardships the men experienced, which were out of our power to redress, we rather connived at it, as we well knew that producing certificates from their officers, if they were so fortunate as to reach New-York, would ensure them a favorable reception with the Commander in Chief. Near an hundred have reached New-York, and about sixty or seventy have been taken up, brought back and confined in a picketed prison near the barracks, where numbers would have actually been starved, had not relief been afforded them by the officers, who furnished them with provisions at their own expence.

Among the deserters, there was a party of twenty who appointed a serjeant at their head to command them, and previous to setting off, swore a most solemn oath, strictly to adhere to a set of rules drawn up by the serjeant, in the nature of the articles of war, but the penalties inflicted in case of breach of any of these articles were singularly curious---being no less than death---immediate instantaneous death---to be hanged upon the next tree, and others equally as tremenduous, the only one tending to mercy was cutting off the offenders ears. The whole party excepting one, who was apprehended as out upon a scout for provisions, got safe to New-York. I should observe to you that this dissertion is among the British troops, the Germans not feeling that *amor patria*, besides they are fully content, being upon the same pay as the British troops, which is near four times as much as they receive in their own country, and for what reason it is impossible to say, but the Americans shew more indulgence to the Germans, permitting them to go round the country to labor, and being for the most part expert handicrafts, they realize a great deal of money, exclusive of their pay, and as the generality of the German troops are only soldiers raised for the war, upon their return to their own country, will become persons of property, excepting the regiments of the Prince of Hesse Hanau's body guards, and General Reidefel's dismounted dragoons, which are two well-disciplined regiments, the rest of German troops were such as little service could be expected from, and when we reflect on the manner they were raised, who could be surprized that they did not act with more alacrity during the campaign; for the mode of obtaining these subsidies, was as follows: When application was made by our court to Germany for troops, the Prince caused every place of worship to be surrounded during service, and took every man who had been a soldier, and to embody these and form them into regiments,

ments, he appointed old officers, who had been many years upon half pay, to command them, or on refufal of ferving, to forfeit their half pay, thus were thefe regiments raifed, officered with old veterans, who had ferved with credit and reputation in their youthful days, and who had retired, as they imagined, to enjoy fome comforts in the decline of life. Only picture to your imagination, enfigns of forty and fifty, commanding of troops not much younger, and judge how proper they are for an active and vigorous campaign, in the thick woods of America.

It being the univerfal opinion throughout the army, that we fhall remain prifoners the remainder of the war, the Britifl officers have contributed to render thei fituation as comfortable as the nature o the country will poffibly allow, and t promote affociation, they have erecte a coffee-houfe, a theatre, and a cold bath

to tenſe up the relaxed ſtate of the body, the intenſe heat of the climate occaſions.

Having repeatedly mentioned to you the barracks, and their ſituation, and as any deſcription would fall exceedingly ſhort, I have ſent you an accurate view of them. To form a juſt conception of the diſtreſſes and ſituation of the army on its firſt arrival, you are not to conſider the place as the drawing repreſents it, but as a thick wood, and not a ſingle tree cut down.

It is with the utmoſt concern I inform you of the death of your old friend W----, of our regiment, the relation of Sir Watkin Williams Wynne, Bart. who I am perſuaded, fell a martyr to the dire effects of that pernicious liquor, peach brandy, the circumſtance attending his death being remarkable, I ſhall relate them. He had
been

been on a visit a few days to some office
and having made a little too free, duri[ng]
that time he became in a state of insani[ty]
the first instance he shewed of it was g[et]ting up in the dead of the night, a[nd]
walking several hours in the snow ba[re]
footed, till his feet were frost-bitten,
had been absent near four hours before [he]
was missed, and upon his companio[ns]
going in search of him, he was found p[a]rading before the door, they conduct[ed]
him into the house, and applying t[he]
usual remedy, all danger of a mortificati[on]
was removed from being frost bit. T[he]
next morning he was frequently asking
a knife to cut a stick, which his compa[ni]ons always contrived to evade giving hi[m]
and on their quitting Charlottesvi[lle]
at which place they had slept, t[hey]
intended to conduct him to the barra[cks]
for advice, but on his expressing a de[sire]
to return to his own quarters, they [in]dulged him in his request. It is said t[hat]

persons laboring under that most calamitous affliction, are possessed of extreme cunning, to deceive those they suspect of watching their actions. He, poor fellow, fully demonstrated it, for keeping up a very rational conversation as they rode along, not discovering the least symptoms of any one insane, till they arrived at an exceeding steep hill, at the foot of which was a rivulet, where they stopt to water their horses, seizing this opportunity, he left them and rode his horse as fast as he could make him go up the hill, his two companions pursued, but he being better mounted, was soon out of sight, they followed the track of his horse in the snow, till it turned into the woods, and concluded any further pursuit would be vain by themselves, they hastened to their quarters, which was not a mile distant, for assistance. By this time night had come on, nevertheless, a party of ten or a dozen with lanthorns, went various roads,
and

446 INTERIOR TRAVELS

and into the woods, which they traver[sed]
beſt part of the night, but could [not]
obſerve the leaſt trace of him; the n[ext]
morning they renewed the ſearch, a[nd]
about five miles off, in a bye pla[ce]
found his horſe faſtened by the bridle t[o a]
fence, cloſe by a rivulet, to which t[hey]
could trace the feet of a man upon [the]
ſnow, they followed the track till t[hey]
came upon the ice, which led them to [a]
bend of the current under a hanging ro[ck]
where the river had not been frozen ov[er]
and which, by the rapidity of the curr[ent]
at that place, ſeldom did, and there i[t is]
imagined he fell in, before he came to [it]
the ice twice gave way, but being ſhall[ow]
he had ſcrambled out. His compani[ons]
could not long remain in ſuſpence, [and]
ſending his ſervant back for one of [his]
ſhoes, on his return they found it exa[ctly]
fitted the track in the ſnow, and from [the]
horſe being ſo near, it left little room [to]
doubt. However, ſome ſhort time af[ter]

all doubts were removed, as the body was found---poor man---I did the laſt ſad office with a heavy heart---but his memory will be ſincerely lamented, by thoſe that knew him,

Yours, &c.

LETTER LXX.

Barracks, Charlottesville, in V[a]
April 18, 1780.

MY DEAR FRIEND,

LITTLE has transpired of intell[igence]
worth relating, unless a repetit[ion of]
grievances and hardships, during [a long]
and severe Winter, and all hopes [or ex-]
pectation of any exchange taking [place:]
there has been a meeting of Comm[ission-]
ers from both armies for that pu[rpose,]
but they could not agree to the di[fferent]
proportions of exchange, as to the [num-]
ber of soldiers in lieu of an officer. [As]
my sentiments upon this head, or a

least tending to politics I am debarred from, as this letter must undergo the examination of the American Commanding Officer; therefore, being confined, I shall give you my obfervations and remarks on the customs of the country, and whatever may concern our army, as they occur to memory, which, though you allow to be tolerable, is not so great as Cæsar's, who forgot nothing but injuries.

Since I have been in Virginia I never could assign the reason why the oxen and sheep should be so small, having such abundance of grass during the summer, in the unlimited range of woods; but the winter has fully demonstrated the cause, which arises from the planters paying such little attention to their cattle during the inclement season, by which means they starve the young ones, or at least stint their growth, so that they but very seldom grow so large as if they were better managed, being content if they can but save their lives; and though they suffer them to be so poor in the winter, yet they presently grow fat again in the spring, which they esteem sufficient for their purpose. This is the reason their beef and mutton is neither so large nor so fat as in England; their flesh, however, is esteemed delicate, and has certainly a fine flavor.

Among the curious plants growing in America, none contribute more to the beauty of the spring than the dogwood, which grows in great abundance, and, when adorned with its numerous white flowers, appears delightful. The wood is very hard, and breaks into small fibres; for want of such necessary implements as tooth-brushes, we substitute this wood. The inhabitants have a custom of tying a branch of this tree round the cattles' neck, when they fall down exhaufted by heat in the fummer, imagining that its virtue contributes to their recovery.

There is another tree rather peculiar to America called the tulip tree, and it creates aftonifhment, in the fpring to behold trees of fuch a magnitude, for they are very large and lofty, bearing a flower for a fortnight together in fhape, fize and colour refembling tulips. The leaves grow in a very peculiar fhape; from whence the tree has, in fome places, the appellation of the old woman's fmock, imagining a refemblance below the leaves.

The log huts in which the foldiers refide, although erected fuch a fhort time, are become extremely dangerous, the timbers being nearly deftroyed by an infect that is in the bark of the tree, which, for want of the nourifhment it receives from the turpentine whilft the tree is growing, preys upon the folid part of the timber; and thefe infects, from the deftruction as well as the noife they make, have the appellation of fawyers, and is certainly a very proper one; for I have feen timber, nearly the circumference of one's waift, which had not been cut down above fix months, that upon ftripping off the bark, there was nothing but the appearance of faw-duft, with a vaft number of thefe infects, refembling a large grub-worm.

The foldiers have been fo indifferently fupplied with provifions, the barracks fwarm with rats of an enormous fize, and notwithftanding each hut has a cat or two, they are very troublefome, and with every precaution, they are continually deftroying the men's cloaths and bedding during the night; it is no very uncommon thing to fee them running fix

or

or feven, one after the other, in the interftices of the logs with which the huts are conftructed.

You may recollect, on our firft arrival in this province, I mentioned that a number of duels were fought, and what partly occafioned them. They have of late been frequent amongft the German officers, but from different motives---difputes at gambling. Their manner of fighting is rather fingular. Each party goes to the field with a fecond, and after ftripping to the fhirt, advancing, fhake each other by the hand, draw their fwords, and cut and flafh each other till one party relinquifhes the conteft; and, unlefs the inveteracy is very obftinate, the conflict is over upon the leaft appearance of blood on either fide; this is deemed a fufficient proof of their courage and juftification of their honor. Moft of the duels among them have ended in this manner except one, where the combatants mutilated one another in a moſt ſhocking manner, as nearly to endanger each other's life.

It is no little pleaſure to me that I am unreſtrained from communicating and opening myſelf freely to you, ſince I began this letter, as an opportunity has occurred of ſending it without inſpection by an officer who has received an account of his being exchanged. By the mode that I intended to ſend this, which was by a flag of truce returning to New York, I wrote ſeveral others; ſome were franked by Col. Bland and others by Col. Sherwood, the American Officers commanding the troops at the barracks. The former behaved with true politeneſs and liberality of ſentiment; he only required an officer to pledge his word and honor, as a gentleman, there was nothing political contained in the letter, on affirming
which,

which, the Colonel defired the letter to be fealed, and on it wrote, Examined, and figned his name. The latter, with an inquifitivenefs, accompanied with rudenefs and impertinence, not only read every letter, fentence after fentence, but made animadverfions on them; the Colonel, like moft perfons poffeffed of an impertinent curiofity, met with a fevere rebuke from Lieutenant Charlton of the 20th regiment, but I am afraid he was too ignorant to take the fenfe of it. After he had read his letter, and feeing the name of Charlton figned to it, the Colonel exclaimed, " Charlton, Charlton! I " recollected a captain of a fhip of that " name, who had a relation that was " a name-fake of mine."---" Very proba- " bly, Sir," replied Charlton, " and there " may be one of that name in my fa- " mily; but I'll venture to fay, if there " is, he poffeffes more liberal ideas and " principles than the American *Sherwoods*."

Some short time since I became acquainted with a Colonel Walker, who has lately been elected a Delegate to represent this State in Congress. The usual hospitality of the country presides at his house; but what renders it unpleasant, the family will chiefly converse on politics, but always with moderation. I was much pleased with a very noble and animated speech of the Colonel's father, a man possessing all his faculties with strong understanding, though considerably above eighty years of age. One day, in chat, while each was delivering his sentiments of what would be the state of America a century hence, the old man, with great fire and spirit, declared his opinion, that " the Ameri-
" cans would then reverence the resolution
" of their forefathers, and would eagerly
" impress an adequate idea of the sacred
" value of freedom in the minds of their
" children, that it may descend to the
" latest posterity; that if in any future
" ages

" ages they fhould be again called forth
" to revenge public injuries, to fecure that
" freedom, they fhould adopt the fame
" meafures that fecured it to them by their
" brave anceftors,"

To you, fo converfant with the world, I need not fay, that there are a clafs of people continually at variance with themfelves and all the world, and whom nothing can pleafe. When one of fuch a defcription gets into the army, you cannot conceive how very unpleafant it is to have any concerns with him, efpecially if he is regardlefs of life. Senfible that an officer muft accept a challenge, he does not hefitate to deal them in abundance, and fhortly acquires the name of a fighting man; but as every one is not willing to throw away his life, when called upon by one who is indifferent of his own, many become condefcending, which this man immediately conftrues into fear,

and

and prefuming upon this, acts as if he imagined no one dare contradict him, but all muft yield obedience to his will.

One of this unhappy difpofition has lately broke forth from the recluse manner in which he lived, having only one affociate, of a fimilar difpofition, and wifhed to ingratiate himfelf with the officers at large. There was no keeping him at a diftance by formal civilities, as he would intrude at all times and feafons. Being a little known to an officer who refides with us, he came one day to dinner; and with the idea that he would lay under no obligation for it, invited the whole mefs to dine with him. On the day appointed, there came on a moft violent fnow ftorm, and in the morning we difpatched a fervant with an apology. He fent word back, " that, by God, he had provided " dinner, and he expected us;" and we
had

had no alternative, but either to encounter a ride of near four miles in a heavy fnow ftorm, or, in all probability, a madman the next morning. The day was, without exception, the moft unpleafant I ever paffed in my life; for after we arrived at his quarters, on his having occafion to quit the room, his companion fhewed us a brace of piftols that lay under his pillow, which he conftantly flept with, and which he had frefh loaded and primed that morning, that if any difpute arofe, it might inftantly be decided without leaving the room.

Such conduct cannot be confidered in any other light than infanity; for a pretended indifference for life does not proceed from true courage; if thefe vaunters meet with one equally as indifferent, and receive a check, they cannot brook it. Such was the fate of this unhappy man, and fo overwhelmed was he with fhame,
that

that he put a period to his exiſtence, in the following ſingular manner.

One Winter's evening, when ſitting round the fire in the coffee-room, having ſome occaſion or other to leave it, he laid his cane in one chair and his gloves in another, and on quitting the room, ſaid, " let me ſee who dare meddle with them before I return." In the interim an officer came in, who being very cold, took one of the chairs and drew near the fire; the company told him that they were Mr. ——'s chairs, and what he had ſaid, when he replied " Damn him, one chair is enough for his cane and gloves, and him too, I think."---- Shortly after his return, he enquired with eagerneſs, who had preſumed to meddle with his cane and gloves, when the officer told him he had, and that he thought in ſuch ſevere weather every man ought to be content with one chair, upon which he began to break out

in

in a moſt violent paſſion, " that his dignity
" and himſelf were inſulted in the groſſeſt
" manner:" when the officer ſtopt him
ſhort, by ſaying, " Mr. ——, I have often
" heard of you as a fighting man, but
" never was in your company before, now
" Sir, I have only to tell you as to fight-
" ing, I care as little about it as you do,
" and, by God, Sir, if you ſay another
" word on the ſubject, I'll throw you be-
" hind the fire." From the moſt violent
paſſion he became inſtantly calm, ſat down
in his chair and never ſpoke another word,
but in about ten minutes left the room.
That he ſhould meet with ſuch a rebuff,
accompanied with a threat, operated ſo
powerfully on his mind, that the next
morning he ſhot himſelf; and his manner of performing that deed was ſingular,
as he was found in a ſhallow ſtream,
where the water did not cover the body,
with a piſtol in one hand and another on
the bank loaded.

Numbers

Numbers of officers have lately been been exchanged; from whence the partiality proceeds I cannot furmife, but am inclined to think it muſt arife from the intereſt of their friends, at head quarters at New York. Notwithſtanding I am deſtitute of any one to make an application for my exchange, I am not without hopes it will ſhortly happen; for not long ſince an American officer, Capt. Van Swearingham, of whom I made mention as being taken prifoner during the campaign, vifited the Barracks. I immediately fought him out, in hopes that, in return for the civility ſhewn him, his gratitude would prompt him to render me a ſervice. Accordingly, on waiting on him, he expreſſed great pleafure at feeing me, but infinite regret at my being ſtill a prifoner, as he fully concluded that both Lieut. Dunbar, as well as myfelf, had long ſince been exchanged; and I had the mortification to find that, ignorant of our names,

he

he had defcribed our perfons to an officer of our army who was going to New York, and wifhing to feize the favourable opportunity of ferving his friends, faid they anfwered the defcription, and giving the Captain their names, they were exchanged in lieu of us. However, as he was going directly to head quarters, it fhould be his firft bufinefs with Gen. Wafhington to effect our exchange. On taking my leave of him, your favorite adage of *Nil defperandum* inftantly occurred to my mind; and I am not without hopes, in a fhort time, of once more vifiting my native fhore.

Yours, &c.

LETTER LXXI.

Winchester, in Virginia, Nov. 20, 1780.

MY DEAR FRIEND,

AT receiving a letter, dated from this place, you will perhaps conceive it is to acquaint you, that shortly after you'll see the person who wrote it. I am not, however, as yet, so fortunate; and not without just cause of apprehension, that the bustle and hurry of the campaign has obliterated from the memory of Capt. Van Swearingham, that such persons as Dunbar and myself exist. And when I inform you this town is not

in

in the extent of our parole, your curiosity no doubt will be excited, as to the cause of my being at it; and your surprize will be no less, on being informed that the whole army are on their march, Congress being apprehensive, from Lord Cornwallis's over-running the Carolinas, that it is his Lordship's intention, by forced marches, to retake our army.

About six weeks ago we began our march from Charlottesville Barracks, the army moving in the same manner as we left New England; but as to the place of our destination, that is yet unknown: we understand it is to some of the northern provinces. At present we remain here, till a matter in dispute is adjusted by Congress between this province and Maryland, as the latter absolutely refused the army's entering that state, apprehensive we were to remain there; in consequence of which such a body of men would greatly distress the inhabitants in fo fmall a province; and they actually, in arms, oppofed our croffing the Potowmack.

You may naturally conclude the murmurs of the officers were great, having been given to underftand that they were to remain at the Barracks till exchanged; and many had laid out confiderable fums to render their log huts comfortable againft the approaching winter, as they had fuffered feverely from the cold during the laft, being unable to keep a fufficient fire without imminent danger, as the chimneys were built, as is the cuftom of the country, with wood; and therefore, to remove all fears of any accident, moft of the officers had ftone ones erected. You will fcarcely credit it, when I tell you my miferable log hut, that was not more than fixteen feet fquare, coft between thirty and forty guineas in erecting. Some officers, who had reconciled

their

their minds, with an idea that they should not be exchanged till the termination of the war, had laid out great sums in making themselves comfortable habitations; for the Barracks became a little town, and there being more society, most of the officers had resorted there. The great objection to residing at them, on our first arrival, was on account of the confined situation, being not only surrounded, but even in the woods themselves. I am apt to think that Col. Harvey, the proprietor of the estate, will reap great advantage, if the province should not; as the army entirely cleared a space of six miles in circumference round the Barracks.

After we quitted the Barracks, the inhabitants were near a week in destroying the cats that were left behind, which, impelled by hunger, had gone into the woods, and being so numerous, they were apprehensive, by their encrease, they would in
a short

a short time be unable to extirpate; exclusive of which, there was reason to suppose they would become extremely wild and ferocious, and would be a great annoyance to their poultry.

We crossed the Pignet Ridge, or more properly the Blue Mountains, at Wood's Gap, and though they are confiderably loftier than those we crossed in Connecticut, termed the Green Mountains, we did not meet with so many difficulties; in short, you scarcely perceive, till you are upon the summit, that you are gaining an eminence, much less one that is of such a prodigious height, owing to the judicious manner that the inhabitants have made the road, which, by its winding, renders the ascent extremely easy.

After travelling near a mile through a thick wood, before you gain the summit of these mountains, when you reach the
top

top you are suddenly surprized with an unbounded prospect, that strikes you with awe and amazement. At the foot of the mountains runs a beautiful river; beyond it a very extensive plain, interspersed with a variety of objects, to render the scene still more delightful; and about fifty miles distant are the lofty Allegany mountains, whose tops are buried in the clouds.

Winchester is an irregular built town, containing between three and four hundred houses. It was last war, as it is at present, the rendezvous of the Virginian troops, in excursions against the Indians. By an inhabitant who resided in this town during the last war, I was informed, that before we reached Fort du Quesne, the country round about it was greatly ravaged by the Indians, who committed horrid barbarities, and the town itself was in great danger, and would certainly have been levelled with the ground, and its in-

H h 3 habitants

habitants maffacred, had not Col. Wafhington (the prefent famous General)
erected a fort upon an eminence at the
north end of the town, that fully protected it; notwithftanding the Indians were
fo bold as to venture in fight of the town,
but never within reach of the fort.

The remains of this fort are ftill to be
traced. It appears to have been a regular
fquare fortification, with baftions at each
angle, and the length of the curtain between eighty and ninety feet. The barracks are ftill remaining, which will contain, with eafe and comfort, near five
hundred men, but upon an emergency
would contain twice as many, as is the
cafe at prefent, there being near that number of our foldiers now quartered in them.
Thefe barracks are conftructed of logs, in
the nature of thofe at Charlottefville, but
upon a far more extenfive fcale. Since
the commencement of the war, the Americans

ricans have picketted them in, and converted them into a place of security for prisoners of war. There appears to have been some attempts to make a dry ditch round the fort; but from the rock being impenetrable, it could not be accomplished.

The water at Winchester is very unpleasant to the taste, which I am induced to believe arises from the limy nature of the soil. It affects strangers with excessive gripings, which we severely felt; and it was laughable enough to observe our morning salutations, accosting each other with faces distorted with pain, and execrating the water and the country in general. The inhabitants say that it is a specific against many diseases.

It was no little mortification to be informed, that within a day's ride of each from Winchester, were a number of natural

tural curiosities, and that we were debarred from visiting them. Therefore I must describe them after the manner they were related to me by one of the inhabitants,

About thirty miles from Augusta Court House, there is a rock, which the inhabitants say was that which Moses struck with his rod, for out of the side of it bursts a torrent of water; and what adds to its beauty, the water, after running some distance through a meadow, rushes down a perpendicular precipice near two hundred feet deep.

Twenty miles from this place there is a most curious cave, running near a mile under a rock, in which are phænomena that I must leave philosophers to account for. These are two springs, the one being equal in heat to the warmest bath, and the other equal to the coldest; they are about a foot asunder, and separated by the natural

natural rock. As both springs possess many medicinal virtues, so each of them is made into convenient baths.

Near these springs is a river, which in some measure resembles the river Mole: the only difference being, that the Mole, although it loses itself under ground, at some miles distant makes its appearance again; whereas this river sinks under a mountain and never more rises, and therefore is very justly called Lost River.

Two natural curiosities, within a morning's ride of Winchester, we did obtain permission to visit. The one was a cave or well, formed by nature; at certain periods a person may descend near two hundred yards, and at others it overflows in great abundance; by the inhabitants it is called the tide well, in allusion to its ebbing and flowing. What considerably adds to this wonderful production of nature is,
that

that for many miles around there is neither mountains, nor any running water, and it is situated in a level country. The other, although considered a curiosity in this country, cannot be deemed so by those who have visited the Peak in Derbyshire; it being six or seven caves in a rock, that communicate with each other.

The Americans, for a length of time, flattered themselves that France would send succours and assist them, which report we considered merely raised to revive the spirit of the people, and to rouse them from their lethargy; for at the commencement of the present year, their affairs were in such a state, that the majority were totally indifferent on which side the contest would terminate, sensible that their situation could not be more distressing. But to those strongly attached to the cause of America, judge how their hopes must have been revived, when intelligence came that
France

France had actually sent them succours, with assurances of assisting them in the most effectual manner. From this period the Americans vauntingly boast, that it is impossible for Great Britain to overcome them, and that in a short time they shall witness the British armies being driven from the continent of America. Equally as this intelligence raised their spirits, so did it depress ours; naturally concluding, that although France might take advantage of our unhappy contest with the Colonies, by seizing on our territories either in the East or West Indies, she would not have been the abettor of Rebellion, especially when it is considered she had territories of her own nearly in the same predicament. But France! France! sorry am I to say it, to gain a superiority in political intrigues, you are indifferent by what arts or means it is accomplished.

In

In a former letter I described what an amazing strong mode of defence block-houses were; and a transaction has lately occurred, that not only reflects the highest encomiums of honor and bravery on those that defended it, but is a very convincing proof of the veracity of my assertion.

This block-house was erected by a party of seventy American Loyalists, that took post on the shore of Hudson's River, opposite New York, to secure them from a surprize, or sudden incursion of Washington's army, and not without just cause of apprehension; for a most furious attack was made upon them by near two thousand of the Americans, with seven pieces of cannon, commanded by Gen. Wayne, and notwithstanding a cannonade of three hours, almost every shot of which perforated the timbers, and several attempts to carry the place by assault, the enemy were

repulsed

repulsed with great loss, leaving behind many killed and wounded; and on their retreat the brave seventy pursued them, took several prisoners, and regained some cattle that they had plundered from the neighbouring plantations.

By an officer just left Washington's camp, we have received the melancholy account of the death of Major André, the Adjutant General of the British army, who was taken as a spy, in negociating a business with Gen. Arnold, which, if it had succeeded, would have nearly been the overthrow of the Americans. This officer was present at his execution, who said, that he met his fate with that courage and manliness of behaviour, that deeply affected every one present, and that his severe destiny was universally lamented: so much was he esteemed, that Gen. Washington shed tears when the rigorous sentence was put in execution. When he
found

found that his fate was inevitably fixed and determined, and that all interceffions and every exertion of Sir Henry Clinton, to fave his life, were in vain, he became perfectly refigned; fo extremely compofed was his mind, that the night previous to his execution, he drew the fituation of the Vulture floop, as fhe lay in the North River, with a view of Weft Point, which he fent by his fervant to a general officer at New York. The only thing that any way difcompofed him, or ruffled his mind, and at which his feelings appeared hurt, was the refufal of Gen. Wafhington to let him die a military death. In regard to this circumftance, the officer informed us, that Gen. Wafhington would have granted his requeft; but, on confulting the board of general officers who figned his condemnation, they deemed it neceffary to put that fentence in force, that was laid down by the maxims of war; at the fame time evincing the fincereft grief, that they
were

were forced to comply with, and could not deviate from, the eſtabliſhed cuſtoms in ſuch caſes.

By the account this officer gave us of his being taken, it appears that Major André was too confident of being out of danger; for when the three men that took him priſoner accoſted him, they enquired whether he was of the Upper or Lower Party, [Here it is neceſſary to explain theſe to you---the Upper Party conſiſted of the partizans of the Americans, and the Lower Party of the American Loyal Refugees, they reſide in New York.] he replied of the Lower Party, naturally conceiving, from the ſmall diſtance he was from New York, they could be no other; upon which they undeceived him, and ſaid he muſt go with them, for he was their priſoner. When too late he perceived his miſtake, and endeavoured to convince them to the contrary, by producing

ducing a passport which he had obtained from Gen. Arnold, in the name of John Anderson.

This seemed to have its intended effect, as they released him, and suffered him to proceed without farther trouble; but he not gone many yards, when one of the young men recollecting that he appeared greatly confused, and that there was something in the stranger's face that struck him forcibly with an impression of some peculiarity, insisted upon his companions returning to examine him more strictly.

This recollection was decisive and fatal to André, who was little accustomed to, or prepared for such encounters, as the officer told us he confessed himself, in his letter to Gen. Washington, where he says, " He " was too little versed in deception, to " practise it with any degree or hope of " success;" for upon these young men returning

returning back, he offered them a considerable purse of gold, a very valuable watch, and innumerable other temptations, with the fascinating offers of permanent provisions for life, if they would either let him pass, or accompany him to New York. In vain was every lure, and every argument; they continued inflexible, steady to their purpose, and conducted him prisoner to Washington's head quarters.

Had Major André, when first accosted, replied " of the Upper Party," he would have met with no hindrance. Had they been, as he supposed, of the Lower Party, he would have been taken prisoner upon making that declaration, and his person would have been easily recognized upon his arrival in New York; but the hasty declaration, that he was of the Lower Party, led to his unhappy destiny.

As it is much eafier to point out errors than correct them, I fhall quit this melancholy topic with obferving, that it is very evident from the time Major André undertook his arduous commiffion, till he met his fevere fate, that he difplayed a refolution and ftrength of mind requifite for great actions, which no doubt would, at fome future day, have rendered him an ornament to his profeffion, and, by fome brilliant atchievement, adored by his King and Country.

What are termed thefe Upper and Lower Parties are moftly known to each other, and poffefs great inveteracy on both fides; and it is no uncommon thing, when two parties meet, to obferve the neareft ties of kindred oppofed to each other. Both parties range at large between the Britifh and American lines, and it has more than once happened, when two parties have met at the fame place, that there has been a ceffation

a ceſſation of hoſtilities, they have ſat down to a good ſupper, and ſpent a jovial evening. At parting they agree to go in different directions, and after a certain ſpecified time have again met and fought moſt deſperately.

The Americans have circulated a report that there has been a great riot in London, that the Members of both Houſes of Parliament had been grofsly inſulted, that a number of houſes had been burnt and all the priſons ſet open, with other reports equally as ridiculous. We give the Americans great credit for raiſing them, as their motives are anſwered by it, that of keeping up the ſpirits of the people, and to impreſs their minds with an idea that Great Britain muſt relinquiſh the conteſt. They are too abſurd to be credited by an Engliſhman. Pray be particular in your next, if ſuch a thing has really happened, which it is almoſt too abſurd to ſuppoſe.

suppose. Surely we have enemies enough to contend with abroad, without any broils at home. It is really too ridiculous and absurd to imagine that such an event has taken place, or to give it a moment's thought.

Yours, &c.

LET-

LETTER LXXII.

Frederick's Town, Maryland, April 12, 1781.

MY DEAR FRIEND,

IN a few days after my laſt letter we left Wincheſter, to proceed on our march to this place, it being ſettled by Congreſs that the army is to remain here till ſome ſituation ſhould be fixed on; but the inhabitants think this only a deception, to grant permiſſion for entering the province, and that we are to remain in this town.

Quitting Wincheſter, we recroſſed the Blue Ridge at Williams's Gap, and in our march

march to this place there was little worthy notice, except the Shennando River, which is exceedingly romantic and beautiful, with a variety of falls; and the water is fo tranfparent, that the pebbles may be feen at the depth of feven or eight feet. There are plenty of trout and other fifh; but it is not navigable even for canoes, on account of the innumerable rocks that are under water; and, in tranfporting goods down the river, the inhabitants make ufe of rafts. When we croffed, it was nearly frozen over.

Upon our arrival in this town, I was not fo fortunate in obtaining fuch comfortable quarters, as when I laft paft through it; being obliged to put up at a miferable dirty tavern, with two other officers, at which we remained till the final determination of Congrefs, as it was fully thought we were to proceed further to the northward.

We

We remained only nine days at this tavern, and upon quitting it the landlord gave us the following curious Bill, which I send you by way of specimen of the American mode of charging.

1780.   Lieut. Anberry,   D^r.

Dec. 19. To 3 breakfastes a 12 dollars   £. 13 10 0
         To 5 ditto for servants a 10 dollars   18 15 0
         To mug syder 30. 8 quarts oats a 1 ½
           dollar 90   -   -   6 0 0
         To 3 diners a 15 dollars £. 16 17 6.
           1 quart beer 45   -   -   19 2 6
         To 3 supers a 12 dollars £. 13 10 0.
           ditto servants £. 18 15 0   -   32 5 0
         To 9 quarts oats 5 1 3. 2 supers ser-
           vants 75   -   -   9 16 3
20. To 1 lodging 30. stabling and hay 3
           horses a 12 dollars 13 10 0   -   15 0 0
         To 9 quarts oats 5 1 3. 3 breakfasts
           13 10 0   -   -   18 11 3
         To 3 breakfasts for servants 11 5 0.
           mug syder 30   -   -   12 15 0
         To 4 diners a 15 dollars 22 10 4. 4 do.
           servants 15 0 0   -   -   37 10 0
         To 9 quarts oats 5 1 3. 2 mugs syder
           60. 2 do. beer 90   -   -   12 11 3
         To 3 supers 13 10 0. ditto for servants
           11 5 0   -   -   -   24 15 0

	To 9 quarts oats 5 1 3 — —	5 1 3
21.	Stabling and hay 3 horses day and night	20 5 0
	To lodging 30 a 15 ds. 3 ditto a 12 ds. 13 10 0 — — —	15 0 0
	To 3 mugs beer 6 15 0. mug syder 30	8 5 0
	To 9 quarts oats 5 1 3. 9 qts. ditto 5 1 3. ditto 5 1 3 —	15 3 9
	To 3 supers a 12 ds. 13 10 0. ditto for servants 11 5 0 —	24 15 0
22.	To lodging 30. stabling and hay 3 horses day and night 20 0 0 —	21 15 0
	Tp 3 quarts oats 5 1 3. 3 breakfasts 13 10 0 — — —	18 11 3
	To 3 breakfasts for servants 11 5 0	11 5 0
	To 18 quarts oats 10 2 6. diners 16 17 6	27 0 0
	To 2 mugs syder 60. mug beer 45	5 5 0
	To 3 supers 13 10 0 — —	13 10 0
23.	To lodging 30. stabling and hay 3 horses day and night 20 0 0 —	21 15 0
	Tp 9 quarts oats 5 1 3. 3 breakfasts 13 10 0 — —	18 11 3
	To 18 quarts oats 10 2 6. 3 diners 16 17 6 — —	27 0 0
	To 1 mug syder 30. mug beer 45 —	3 15 0
	To 3 supers 13 10 — —	13 10 0
24.	To lodging 30. stabling and hay for 3 horses day and night 20 0 0 —	21 15 0
	To 3 breakfasts 13 10. 15 quts oats 8 14 3 — —	21 11 3
	To corn 10 quts 7 10 0. Diners 16 17 6 — —	24 7 6

To 2 mugs beer 90. 1 mug fyder 30	6 0 0
To 4 fupers 18 0 0 - -	18 0 0
25. To lodging 30. ftabling and hay 3 horfes day and night 20 0 0 -	21 15 0
To 3 breakfafts 13 10 0. 3 diners 16 17 6 - -	30 7 6
To 32 quarts oats 18 0 0. 3 fupers 13 10 0 - -	31 10 0
26. To lodging 30. ftabling and hay 3 horfes day and night 20 0 0 -	21 15 0
To 3 breakfafts 13 10 0. 2 diners 11 5 0 - -	24 15 0
To 3 mugs beer 90. mug fyder 30 yefterday - -	6 0 0
To mug fyder 30. diner 5 12 6. Bowl tody 60 - -	10 2 6
To 2 quarts oats 22 6 -	1 2 6
	730 10 0
To 4 quarts ditto 45 -	2 5
True balance £. 732 15 0
To the hier of the dineing room, hard money - -	1 15

Errors excepted,
Per ROB. WOOD.

Jan. the 3d, 1781. Recd of Mr. Thos. Amberry, Seven hundred and thirty-two Pound fifteen Shillings, in full for the Paper Currency Account above.

Per ROB. WOOD.

After perusing the articles of the bill, and finding them just, as was customary, I asked the landlord what he would allow in exchange for hard money. He, being a staunch American, flew into a violent passion, saying, "He was surprized I "should make him such an offer; that "there were rascals enough already to "ruin their country, by selling and traf- "ficking in paper; and that, for his part, "he knew no difference between Con- "gress money and King George's." I begged him to be pacified; that in half an hour I would settle his bill; when, with the utmost insolence, he replied, " I "swear now, if it an't settled by twelve "o'clock, I swear I'll send the sheriff af- "ter you, and you'll soon see the inside of "that place," pointing to the prison op- "posite his house."

You'll no doubt be surprized, that, for the fellow's impertinence, I did not give him
a horse-

a horfe-whipping, which, had it been in England, a landlord would hardly have efcaped. But, my dear Friend, we are become perfect Stoics, and it requires an infinite torture to ruffle our temper in the leaft. We have fo long been accuftomed to ill language and infolence from the inferior fort, that we really pay no more attention to it, than Gen. Phillips obferved we fhould to the cackling of fo many geefe.

On my quitting the fellow to go in fearch of paper money, it occurred to me that he might employ fome one to watch over me. I therefore went to the barracks and fent a ferjeant, who foon came back, when I returned and paid him his bill of feven hundred and thirty-two pounds fifteen fhillings; and obferving the item of one pound fifteen fhillings in hard money, I tendered him the fum in paper, retorting upon him his own words, that he knew

knew of no diftinction. The fellow appeared much confounded and afhamed; but as the charge was an agreement with his wife, who was to have it as a perquifite, for the entire ufe of the room, I paid the half-joe exclufive of the bill: no doubt the fellow would not have made the leaft fcruple of confcience to have taken the whole amount in fpecie,

Your curiofity is raifed to know at what rate I purchafed the paper money to difcharge the bill. Know then, that the enormous fum of feven hundred and thirty-two pounds fifteen fhillings, I difcharged for about four guineas and a half. After this I think I need not mention any thing more of the depreciation of paper money.

It being determined by Congrefs that the army is to make fome refidence in this town, the men are quartered in very
comfortable

comfortable barracks, that were built by the Americans since the commencement of the war, are better supplied with provisions, and allowed many privileges, such as working for the inhabitants permitted to go into the country to purchase vegetables, &c. and since the men have been prisoners they have never enjoyed so many comforts. Such treatment is more likely to have the desired effect of Congress than ill usage, in tempting them to desert. So prevalent, indeed, has been desertion in our regiment, that it is now reduced to sixty men, including non-commissioned officers, and the other regiments are in proportion, all of which, in Canada, mustered four hundred and fifty.

The officers are quartered in the town and plantations around. My quarters are at a Col. Beattie's, of the militia, who, though strongly attached to the American cause,

cause, having a son in the Maryland regiment, in General Greene's army, is not without a penchant for a little of the *true touchstone*. The plea he makes to his countrymen for admitting us into his house is, that as he has a large family and must provide for them in the best manner possible.

Since our arrival in this province a person has introduced himself to the officers as a clergyman, and as one strongly attached to the British government. The inhabitants say that he was never ordained, and that he has created much confusion in various families by disavowing their marriage, he having no right to perform the ceremony. This has cut out abundance of work for the limbs of the law. He still performs Divine service at various churches, with all their regular duties. Whether his political principles are put on for the sake of our company

pany and a little conviviality, I cannot pretend to fay; but this much I can affirm as to his religious ones, that he follows St. Paul to a tittle, being " *all things to all men:*" for he will fwear with thofe that fwear, and drink with thofe that drink.

Yours, &c.

LETTER LXXIII.

Colonel Beattie's Plantation, near Frederick Town, in Maryland, July 11, 1781.

MY DEAR FRIEND,

NOTHING will more fully illustrate the tyranny and oppression of Congress and its upstarts in power, than reciting two of the most flagrant acts of injustice, at the house of one Taylor, a Quaker, where Capt. Jameson, of our regiment, is quartered. One of the collectors, for a tax of forty-eight shillings, took from the stable a beautiful horse, worth near thirty guineas; and for another of about five or six pounds, they brought

brought carts, and conveyed away a large ſtack of hay, of near forty pounds value. This paſſive man (who, I ſhould inform you, was a true friend to Government, and in conſequence greatly perſecuted) made no other complaint than, " Well, " let them take---let them take all my " ſtock, my farm, and turn me out of my " houſe, I have that by me that will never " let me want in my old age."

From his attachment to his Sovereign, and ſpeaking his ſentiments, he was continually threatened with impriſonment; but that, and every other perſecution, he would bear with the utmoſt chearfulneſs and reſignation, concordant to the principles of his religion. Nevertheleſs, at times, the poor old man would fetch a heavy ſigh, as if his heart was burſting with grief, and exclaim, " Ah, well-a-day! " little did I think, after the labor of my " youth,

" youth, and training up a large family in
" the fear of the Lord, this would have
" been the reward of my old age. There,
" friend, (pointing to some extensive mea-
" dows that were before his house) with
" these hands did I clear that ground, and
" many a weary night have I worked by
" light of pine wood, to leave my chil-
" dren an inheritance, which is daily threa-
" tened to be taken from me." Here his
fortitude would be overcome; and, after
a little respite, his final exclamation was,
" The Lord's will be done."

Oh, Americans! if this is the basis on which you are to establish your independence, surely you must think there will be a day of retribution! And though it may not fall on your heads, the next generation may have cause to curse the calamities their forefathers have brought on them.

We

We daily expect to remove from this province, on account of the movements of Lord Cornwallis's army, which we underſtand is forming a junction with the troops landed in Virginia, under the command of Gen. Phillips and Gen. Arnold, and this ſtate are not without apprehenſions of a deſcent being made by the King's forces. Therefore to impede this progreſs, Gen. Waſhington has detached two ſtrong bodies, one of continental troops, under the command of the Marquis de la Fayette, and the other confiſting of the Penſylvania line, under Gen. Wayne. They paſſed thro' Frederick Town laſt month, and appeared to be moſtly Scotch and Iriſh, with a great number of blacks. They were badly cloathed, and ſo extremely mutinuous and difcontented, that their officers were afraid to truſt them with ammunition. I obſerved that they wore black and white cockades; the ground being the firſt color and the relief of the other.

other. On enquiring the cause, a very pompous American replied, " It was a " compliment to, and a symbol of affec- " tion for, their generous and magnani- " mous allies the French."

Our quarters have been rendered very disagreeable to us by an unpleasant cir- cumstance, the death of the Colonel's son, who was killed at the battle of Camden, in the Carolinas. He, as well as the whole family, have taken it much to heart, and the house has been ever since a scene of lamentation. What renders it still more disagreeable is, whenever we meet the Co- lonel, he seems extremely anxious to be revenged upon us. We are seeking out for other quarters, but they are very difficult to be obtained.

At Easter holidays the young people have a custom, in this province, of boil- ing eggs in logwood, which dyes the shell crimson,

crimſon, and though this colour will not rub off, you may, with a pin, ſcratch on them any figure or device you think proper. This is practiſed by the young men and maidens, who preſent them to each other as love tokens. As theſe eggs are boiled a conſiderable time to take the dye, the ſhell acquires great ſtrength, and the little children divert themſelves by ſtriking the eggs againſt each other, and that which breaks becomes the property of him whoſe egg remains whole.

To impreſs the minds of his children with their glorious ſtruggle for independence, as they term it, the Colonel has an egg, on which is engraved the battle of Bunker's Hill. This he takes infinite pains to explain to his children, but will not ſuffer them to touch it, being the performance of his ſon gone to camp; but now being ſlain, he preſerves it as a relic. The Colonel favoured us with a ſight of it,

it, and, considering the small space, the
battle is very accurately delineated.

As we imagined, orders are arrived for
the removal of the army to York Town
and Lancaster, at which places the officers
are to be separated from the soldiers, and
are to be quartered at East Windsor in
Connecticut. Brigadier Gen. Hamilton
has expressed great displeasure at this separation, which is directly against the
terms of the convention; but after Congress have broke the most essential point,
it is vain to remonstrate against such proceedings. We are now in their power,
and they act with us as best suits their
plan. The General gave out in orders,
that if it was the desire of the troops, he
would protest to Congress against the separation; at the same time adding, he well
knew it would be in vain. He strongly
recommended the soldiers to behave in
every respect the same as if their officers
were

were present, and, though separated, they should remember that subordination was due to the non-commissioned officers, who still had authority over them. The General lamented that he was unable to furnish supplies of cloathing and other necessaries; therefore directed officers who had the payment of companies, to settle the men's accounts, and give them their balance to provide themselves, which most of them will be enabled to do, as the generality have twenty or thirty pounds to receive. To military men it will appear surprizing, but there was a private in the company I paid who had forty-five pounds due to him.

The troops have greatly diminished since they came to Frederick Town, not only by desertion but death, as numbers have fell a sacrifice to spirits, which are easily procured and at a cheap rate, as there are abundance of stills around the coun-

try,

try, and the soldiers were in a continued state of intoxication. I need not tell you of the inordinate paffion that foldiers in general have for liquor, and what a difficult matter it is to reftrain them from it; but where it is continually before them, next to an impoffibility. Within this fortnight we have loft two in a moft melancholy way, who, during the abfence of the man that attended a ftill on the Colonel's plantation, drank the liquor hot out of the pipe, and the next morning were found dead in their beds.

In a few days we fet out on our march. If an opportunity occurs, I will write to you from Lancafter; but you may depend, upon my arrival in Connecticut, to hear from

Your's, &c.

I have

I have unsealed this Letter, just to add a melancholy Postscript, of which we have this moment received tidings, the loss of that brave officer General Phillips; who died last month of a fever at Richmond. His skill and knowledge in all military concerns, not only in his early days received the approbation of that great commander Prince Ferdinand of Brunswick, on various occasions in the last war in Germany; but justified such commendation by every part of his subsequent conduct: particularly in the unequalled duties, toils, dangers and hardships of our campaign. A circumstance attended his death, similar to the inhumanity that the Americans displayed at the interment of General Frazer. For them, whom we suppose were exasperated, some excuse may be pleaded; but that the Marquis de la Fayette, whose nation is so conspicuous for the quintessence of *les petits attentions*, should be guilty of such conduct, is astonishing.

For

For notwithſtanding a flag of truce was sent to inform him, that acroſs the river, at ſuch a houſe, General Phillips lay dangerouſly ill, and at the point of death, and to ceaſe cannonading. This requeſt was denied; an inceſſant fire was kept up, ſeveral balls went through the houſe, and one through the adjoining room to where General Phillips lay, juſt as he was breathing his laſt, which diſturbing him, he exclaimed, "My God, 'tis cruel, "they will not let me die in peace."

LETTER LXXIV.

East Windsor, in Connecticut, Sept. 2, 1781.

MY DEAR FRIEND,

DISTRESSING and humiliating as the scene was, when we commanded our men to pile up their arms and abandon them on the plain of Saratoga, still much greater was the separation of the officers from the men at Lancaster. On the morning it took place the regiments were paraded near the barracks, which are picketed in, and converted into a prison. At a small distance was drawn up a regiment of continental troops, the Colonel of which

behaved

behaved extremely polite, saying, he should not march the British troops to the barracks, till their officers informed him they were ready. When the Colonel was informed he might march the men, the American troops, forming a square around the British soldiers, conducted them to the prison.

The sight was too deeply affecting, and we hastened from the spot. Could you have seen the faces of duty, respect, love and despair, you would carry the remembrance to the grave. It was the parting of child and parent, the separation of soul and body--- it effected that which the united force of inclement seasons, hunger and thirst, incessant barbarity, adverse fortune, and American insults heaped together, could never have effected---it drew tears from the eyes of veterans, who would rather have shed their blood. As far as sounds could convey, we heard a reiteration of " God
" bless

"blefs your Honors." It was fuch a fcene as muft leave an everlafting impreffion on the mind. To behold fo many men, who had bravely fought by our fide---who in all their fufferings looked up to us for protection, forced from us into a prifon, where, experiencing every feverity, perhaps famifhing for want of food, and ready to perifh with cold, they had no one to look up to for redrefs, and little to expect from the humanity of Americans.

It was extremely vexatious to be again difappointed in vifiting Philadelphia, efpecially when in fight of it; but all entreaties to the Major who efcorted us, for indulgence, were in vain. However we received fome little compenfation in paffing through Bethelem, at which place is a fettlement of the Moravians.

The tavern at Bethelem is upon an exceeding good plan, and well calculated
for

for the convenience and accommodation of travellers. The building, which is very extenfive, is divided throughout by a paffage of near thirty feet wide. On each fide are convenient apartments, confifting of a fitting room, which leads into two feparate bed-chambers. All thefe rooms are well lighted, and have fire-places in them. On your arrival you are conducted to one of thefe apartments, and delivered the key, fo that you are as free from interruption as if in your own houfe. Every other accommodation was equal to the firft tavern in London. You may be fure our furprize was not little, after having been accuftomed to fuch miferable fare at other ordinaries, to fee a larder difplayed with plenty of fifh, fowl and game. Another matter of equal furprize, as we had not met with fuch a thing in all our travels, was excellent wines of all forts, which to us was a moft delicious treat, not having tafted any fince we left Bofton;

Boston; for notwithstanding the splendor and elegance of several families we visited in Virginia, wine was a stranger to their tables. For every apartment a servant is appointed to attend, whose sole business is to wait on the company belonging to it, and who is as much your servant, during your stay, as one of your own domestics. The accommodation for horses is equal, with servants to attend them. In short, in laying out the plan of this tavern, they seem solely to have studied the ease, comfort and convenience of travellers, and is built upon such an extensive scale, that it can with ease accommodate one hundred and sixty persons. General Phillips was so much delighted with it, that after he quitted Virginia, not being permitted to go to New York, on account of some military operations that were on foot in the Jerseys, he returned back near forty miles to take up his residence at it, merely on account of the accommodations.

The

The landlord accompanied us to the intendant, or the head of the society, who with great politeness shewed us every thing worthy of observation on the settlement.

The first place he conducted us to was the house of the single women, which is a spacious stone building, divided, similar to the tavern, into large chambers, which are, after the German mode, heated with stoves. In these the young women pursue various domestic employments, and some are employed in fancy and ornamental work; in all their apartments are various musical instruments. The superintendant of these young women conducted us to the apartment where they slept, which is a large vaulted room the whole dimension of the buildings, in which were beds for every woman. The women dine in a large hall, in which is a handsome organ, and the walls adorned with scripture pieces, painted by some of the

women

women who formerly belonged to the society. This hall anfwers the purpofe of a refectory and chapel: but on Sundays they attend worfhip at the great church, which is a neat and fimple building.

The houfe of the fingle men is upon the fame principle as that of the women; upon the roof of which is a Belvidere, from whence you have not only a moft delightful profpect, but a diftinct view of the whole fettlement. We obferved that the building was much defaced, which the fuperintendant informed us was occafioned by the Americans taking it from the young men, and converting it into an hofpital for the fick and wounded, after the battle of Germantown; and, added he, " it is incredible what numbers pe-
" rifhed for want of proper care and at-
" tention, and the hofpital being ill fup-
" plied with drugs." Pointing to an adjoining field, he faid, " There lie buried
" near

" near seven or eight hundred of the A-
" merican soldiers, who died here during
" the winter."

All manner of trades and manufactures are carried on in this place distinctly, and one of each branch; at these various occupations the young men are employed. Every one contributes his labor, and the profits arising from each goes to the general stock. These young men receive no wages, but are supplied with all necessaries from the various branches of trade. They have no cares about the usual concerns of life, and their whole time is spent in prayer and labor; their only relaxation being concerts, which they perform every evening.

These people, who are extremely shrewd and sensible, in a manner foreseeing the ill consequences attending a civil war, had before its commencement, laid in grea
quantitie

quantities of European goods, which they sent to their various farms interspersed around the settlement.

The Moravians are not only very assiduous, but ingenious too. They have adopted a sort of marriage, but from the manner of its celebration you cannot suppose that mutual tender endearments and happiness to subsist between the parties united as with us. A young man feels an inclination to marry, which does not proceed from any object he is enamoured with, for he never sees his wife but once before the ceremony takes place; it being contrary to the principles of their religion to suppose it is from the passions of nature, but merely to uphold the society, that it may not sink into oblivion. The young man communicates his inclination to their priest, asking of him a girl to make his wife, who consulting with the superintendant of the young women, she produces her who is next in rotation for marriage. The prieſt preſents her to the young man, and leaves them together for an hour, when he returns. If they both conſent, they are married the next day. If there is any objection, both their caſes are very pitiable, but eſpecially the woman's, as ſhe is put at the end of the liſt, which amounts to near ſixty or ſeventy; nor does the poor girl ſtand the leaſt chance of a huſband till ſhe arrives again at the top, unleſs the man feels a ſecond inclination for marriage, for he never can obtain any other woman than the one with whom he had the firſt interview. This, I am induced to think, was the reaſon of there being ſuch a number of old women among the ſingle ones. Thus you ſee, my friend, that marriage and its inexpreſſible enjoyments, are not the reſult of the paſſions, but a mere piece of mechaniſm, ſet to work by chance and ſtopt alone by neceſſity.

When

When two parties meet and are united in marriage, a houfe is provided for them by the fociety, of which there are great numbers around the town; very neat habitations, with pleafant gardens. Their children of either fex, at the age of fix, are taken from them, and placed in the two feminaries, confequently they can have little affection for them. When either of the parties die; if the woman, the man returns to the apartments of the fingle men, and if the man, the widow retires to a houfe that is built for that purpofe.

The religion of the Moravians refembles more that of the Lutherans than the Calvinifts; in one point it greatly differs from both, by admitting of mufic and pictures in their places of worfhip. Prayer conftitutes almoft a third of their employment; for exclufive of the daily public devotions in their great church, they attend service in their own chapels morning, noon and evening.

Setting aside their ridiculous mode of entering into the marriage state, and which to them is of little moment, I could not but reflect, if content was in this life they enjoy it. Far from the bustle of a troublesome world, living in perfect liberty, each one pursuing his own ideas and inclination, and residing in the most delightful situation imaginable, which is so healthy, that they are subject to few, if any diseases.

As want is a stranger, so is vice. Their total ignorance of the refined elegancies of life, precludes any anxiety or regret that they possess not wealth to enjoy them. Nevertheless they possess what many are entire strangers to, who are surrounded with what are termed blessings, those

true

true and essential ones---health and tranquility of mind; and that you may ever enjoy them, though no Moravian, in a high degree of refinement, is the sincere wish of

Yours, &c.

LETTER LXXV.

Hartford, in Connecticut, Sept. 14, 1781.

MY DEAR FRIEND,

THIS is deemed the capital of this province. It stands on the west side of the Connecticut River, and is situated about forty miles from the sea-coast.

We were shewn, among other things, the following curiosities, an house built in the year 1640 of American oak, the timbers of which were yet sound, and almost in a state of petrefaction. In it was born a Jonathan Belcher, Esq. who was
Governor

Governor of this province as well as of New Jerſey, and, by his upright adminiſtration, idolized by both ſtates. The ſecond was an elm tree, held as ſacred as ever the oak was in the days of the antient bards of our own country the druids; as this elm, in ſome time of imminent danger, concealed the charter of the province. The third was a moſt wonderful well, which being dug near ſeventy feet, without the leaſt appearance of water, the labourers met with a large rock, and on the miners boring this rock, in order to blaſt it with powder, they drove the auger through it, upon which the water ſpouted up with ſuch amazing velocity, that it was with the utmoſt difficulty, with the aſſiſtance of a number of pumps and a fire-engine they could keep the well dry till it was ſtoned, which was no ſooner accompliſhed than it filled and ran over, and has ever ſince ſupported, or rather

formed,

formed, a brook, for above one hundred years.

The inhabitants of Hartford relate a ludicrous ſtory of Whitfield, who travelled America in the hopes of ſowing the ſeeds of Methodiſm upon this continent; and, from a ſermon he preached at the great meeting in this town, you may be ſure did not gain over the female part of his congregation; but was inſulted, and obliged to take ſhelter in the firſt houſe that would admit him. The text he had ſelected was, " Anoint my eyes with eye-" ſalve." After expatiating for a conſiderable length of time, to point out what was *not* the true eye-ſalve, he, in the uſual cant of thoſe fanatic preachers, ſays, " Now I'll tell you what *is* the real eye-" ſalve—it is faith—it is grace—it is ſimpli-" city—it is virtue—it is virgin's water. " But, ah Lord, where can that be found? " Perhaps not in this grand aſſembly."

At

At a place called Symſbury are ſome copper mines that are exhauſted of their ore, which are converted to a ſtate dungeon; where, formerly, ſuch offenders as the General Aſſembly did not chuſe to puniſh with death were ſent, ſhewing the humanity and mildneſs of the law; not but, in my opinion, they would have ſhewn it more conſiderably, by hanging up the unfortunate wretch; for in the courſe of a few months, after lingering out a miſerable exiſtence, the diſſolution of nature puts a period to their pain. Theſe mines were worked many years ago, the miners boring near half a mile through a mountain, making large cells that are forty yards below the ſurface. The priſoners are let down by a windlaſs into this diſmal cavern, through a hole, which anſwers the purpoſes of conveying their food and air; as to light, it ſcarcely reaches them. This place, ſince the commencement of the war, has been converted to the infamous purpoſe

pose of imprisoning Loyalists, to make them renounce their attachment to their Sovereign, and yield obedience to Congress; and I am informed that numbers have been taken from their houses, by order of the Assembly, and after a slight examination where witnesses were easily procured, either through malice or interest, they have been hurried away to this dungeon, to drag on a short period of pain and misery, which, from the number of steady spirits who have been imprisoned and expired in it, may, with great propriety, be called the catacomb of loyalty.

There is an animal supposed to be peculiar to New England, called the cuba. This animal, as if sensible that his family rely on him for protection, is extremely tender of them, and never forsakes them till death dissolves the union. What further displays his magnanimity is, he never indicates the least anger to the

the female, though ever so provoked by her. What a charming lesson from nature is this to mankind; and how happy would the rational part of the creation become, if they did but pursue the examples of irrational animals.

Yours, &c.

LETTER LXXVI.

New York, Sept. 25, 1781.

MY DEAR FRIEND,

NEW Haven is remarkable for having given the epithet of pumpkin-heads to the New Englanders, which arose from a severe and religious code of laws, made at the first settlement of Connecticut; which enjoin every male to have his hair cut round by a cap, and when caps were not readily at hand, they substituted the hard shell of a pumpkin, which being put on their head every Saturday, the hair was cut by it all round the head.

head. What religious virtue may be derived from this custom, it is difficult to find out; certainly there is much prudence in it, for it prevents the hair from entangling, saves the use of bags and ribbons, and prevents it from incommoding the sight by falling over the eyes. I am induced to think the custom arose from this cause, that as they were such enthusiasts in religion, and at the same time a lawless and profligate people, those who had lost their ears for heresy, should not conceal their misfortune and disgrace.

We passed by a meeting that was situated close to the sea shore, which about three Sundays since was surrounded by a party from Long Island, at the time of divine service, and the most notorious rebels, with the clergyman, were taken prisoners. Upon the alarm the confusion was great, the congregation getting out as faſt as they could, each man taking the firſt horſe he met with, rode away full gallop. Some of our party, having mounted other horſes, riding after them. An inhabitant, who reſides near the meeting, informed us that it was a ludicrous fight; ſome galloping off with their neighbours horſes, the owner running after to ſtop him; others ſeeking refuge in an adjoining wood; women ſcreaming, ſhrieking and fainting; and as no miſchief aroſe from it, it muſt have been truly laughable.

Upon our arrival at King's Bridge, it is impoſſible to deſcribe the emotions of joy depicted in the countenance of every one; when we had paſſed the barrier, we felt ourſelves once more at liberty and ſafe out of the hands of barbarians; for ſo many fortuitous circumſtances had taken place from the time we were made priſoners, that, notwithſtanding we received an official

official accounts of our being exchanged from the commiffary of prifoners, and obtained our paffports, ftill we did not conceive ourfelves altogether emancipated, till we had got within the Britifh lines.

The ifland of New York, at King's Bridge, is joined to the continent by a fmall wooden bridge, and the country around is very rocky and mountainous. The river, which feparates the ifland from the continent, is a fafeguard againft any fudden invafion of the enemy, and the works that are thrown up, which are exceedingly ftrong, are on fuch commanding fituations, that an army would be cut to pieces in attempting to pafs it. This poft is fourteen miles from the city of New York.

Our fleet is repairing after the action they have had with the French off Chefapeak Bay, and, when in a condition, are to fail with a confiderable body of troops, which Sir Henry Clinton is to command himfelf, in order, if poffible, to fave Lord Cornwallis's army. I cannot defcribe the eagernefs of both navy and army to effect it, particularly the former, who are ufing the utmoft diligence and labor in the neceffary repairs.

A day or two before we came here, Prince William Henry arrived from England, in the Lion of feventy-four guns, under the care of Admiral Digby. The Prince has been on fhore, and vifited moft of the places in the city and the pofts around it. He is very fhrewd and fenfible, making many pertinent remarks and obfervations. Not long fince he accofted Lieut. Bibby, of our regiment, in the following manner: " Well, Captain Bibby, " fo you are in the Adjutant General's " office. I fuppofe there are handfome " perquifites." Bibby replied, " Upon my
" word,

"word, your Royal Highness is misin-
"formed; for no one in that office has
" more than his bare salary."---" Indeed!"
exclaimed his Royal Highness, with surprize: " Well, well, then you should par-
" take of those of the Commissaries and
" Barrack Master Generals; for, let me
" tell you, they have emoluments enough
" for both."

The city of New York stands on the southern extremity of the island, and its situation is extremely delightful; commanding such a variety of prospects, as are the most charming that can be conceived. The city is mostly built upon the East River, on account of the harbour. In many of the streets are rows of trees on each side, for shelter from the amazing heats in summer. Most of the houses are built with brick, very strong and neat, and several stories high; many of them have balconies on the roof, where company sit in the fummer evenings, to enjoy the profpect of the oppofite fhores and harbour; and the roofs are covered with fhingles. The ftreets are paved and clean, but in general very narrow; there are two or three, indeed, which are fpacious and airy. The length of the town is fomewhat more than a mile, and the breadth of it about half a mile. The fituation is reckoned healthy, but fubject to one great inconvenience, which is the want of frefh water.

There are feveral public buildings, tho' but few deferving attention. There were two churches, the Old or Trinity Church, and the New one or St. George's Chapel, both very large; the former was deftroyed by fire: by the remains it appears to have been in the Gothic tafte. The latter is built upon the model of fome of the new churches in London, and oppofite to it is a fpacious fquare, where ftands the park of artillery. Befides thefe two, there are

feveral

several other places of worship, consisting of two Low Dutch Calvinist churches, two High, one French; meeting houses for Lutherans, Presbyterians, Quakers, Anabaptists, Moravians, and a Jews synagogue. There is a very handsome charity school for sixty boys and girls; a good workhouse, barracks for a regiment of soldiers, and an exceeding strong prison. The courthouse is not so considerable as might be expected for such a city, and is now converted into a guard-house for the main guard.

The original fort was quadrangular, capable of mounting sixty pieces of cannon, but now there are great additions. In this fort stands the governor's palace, and underneath the fort is a battery capable of mounting ninety-four guns, and barracks for two companies of soldiers. Upon a small island, opposite the city, is an hospital for sick and wounded seamen.

The North River is somewhat more than two miles over to Paulus Hook, where there is an exceeding ſtrong work oppoſite New York. On account of the expoſure to the north winds, and to the driving of the ice, in the winter, ſhips cannot anchor there at that ſeaſon of the year, and therefore lay up in the Eaſt River, it being the ſafeſt and beſt, though the ſmalleſt, harbour.

The ſea near New York affords great quantities of oyſters, as well as variety of other ſea fiſh. Lobſters were extremely plentiful, of an enormous ſize; but after the cannonade at Long Iſland they forſook the coaſt, and not one has been ſeen ſince. The manner they firſt came upon the coaſt is rather ſingular, for although New England abounded with them, none were ever caught here; but this city was ſupplied by the New Englanders, who brought them in great wellboats.

boats. One of thefe boats coming thro' the Sound, and paffing Hell Gates, a very dangerous rocky part, ftruck and fplit to pieces, and the lobfters efcaped; after which they multiplied very faft, and were caught in great abundance, till frightened away by the noife of the cannon.

Having mentioned a place with fuch a tremendous name as Hell Gates, it may not be amifs to defcribe it, which I am enabled the more fully to do, having one afternoon, with a party, made a trip up the Sound and paffed this dangerous fpot. We left New York, with a fair and ftrong breeze, near upon the height of tide, as at any other time it is impaffable, and in about two hours paffed through Hell Gates. It is really impoffible to do this, without calling to mind the defcription of Scylla and Charybdis. The breadth of the Sound at this place is about half a mile, but the channel is very narrow,

row, not exceeding eighty yards. The water rushes with great rapidity and in various currents, only one of which will carry a vessel through with safety; for on one side there is a shoal of rocks, that just make their appearance above the water, and on the other a dreadful vortex, produced by a rock lying about nine feet under the surface, which is termed the pot, and draws and swallows every thing that approaches it, dashing them to pieces upon the rock at the bottom; at stated times of the tide this tremendous whirlpool boils furiously like a pot, and at others sucks every thing into it like a funnel.

Nearly oppofite to Hell Gates lies another reef of rocks, which, that it may bear some resemblance of horror, is named the Devil's Frying Pan. The noise made by the water in rushing over them, may be compared to that of water poured upon

upon red hot iron. This alfo draws veffels towards it, to their inevitable deftruction.

There are exceeding fkilful pilots to navigate through thefe dangerous ftraits, notwithftanding which fhips are frequently loft. Before the war, it was deemed an impoffibility for a top-fail veffel to pafs; but fince the commencement, fleets of tranfports, and the frigates that convoyed them, have ventured and accomplifhed it.

But what is ftill more extraordinary, and difplays a noble inftance of courage and intrepidity, that gallant feaman, Sir James Wallace, conducted his Majefty's fhip the Experiment, of fifty guns, through this dreadful channel.

At the time d'Eftaign lay off Sandy Hook with a fuperior force, and blocked up the harbour of New York, he difpatched
fome

some ships of the line round the east end of Long Island to cruize in the Sound, and to intercept any of the King's ships. At that time Sir James Wallace was cruizing at the mouth; and perceiving the French vessels, sailed back into the Sound. The French pursued, certain of the prize. Sir James saw his danger, and being unable to engage such a superior force, rather than the ship should fall into the enemy's hands, made the bold attempt to pass through Hell Gates; which was the wonder and astonishment not only of the French, who were obliged to return much chagrined, but of all the captains of our fleet; as it was ever deemed a rashness to attempt, but was accomplished by an act of necessity.

This afternoon I went down to the beach, to see the whale boat set off with dispatches for Lord Cornwallis's army, and you cannot conceive how elated the
crew

crew were; entertaining an idea of conveying tidings that would make them joyfully received.

As thefe are open boats, and have fo many leagues to fail before they reach the Chefapeak, you muft neceffarily conclude the voyage to be attended with imminent danger. Their intention is to coaft along fhore, but may be frequently driven out of fight of land; the laft boat that came from Lord Cornwallis, was in that fituation for three days. They eafily evade being taken, as they can fail in fhallow water, and keep clofe in fhore. The boats that pafs between the two armies have little apprehenfion of being captured, except in paffing through the French fleet at the mouth of the Chefapeak.

Your's, &c.

LETTER LXXVI.

New York, Oct. 30, 1781.

MY DEAR FRIEND,

THOUGH Long Island is in our possession, still towards the east end there are continual scouting parties of the Americans, that cross the Sound from the Connecticut shore, whose sole business is to plunder the inhabitants, and pick up prisoners.

On crossing the East River from New York you land at Brooklyn, which is a scattered village, consisting of a few houses.

At this place is an excellent tavern, where parties are made to go and eat fiſh; the landlord of which has ſaved an immenſe fortune this war. At a ſmall diſtance from the town are ſome conſiderable heights, commanding the city of New York. On theſe is erected a ſtrong regular fort, with four baſtions. To deſcribe the works thrown up by the Americans upon this iſland, would be beſtowing more attention on the ſubject than it deſerves, as they actually cover the whole. They are not only on grounds and ſituations that are extremely advantageous and commanding, but works of great ſtrength, that I am at a loſs to account for their ſo haſtily abandoning them, as they were certain by ſuch a ſtep to give up New York. I am induced to believe, that Gen. Waſhington thought the Americans were ſo panic-ſtruck after the engagement, as our troops purſued them cloſe to their lines, that they would not ſtand an aſſault; and if

his

his lines were carried he was sensible there was no place of retreat, and that his army must inevitably have been destroyed.

Long Island is the largest island from Cape Florida to Cape Sable. It is one hundred and thirty miles in length and about fifteen miles in breadth, and from its formation derives its name. The south side, next to the Atlantic, is low, level and sandy, with extensive bays within the land, near the length of the island; on that side opposite the continent, the lands are high, hilly and broken, but with a number of fine bays and harbours. A chain of hills runs through the middle of the island, the whole length of it, from which there is an extensive view of the ocean and the adjoining continent.

The Plain is a perfect level, and what is a phænomenon in America, has not a tree growing upon it. The soil is said to be
incapable

incapable of producing trees, or any vegetation except a coarse grass, and a kind of brush-wood or shrub which seldom grows higher than four or five feet, and that only on a particular part of the plain.

The soil of this plain is a black earth, covered with a kind of moss, and under the earth, which is of a spongy quality, is a bed of gravel, which, consequently absorbing the heaviest rains, prevents the water from remaining on the ground; it therefore naturally follows, that in wet seasons there is abundance of grass, and in dry ones it is entirely parched up.

The plain supports great quantities of cattle, sheep and horses, which are supplied with water from the ponds made by the inhabitants in different places, and, that they may retain the rain, have clay bottoms; for what is equally as remarkable

markable as the plain itself, there are no springs or running water throughout its whole extent. This plain is of the nature of our commons in England, having no inclosures, and almost uninhabited, except a few public houses for the convenience of travellers.

It is impossible to describe the anxiety of every one when the fleet left this place, in full hopes and expectation, although it had to fight its way through a much superior force, it would have been the means of saving the gallant and brave army under Lord Cornwallis; but language is unable to describe the feelings of every loyal subject, when the fleet returned, unable to effect so noble a purpose; for three days before the fleet made the Chesapeak, that gallant army had surrendered to the combined forces of France and America.

When

When the British fleet left Sandy Hook, Gen. Washington had certain intelligence of it, within forty-eight hours after it sailed, although at such a considerable distance as near six hundred miles, by means of signal guns and alarms. A very notorious rebel in New York, from the top of his house, hung out the signal of a white flag, the moment the fleet got under way, which was immediately answered by the firing of a gun at a small village about a mile from our post at Paulus Hook; after that a continual firing of cannon was heard on the opposite shore; and about two days after the fleet sailed, was the period in which Gen. Washington was so pressing for the army to surrender. There is a secresy to be observed in war, necessary to the well-conducting of plans, and the execution of any particular measure that is concerted, which, being disclosed, all is frustrated. This was the case in the present instance: the sailing of the fleet, by a villain under the mask of a Loyalist, was revealed to the Americans; and to similar causes may be accounted the many fatal calamities attending our army upon this continent.

The loss of Lord Cornwallis's army is too heavy a blow to be soon or easily recovered; it evidently must change the face of affairs: for the war which commenced in this country, and ought to have been maintained in the offensive, must now degenerate into a dishonorable defensive; and if Great Britain is determined to overcome the Colonies, she must send out a very numerous reinforcement in the spring, or the surrender of Lord Cornwallis may be considered as the closing scene of the whole continental war in America.

I have taken my passage in the Swallow Packet, which the latter end of the week sails for England. I preferred coming home

home in the packet rather than a transport, not only as it is a better sailing vessel, and having more hands is in less danger of being captured; but the transports in general are so exceedingly crazy, and their bottoms so very bad, owing to their laying up such a length of time in rivers, that they are unable to withstand the boisterous winds and waves of a winter's passage.

As this is the last letter you'll receive from me in America, permit me, before I bid a final farewel to it, to make some few reflections on this unfortunate contest.

Although America, through France and her naval power, may gain independence, she will find in what an aukward predicament she has involved herself, and how convulsed the provinces must be for a length of years. As a new ftate fhe muft maintain or eftablifh her public character, and is bound, by every tie of policy, not to defert her allies.

Alas, deluded Americans! When too late, you'll repent your rafhnefs. Let me impartially afk the moft fenfible among them, When the Independency is eftablifhed, will they poffefs that freedom and liberty as under the Englifh government? If their anfwer is impartial, they muft declare, Certainly we fhall not; but in a few years *perhaps* we may. That period, I am afraid, is at a great diftance.

Much, indeed, are they entangled in the cabals of a French court, which will, fooner or later, not only endeavour to enflave them in reality, but difpoffefs them of their fouthern provinces. It is not without juft grounds I affert that e'er half a century elapfes, America

America will be suing that protection from the mother country, which she has so ungratefully despised, to screen her from the persecutions and tyranny of France. They are conscious of being happy before this unfortunate revolution, and will feel that they are no longer so; they must inevitably regret the change in sullen silence, or, if they have any thing like spirit left, rouze into arms again.

Yours, &c.

LETTER LXXVIII.

On board the Swallow Packet, St. Mary's Harbour, in the Iflands of Scilly, Dec. 8, 1781.

MY DEAR FRIEND,

ON the day after our arrival here, Lord Dalrymple, who had the charge of Sir Henry Clinton's difpatches, apprehenfive that the packet might be detained for a confiderable time by contrary winds, and anxious to deliver difpatches of fo much importance to the nation, hired a fmall fifhing boat, and, notwithftanding it blew a hard gale, regardlefs of the imminent dangers of the feas and furrounding enemies, fo much had he the public fervice service at heart, that, nobly braving them, he, at the utmost risk of his life, set sail in it from this place, accompanied by the Earl of Lincoln, who was a passenger on board the packet. From a lofty eminence we saw the boat leave these islands, while the sea ran so tremendous high, that it was thought by every one they never could reach the English coast.

Strangers who land here, are conducted to the spot where the body of that famous Admiral Sir Cloudesley Shovel was found, after his shipwreck in the year 1707. It was in a small cove called Porthelisk near what is termed the Tolmens; and it is handed down by tradition that he was discovered naked, and only distinguished from the most ordinary sailor under his command, by having round his neck a portrait of his royal mistress, on the reverse of which was engraved his name.

A sand-

A sand-bank offering itself very opportunely, as if for the very purpose, he was interred under it. Whoever has seen the place, will allow it would have been doubly inhuman not to have buried him, whoever he was. For my own part, it recalled to my mind the argument that Archytas makes use of to bespeak the like friendly office.

> At tu nauta, vagæ ne parce malignus arenæ,
> Ossibus & capiti inhumato,
> Particulam dare.
> Hor. Od. xxviii. lib. 1.

History informs us, that the body of this great man was afterwards taken up, and conveyed to Westminster abbey. A small pit on this sandy green, is still visible.

> Pulveris exigui parva munera.   Ibid.

These islands are of great utility in time of war, as they afford protection to trading

ing veffels and homeward-bound fhips, which would by contrary winds, without this refuge, be obliged to beat about in the Channel, expofed to the danger of being captured by the enemy.

The not eftablifhing a packet between thefe iflands and the main, is an inconvenience to be lamented and a ground for cenfure. I am confident it would bring in a great revenue; for, during our ftay, a packet of letters was given to the Captain of our fhip, nearly as large as that he has brought from New York. You would fcarcely believe it, but they have been feventeen weeks without any intercourfe with the country. Such an intermiffion of correfpondence muft be extremely detrimental to trade. A fmall fhip of about forty tons, to pafs and repafs as the weather permitted, would, by freight and trade, not only repay expences, but be a handfome income to the owners.

The

The utility of a frigate being stationed here, was noticed to me by several of the inhabitants; for, during this war, a French cutter came into the harbour, with a view to cut away the ships at anchor; but a frigate happening to be there at that time, the cutter sheered off, and no other has since made its appearance; which must arise from the idea that a frigate is actually stationed in these islands.

The wind coming favorable, the Captain has desired the passengers to repair on board.

Yours, &c.

LETTER LXXIX.

Falmouth, Dec. 15, 1781.

MY DEAR FRIEND,

YESTERDAY afternoon we left Scilly Islands, and arrived at this place about one o'clock this morning. On going ashore, description would fall exceedingly short of the transports I felt on setting my foot once more on my native land.

We here learnt, that after a very dangerous passage, and being nearly captured by a French cutter, Earl Lincoln and Lord Dalrymple arrived safe at Penzance, and a few days ago paſſed through this place for town.

The former of theſe noblemen received a ſhock that muſt have ſunk deep indeed. While they were changing horſes, a hearſe was ſetting off from the ſame inn for London; and on his Lordſhip's enquiry concerning it, he was told it was a corpſe that had arrived a few days ſince in the Liſbon packet. His curioſity and his fears were awakened. It was the corpſe of his brother, Lord John Pelham Clinton, who, a few months ſince, had gone over to Liſbon for the recovery of his health. A brother whom he panted to meet with---whoſe affection was his joy and his pride. Thus are our proudeſt hopes, like a tower, propt but by a broken reed, which is ever ready to break! Your own feelings can better exprefs the ſituation of his heart, on receiving the melancholy

melancholy information than my pen is able to defcribe.

It is remarkable on the very day before we put into Scilly Iflands, while we were in purfuit of the fhip a-head of us, he expreffed vaft anxiety about his brother, as he had not had letters from him for fome months, adding, with a gloominefs, that he hoped he fhould have fome accounts by the next packet. The fhip then in fight proved to be the Lifbon Packet, which had his brother's dead body on board.

Having fully complied with your requeft, on my leaving England, of embracing every opportunity to let you hear from me, and as this will be the laft of our literary correfpondence, permit me, before I conclude, to apologize for any inaccuracies of expreffion, and every little
fault

fault that may have occurred. And if you can believe me diffident enough to diftruft my own talents, cautious of affuming merit from your too indulgent opinion, and anxious to throw myfelf into your arms, it will evince the clearnefs of your judgment, and the fincerity of your friendfhip for

Yours, &c.

FINIS.

www.ingramcontent.com/pod-product-compliance
Lightning Source LLC
Chambersburg PA
CBHW031938290426
44108CB00011B/604